Assessing and Stimulating a Dialogical Self in Groups, Teams, Cultures, and Organizations

Hubert Hermans
Editor

Assessing and Stimulating a Dialogical Self in Groups, Teams, Cultures, and Organizations

Editor
Hubert Hermans
Emeritus-professor of psychology
Radboud University of Nijmegen
The Netherlands

ISBN 978-3-319-32481-4 ISBN 978-3-319-32482-1 (eBook)
DOI 10.1007/978-3-319-32482-1

Library of Congress Control Number: 2016941335

Printed on acid-free paper

This Springer imprint is published by Springer Nature
The registered company is Springer International Publishing AG Switzerland

Preface

What is the origin of this book? Together with my colleagues, I published the first article on the dialogical self in the *American Psychologist* in 1992. This article marked the beginning of a period of more than 20 years of research, which led to the production of several hundreds of books and articles in a wide variety of scientific journals. At the same time, some practice-oriented psychologist did the painstaking and laborious job to develop new and original methods for assessing and stimulating a dialogical self and applied them systematically in their own coaching and counselling settings. With some of these colleagues I stayed in close connection and followed them over the years. I noticed that their work was not only inspired by Dialogical Self Theory but also powerful enough to enable clients to change their life or career situation. After studying my colleagues' work and discussing it with them, I decided to select nine methods of high theoretical significance and practical utility for publication in this book. I invited the authors of these methods to describe their techniques in detail, to sketch their protocols, to show how the method works in a realistic case study and to explain when and where to apply it. In their systematic theoretical scope and practical relevance, all methods can be considered as emerging from a scientist-practitioner paradigm.

I'm proud to have the opportunity to bring these imaginative methods together in one book. What do they have in common? They have three main features. First, they appeal to the *self-organizing capacity* of the person. They are not simply assessing a trait or personality characteristic, but they invite the participants to bring their hidden, neglected or suppressed energies to the surface in profound processes of self-reflection and self-dialogue. Second, *assessment and change coincide* in all procedures. That is, the methods are not only intended to create a picture of the organization of the different self-parts but also, and at the same time, give this organization an impulse in the direction of the desired change. Third, the professionals who apply these methods are not expected to take a stance as 'distanced observers' but as dedicated professionals who realize a *cooperative relationship with their clients*. In other worlds, the methods are explicitly relational procedures, stimulating a dialogical space to emerge between counsellors and their clients and, at the same time, creating a similar generative space in the selves of the clients.

My purpose with this book is to inspire both scientist and practitioners and those who combine both scientific and practical interest in themselves, to apply one or more of the presented methods, including their combinations, in their own setting and to adapt them in the service of their own purposes. The book will primarily be useful to social, cultural and organizational psychology practitioners and to young researchers worldwide for master and doctoral dissertations. Research and method courses within industrial/organizational psychology master programs are ideal settings for a systematic use of the book. It will be relevant also for undergraduate students interested in understanding how Dialogical Self Theory could be grounded in empirical/practical contexts. Educators can find this work of interest for their practices.

Finally, I warmly thank all authors of the book for their stimulating enthusiasm, for their dedicated effort and for their persistence to survive an editor who did not give up his attempts to create the necessary coherence in a broad variety of dialogical approaches.

Pragmatism is perhaps America's most distinctive contribution to philosophy. Developed by Pierce, Dewey and James in the late nineteenth and early twentieth centuries, pragmatism holds that both the meaning and the truth of any idea are the functions of its practical outcome. The pragmatists rejected all forms of absolutism and insisted that all principles be regarded as working hypotheses that must bear fruit in lived experience. See more at http://www.philosophytalk.org/shows/american-pragmatism#sthash.x8MTNfwI.dpuf

The Netherlands Hubert Hermans
26 February 2016

Contents

Author Bios

Kate Clarke has a Master's degree in Theoretical and Life-Span Psychology from the University of Leiden in the Netherlands. She is a certified coach in the self confrontation method and has been using this method and the concepts of the dialogical self intensively since 1997. As a young adult, she emigrated from the United States to the Netherlands. After establishing her career as a psychologist and coach, she started her bureau Clarke & Esser in Rotterdam. She developed a narrative coaching approach for persons who have multiple cultural backgrounds. By using the stories of each cultural voice within a person, inner dialogue becomes possible, enhancing one's purpose in life and work.

Hubert Hermans is emeritus professor of psychology at Radboud University of Nijmegen, the Netherlands. He developed a Self Confrontation Method, an idiographic procedure for assessing a person's meaning system. He is most known as creator of Dialogical Self Theory. Among his books are *The Dialogical Self: Meaning as Movement,* with Harry Kempen (Academic Press, 1993); *Self-Narratives: The Construction of Meaning in Psychotherapy*, with Els Hermans-Jansen (Guilford Press, 1995); and *Dialogical Self Theory: Positioning and Counter-Positioning in a Globalizing Society,* with Agnieszka Konopka (Cambridge University Press, 2010). He is President of the *International Society for Dialogical Science* (ISDS). E-mail: HHermans@psych.ru.nl. Homepage: www.huberthermans.com

Jutta König is specialized in acculturation processes and how this affects identity development. She published *Moving Experience: Complexities of Acculturation in 2012* in which she developed the PEACE methodology to explore hybrid identities. Working in private practice as a career coach, psychotherapist, writer, public speaker and researcher, she has years of experience with people of different cultural backgrounds in Singapore, Belgium and the Netherlands. She is chair of the International

Career Certification Institute, board member of CMI and a member of the programme committee of the Dialogical Self Academy. Highly skilled in recognizing people strengths, her passion is to support clients to find fulfilment and live their dreams.

Agnieszka Konopka holds a PhD in psychology of emotions. She is co-founder of Compositionwork and a Cambridge University Press author and co-author of *Dialogical Self Theory: Positioning and Counter-positioning in a Globalizing Society* (together with prof. Hubert Hermans). Agnieszka coaches and trains internationally psychologists and those who are interested in personal development. She is specialized in contemplative, present oriented ways of working with feelings and awareness.

Joanna Krotofil is a Research Associate at the Division of Psychiatry, UCL. She studied Psychology at Jagiellonian University, and in 2012 she obtained her PhD from the Institute for the Study of Religions (Jagiellonian University). Her PhD thesis focuses on the relationship between religion and identity among recent Polish migrants in UK, and the dialogical relationships between institutions and individuals undergoing identity re-negotiation. She has published a number of papers exploring the application of the Dialogical Self Theory in research on migration. E-mail: j.krotofil@ucl.ac.uk.

Reinekke Lengelle PhD, is a visiting graduate professor with Athabasca University (Canada's Open University) and a researcher at The Hague University, the Netherlands. She is also the co-creator of the method 'Career Writing' and created a set of *career cards* to get people writing about their lives and vocations. She is also a published poet and playwright and the author of various international peer-reviewed journal articles. Her graduate courses for personal development, 'Writing the Self' and 'Narrative Possibilities', continue to be popular year after year. Homepage: www.blacktulippress.com

Dina Nir has a PhD from the Hebrew University of Jerusalem and holds a lecturer position at the Ono Academic College of Israel affiliated with the Interdisciplinary Center (IDC). Dina's research focuses on developing and empirically validating positive interventions that boost well-being and human flourishing. Dina has developed the Negotiational Self Theory (NST) – a mindful approach to making everyday decisions and has created and empirically validated the Negotiational Self Method (NSM), which offers a means of steering one's inner conflicts towards integrative 'win-win' decisions. Dina has many years' experience in public speaking and conducting positive psychology workshops in organizations.

Wim van Beers (1947) studied psychology in Nijmegen and got his PhD in 1982. From 1982 to 1987, he worked as an internal consultant for Philips in the Netherlands. From 1989 to 2010, he worked for Schouten & Nelissen first as a unit manager and then also as a member of the board of directors responsible for quality knowledge and competence management. In 2010, he became a private entrepreneur specialized in management consultancy, coaching and mediation. He wrote several books on result-oriented management and performance management. Since 2013 he works together with Dr. Agnieszka Konopka in their company Compositionwork. Together they wrote several publications on Compositionwork.

Tessa van den Berg is a manager at Deloitte Consulting and a senior consultant specialized in corporate learning in the context of organizational change and transformation. She graduated from the Free University of Amsterdam in the Netherlands with a degree in Organizational Anthropology. Tessa works with clients to align their corporate learning to business objectives, driving continuous improvement. She has been a consultant for 12 years, of which she spent 7 years in China and Japan. She is currently based in the Netherlands. She is a member of the Association for Talent Development (ATD, formerly ASTD).

Richard van de Loo is an associate at Meijer Consulting Group (Utrecht, the Netherlands). He specializes in individual and team coaching and in management and leadership development in organizations. His work as an applied psychologist inspired him to regularly reflect on and publish about personal and team development. An example of this is his PhD thesis on the development of a programme for career orientation based on the Self Confrontation Method (SCM). He trains consultants in the application of the SCM Organization. Since 2012, he has been the president of the Dutch Association of SCM practitioners (*ZKM vereniging*). E-mail: richard@meijercg.nl

Rens van Loon is a professor of Dialogical Leadership at School of Humanities, Tilburg University, and a director at Deloitte Consulting. He is specialized in leadership and organizational change and transformation. Rens is a board member of the International Leadership Association (ILA), member of TAOS and active in the International Society for Dialogical Science (ISDS). Next to several Dutch books on leadership, he published 'Dialogical Leadership: Dialogue as Condition Zero' in the *Journal of leadership Accountability and Ethics* (2015); 'Dancing Leader: Leading and Following' in *Followership in Action: Cases and Commentaries*, edited by Rob Koonce (2016).

Harmien Visser owns, since 1994, an agency for educational and career guidance and counselling. She is coaching scholars, young adults and elder people, focusing on personal development and empowerment. Their requests for help are mostly about career or educational choices, personal performance, outplacement, burnout, fear of failure or just the need for reflection on their own life and career. From 1998 till 2009, she was teacher at the trainings institute for Valuation Theory and Self Confrontation Method in Nijmegen. She published some articles in professional journals about the value of the SCM in career counselling.

Peter Zomer graduated in 1992 as an industrial and organizational psychologist and obtained in 2006 his doctorate with the thesis *The Team Confrontation Method (TCM): Design, Grounding and Testing*. He has been a practitioner of leadership development and team building for years, in both the corporate and public domain. In his research, he has been developing ways of working with teams based on Dialogical Self Theory. Email: peter@zomer-cornelissen.nl. Website: www.zomer-cornelissen.nl; see also his profile on Linked-in.

Introduction

More than ever, the contemporary world confronts us with two challenges: to develop ourselves as autonomous individuals and, at the same time, to find an adaptive response to a social and societal environment that is becoming increasingly complex. These contradictory demands require the self to function as a 'part-whole': it is both a whole on itself and part of a broader system. We have to find our way in work and life as *independent* persons who are increasingly *inter-dependent* in our relationship with significant others, groups, teams, organizations and cultures. This special situation places us in a field of tension in which we are confronted with both challenging possibilities and hindering obstacles. With regard to our autonomy, the self has become a 'project' that requires care, wisdom, planning and a sense of direction in order to make effective use of its strengths and weaknesses in changing and unpredictable environments. At the same time, this project can only be realized in close cooperation with others, or at least with the support of others, who create the conditions to feed and stimulate the self but also have the power to frustrate it and even let it fail. The central idea of this book is that we need dialogue, dialogical capacities and dialogical methods to achieve this task.

Before describing the different chapters in this book, an introduction of their theoretical foundation is needed. Therefore, I will start with the core message of the book and the main assumptions of the guiding theory.

The Necessity of Dialogue in Fields of Tension

The core message of this book is that, in order to find our way in the field of tension between independence and inter-dependence, we profit from dialogical relationships not only with the actual others but also with the internal parts of our self. Dialogical relationships allow the construction of new and empowering meanings – they serve as an interface between self and society. Yet, such a constructive relationship with ourselves, is not at all self-evident. Just as in our connections with actual others who confront us with both prospects and problems, we are confronted with opportunities and obstacles in ourselves. The roots of this similarity stem from the social nature of the self. Almost all relationships that we have with actual others have their parallel in the relationship with ourselves. We love, esteem, help, consult, support, admire, reward, control, manage, command or celebrate ourselves. But we may also hate, depreciate, despise, frustrate, punish, neglect, suppress, ridicule, harm or even destroy ourselves. In this wide array of self-to-other and self-to-self connections, dialogical relationships have a special place and are worth being fostered and developed. But, what do we mean when speaking about 'dialogue'?

'Dialogue' comes from the Greek word dialogos. *Logos* means 'the word' and *dia* means 'through.' However, logos includes more than 'word' in a grammatical sense. It derives from the verb *legein* meaning 'to tell, say, speak'. So, dialogue, in its most basic sense, is actually a 'dialogical activity' that enables people to *address* each other in order to convey messages, tell their stories and share their experiences. When participants address each other, they do so from a particular *position* (e.g., I as taking a critical stance towards you) and, at the same time, they place the other in a position as well (you as criticized and challenged to give me an answer). When we introduce the notion of position, we take into account the assumption that dialogue is basically a *spatial-relational activity*. The difference between logical and dialogical relationships may help clarify this claim.

Difference Between Logical and Dialogical Relationships

Consider two phrases that are completely identical, 'life is good' and again 'life is good' (Bakhtin, 1984). When we consider these phrases from the perspective of Aristotelian logic, they are related in terms of *identity*; they are, in fact, one and the same statement. From a dialogical point of view, however, they are different because they are utterances expressed by the voices of two spatially separated people in communication, who in this case entertain a relationship of *agreement*. They are identical from a logical point of view but different as utterances as the first is a statement, the second a confirming statement. In a similar way, the phrases 'life is good' and 'life is not good' can be analyzed. Within a logical framework, one is a *negation* of the other. However, as utterances from two different speakers, a dialogical relation of *disagreement* evolves. Agreeing and disagreeing are, like questioning and answering, basic dialogical forms. Being involved in such communications, participants position themselves towards each other. In this process of positioning and counter-positioning, participants may learn from each other and new meanings may emerge which contribute to the innovation of both self and other.

For a proper understanding of the theory underlying the methods presented in this book, it has to be emphasized that dialogical relationships also exist within the self. Sometimes I may experience life as good, at other moments as not good. An internal dialogue emerges when the two phrases are brought together as coming from contrasting voices in an inner talk. Suppose that I'm sometimes optimistic and sometimes pessimistic. When the position 'I as optimistic' prevails, I may say to myself that my project is going well. When this position recedes to the background, 'I as a pessimist' comes to the fore and might say that my project is not going well. From a dialogical point of view, these positions are not entirely independent mechanisms. In situations where I am overly optimistic, my more pessimist position may correct this 'over-positioning.' When, on the contrary, my pessimist position becomes more dominant, it may learn from the possibilities offered by my optimist position. Moving back and forth between the two positions and their voices, they learn from each other and build new meanings.

The difference between logical and dialogical relationships is also helpful to articulate the highly dynamic nature of the process of positioning. Whereas logical argumentation leads to a final conclusion that completes the reasoning process, positioning in the context of a dialogue invites taking a next step in an ongoing stream of events that evolves as a process of repositioning and counter-positioning.

To avoid misunderstandings, it must be added that, although logical and dialogical relationships are different, they don't exclude one another. Dialogical relationships are not reducible to logical relationships, but assume the existence of a social context. Logical relationships produce order and organization in thinking and are needed for consistency of argumentation. By providing clarity with regard to relevant distinctions and consistency of reasoning, they contribute significantly to dialogical relationships.

Emergence of a Dialogical Space

When we look at our own experiences, we may witness that external dialogues (with others) and internal dialogues (with ourselves) are closely intertwined. We rehearse exchanges with others at the moments we are alone and build on them so that we are better prepared for the next conversation. When being involved in communication with others, we listen to ourselves at the same time in order to select the answer that is most suited to contribute to the ongoing interchange. In an exchange where participants feel that they can express and share their experiences, a 'dialogical space' emerges as an in-between space that was not there before the dialogue started. This can happen in situations where a new insight or new meaning is growing as a common construction that is felt as a link created between you and the other. When two or more people are involved in a generative dialogue, they feel the emergence of an invisible common space in which they feel respected as dialogical partners and feel the freedom to express their views and experiences from their own point of view. In this space, participants are open to sharing and listening to each other's experiences, even when these may be very different from each other. The bandwidth of such a space is broad and a diversity of positions and experiences can be expressed. The participants typically feel a strong sense of sharing and have the impression that the space is not only between them but is also connecting them. The emergence of a dialogical space is an optimal condition for the construction of new and common meanings. Such a space can also arise in the self when, for instance, a person is engaged in expressive writing, creative self-reflection and self-investigation, when openly listening to the voices in oneself and during moments of inner silence.

Self as a Micro-society of *I*-Positions

The central conceptual framework, Dialogical Self Theory (DST) (Hermans & Gieser, 2012; Hermans & Hermans-Konopka, 2010), weaves two concepts, self and dialogue, together in such a way that the intimate interconnection of self and society becomes apparent. Typically, the 'self' represents something 'internal,' which occurs within the mind of the individual person, while 'dialogue' is typically associated with something 'external,' happening between participants involved in communication.

The composite concept 'dialogical self' transcends this dichotomy by creating direct linkages between the internal and external so that self and other and, in a wider context, self and society can directly influence each other in mutually enriching ways. The dichotomy is transcended by considering the self as a process of positioning towards oneself and the other. Such a theoretical construction creates direct avenues between the self and society and back again. This allows people to create productive linkages between their position in a group or organization (e.g., I as leader, I as professional, I as coach) with positions in the self (e.g., I as ambitious, I as a dreamer, I as an enjoyer of life). This self-society connection allows one to abandon a conception of the self as essentialized and encapsulated in itself. Moreover, it abandons the idea of a 'soul-less' society that lacks the opportunity to profit from the richness and creativity of the individual human mind and its potentials to innovate existing social practices.

Dialogical Self Theory emerged at the interface of two traditions: American Pragmatism and Russian Dialogism. As a theory of the self, it is inspired by James's (1890) and Mead's (1934) classic formulations on the self, conceptualized as an *I* which is able, as a subject, to reflect on the *Me* as an object. As a dialogical theory, it builds on the fertile insights in the dialogical nature of the mind as proposed by Bakhtin (1984). Elaborating on the views of these theorists, Dialogical Self Theory aims to create an interface for the construction of methods and practices that are both theory-based and valuable in their pragmatic implications.

Main concepts of Dialogical Self Theory

In a most succinct way, the dialogical self can be described as a *dynamic multiplicity of I-positions in the inner space of the self.* Conceived in this way, the self functions as a micro-society as part of the society at large. The I is intrinsically connected with the social and societal environment and is bound to particular positions in time and space. As embodied in time and space, the I has the possibility to move from one position to the other in its response to changes in the situation and time. From a spatial perspective, the I is involved in a process of positioning and counter-positioning. From a temporal point of view, it moves forward in the form of positioning and repositioning. In this way, the I fluctuates among different and even opposing positions not only in the self but also between self and real or imagined others. Like in the society at large, these positions are involved in relationships of relative dominance and social power. Some positions are, temporarily or more structurally, more powerful in the self than other ones and their needs, wishes and values receive priority over those of other positions. As part of sign-mediated social relations, positions can receive a voice so that dialogical exchanges among them develop. The voices behave like interacting characters in a story or movie, involved in the processes of question and answer, agreement and disagreement, conflicts and struggles, negotiations and integrations. In agreement with James's (1890) distinction between I (self as subject) and me (self as object), each of the positions has a story to tell about their own experiences from their own perspective. As different voices, these characters exchange knowledge and information about their respective Me's, creating a complex, narratively structured self (Hermans & Hermans-Konopka, 2010).

All methods presented in this book are based on the subject-object-project triad. They offer specific procedures for self-investigation and self-dialogue for changing and developing different *I*-positions in the self in the context of the wider social and societal environment. They have in common a gradual transition between assessment and change. They offer procedures for examining the content and organization of the self and, based on the results, they produce guidelines useful for changing the existing organization of the self. Before I turn to the different methods, some further explanation of their theoretical basis is needed. In the following sections, I discuss three concepts of the theory that play central roles in most or all of the chapters, *I*-position, meta-position and promoter position and their implications for change in the self.

The Meaning of *I*-position

An *I*-position is a spatial-relational act. It always exists in the context of other positions (e.g., I position myself as competitive towards a rival and as cooperative towards a close colleague). The act of *I*-positioning always has two sides: it is a way of placing oneself vis-à-vis with somebody else in the literal societal space and, at the same time, towards oneself in the metaphorical space of the self. Positioning means taking a stance towards somebody, either physically or virtually, and is to be understood as a way of addressing the other and oneself via verbal or non-verbal orientations and communications. I can become tender-hearted towards another person and, at the same time, more open in the relationship to myself. Or, in a different case, I take a permissive stance towards another person, but, at some later moment, I criticize myself for going too far in my openness. Given its spatial nature,

I-positioning always implies a 'here' and a 'there', in the communication with the actual or imagined other. Between this here and there, a field of tension is stretched in which I make, physically or virtually, dialogical movements from myself-here to the other-there and back. Taking a stance towards, from or against the other, there is always a similar or dissimilar movement in the metaphorical space of my own self. I appreciate myself when I made a good deal and I criticize myself when I made a stupid remark during a conversation with a colleague. There are fields of tension not only between people but also between different *I*-positions in the self.

Difference with self-definition and self-categorization. Positioning is not to be confused with self-definition or self-categorization. When I *define* myself as friendly, I consider myself a person to whom I attribute a particular personality trait (friendliness). In contrast, when I *position* myself as friendly, I take a stance towards another person, orienting myself as a kind embodied being to him or her. When I *categorize* myself as a psychologist, I see myself as a representative of a particular class of people. When I *position* myself as a psychologist, I place myself as an investigator or adviser in a relationship with others. Positioning is a form of addressing a spatially located other. As a consequence of this addressing act, a position is always questioned, confirmed, modified or rejected by other positions in the self or other in a relational way. As a spatial-relational act, it can never escape a dynamic relationship with other positions and is more context-bound than a static definition or categorization. Similar remarks can be made about the popular but rather static notion of 'self-image', which lacks the dynamic nature of positioning and counter-positioning.

Difference with Self-Presentation *I*-positioning is not identical to self-presentation. This can be clarified by referring to an example in Goffman's (1959) classic work *The presentation of Self in Everyday Life*. A girl living in a dormitory wants to impress the other girls with her popularity by the number of telephone calls she receives. Goffman describes this example with the intention of demonstrating that self-presentation aims to convey an image of oneself to the outside world in such a way that the addressee perceives this image as reality. *I*-positioning, however, not only refers to the positions people wish to present to the outside world but also to positions they take in the internal domain of the self. An internal positioning may be entirely discrepant from the impression one wants to convey to the outside. The dormitory girl in the example may send out impressive signs of her popularity to the environment, but internally she may position herself as 'somebody in whom boys are not really interested' or even as 'not worth a date'. As this example suggests, internal and external forms of positioning are dynamically related as the presented position may function as an overcompensation for a problematic positioning towards oneself. The act of positioning is closely connected to the events taking place in the field of tension between self and environment and between the self and itself. The two forms of relationships may be symmetrical but also opposed and even contradictory.

Internal and External Positions As extended to the environment, as James (1890) would have it, the dialogical self includes not only *internal* positions (e.g., I as an ambitious worker, I as a sports fanatic, I as a lover of classical music) but also *external* positions (e.g., my trustworthy colleague, my stubborn opponent, my always hesitating friend). Moreover, not only internal but also external positions can have the quality of *I*-positions, that is, the other is conceived as another subject or another I. This point of view is consistent with Bakhtin (1984) who proposed to see the other as 'another full-fledged I'. Indeed, we can identify with another person, animal or even an object (e.g., a piece of art in which I recognize myself) or with nature (e.g., 'I as a piece of earth that becomes aware of itself'). This identification can reach the point that the other is seen as part of an *extended self.*

A position is broader than the sociological concept of 'role'. It includes both social positions or roles (e.g., I as a father, I as a scientist, I as a leader) and personal positions (e.g., I as a dreamer, I as pessimistic, I as a joker). Typically, social positions receive a personal touch as merging with personal positions. The 'same' role may receive very different personal expressions on the basis of one's personal preferences, capacities or histories (e.g., the inspiring teacher, the humorous teacher, the rational teacher). (For the combination of personal and social positions, see Leijen and Kullasepp, 2013.)

Meta-position as an Over-Arching and Long-Term Perspective

Society is full of committees, cross-disciplinary teams for doing research into future trends or ombudspersons who review requests from individuals and groups. Typically, their aim is to get an overview of the complexities of a particular problem area as a basis for giving advice or taking actions. Ideally, they try to reach beyond the present state of affairs by taking a long-term view of the situation at hand. They are, in fact, taking a 'meta-position' that provides an overview of more specific social and societal positions, including their patterns and inter-relationships. This overview prevents the different parts of a social system from becoming fragmented and incoherent in its purposes. A meta-position is also indispensable for any theory of the self as it offers a 'distance view' on the diversity and complexity of specific *I*-positions and their dynamic relationships. In its most typical form, a meta-position can be described as an overview of a greater variety of specific positions, their mutual linkages and their associated voices and narratives (e.g., when reflecting about myself, I noticed that when I shared my experiences with my partner, I discovered things that I simply did not see when I discussed them with my colleague).

The main features of a meta-position are the following: (a) it creates an optimal *distance* towards other more specific positions, although it may be attracted, both cognitively and emotionally, towards some positions more than others (e.g., a critical meta-position or a compassionate one); (b) it provides an *overarching view* of a multiplicity of positions, both internal and external ones, so that they are perceived in their dynamic interconnections; (c) in linking past, present and future, a meta-position permits a *long-term view* of the self so that linkages among positions as part of one's personal history and the collective history of one's group or culture become visible; (d) it leads to an *evaluation* of the several positions and their organization; as a result of this evaluation, some positions receive priority above others and the degree of automaticity of positions is reduced; (e) a person becomes aware of the differences in their *accessibility*. Each position has an entrance and an exit. When the entrance is closed, it is difficult for the meta-position to get familiar with the specific needs, wishes and values of this position. In reverse, a well-developed meta-position creates an open entrance to a broad variety of specific positions so that they can share their experiences and stories with the meta-position (e.g., when writing about my experiences, I have access not only to my position as 'successful' but also as 'failing' so that I let them come together and learn from their interplay); and (f) the *direction of change* and the importance of one or more positions for the future development of the self becomes apparent. In summary, the development of a meta-position with a broad scope and long-term perspective contributes more than the other positions, to the cohesion and continuity of the self as a whole (Georgaca, 2001; Hermans & Hermans-Konopka, 2010).

Promoter Positions: Stimulating Change and Development

In a group or society, particular people are appreciated and considered as particularly inspiring and they are granted respect, admiration, influence and even social power. Typically, we perceive them as giving a significant push to the development of a group or organization. Such people function as 'promoters' because they are seen as adding value to the community, giving it a sense of direction and contributing to its further development. Promoters work not only in society at large but also in the mini-society of the self. As promoting *I*-positions they can be adopted and further developed as parts in the extended domain of the self. For some it may be a well-known person who reaches the status of a hero or heroine, like a Mandela, a Gandhi, a Malala Yousafzai, a pop artist, an admired film actor or an imaginary figure from a book. For others a person living in their immediate environment may function as a promoter: a parent, a grand-parent, a dedicated friend or a psychotherapist. Such people may enter the metaphorical space of the extended domain of the self and become established as valuable sources of energy.

A promoter position may inhabit not only the external domain of the self but also its internal domain. External promoters in the self (e.g., my most important teacher) may transform into similar promoters in the internal domain (e.g., I as a dedicated professional identifying with my teacher) or become promoters that develop in the opposite direction (e.g., I as wanting to overcome the limitations that spoiled the lives of my beloved parents). Usually, promoters show a great variation of possibilities. They may include positions like 'I as never giving up' 'I as spiritual' or 'I as artistic', for other people they be 'I as caring for the unprivileged', 'I as becoming a creative author' or 'I as supporting my children'. Even over the life-course promoters may change and show up as remarkably different, particularly when people go through a turning point in their lives (e.g., from 'I as an upward climber' to 'I as a mentor of young people').

Promoters in the self (Valsiner, 2004) have a number of characteristics that are analogous to inspiring leaders in society: (a) they imply a considerable *openness* towards the future and have the capacity of producing a diverse range of more specialized positions that are relevant to the further development of the self; in this way they operate as innovators of the self; (b) they *organize* and give direction to a diversity of more specialized *I*-positions that otherwise would fragment the self if they went their own way; they provide a sense of direction: they have a 'compass function' for the self-system as a whole; (c) they *integrate* a diversity of new and already existing positions in the self by bringing them together in the form of adaptive and productive combinations; (d) if sufficiently dialogical, they have the potential to contribute to the *democratic organization* of the self (giving each specific position an opportunity to express and develop itself and not allowing any position to play a dictatorial role in the self).

Note that 'meta-position' and 'promoter position' are different concepts. Whereas a meta-position is a spatial concept providing an overview of a greater variety of *I*-positions, a promoter has temporal focus as it gives an impetus to the future development of the self. While a meta-position works as a vertically ascending and descending 'helicopter' allowing various distance views on the landscape of the self, a promoter functions like a motor pushing the 'machinery' of the self into a desired direction at a horizontal plane.

Together, the concepts of *I*-position, meta-position and promoter position are at the heart of Dialogical Self Theory and have a prominent place in the different chapters of this book. While the multiplicity and diversity of *I*-positions are the basic ingredients of self-knowledge and self-dialogue, the development of meta-positions and promoters are essential to the organization and further development of the self as a whole.

What Is 'Change' in This Theory?

It is generally assumed that the self is always involved in change and development. However, this self-evident assumption does not automatically take into account the important phenomenon, generally discussed under the label 'resistance to change'. In their innovative book *Immunity to Change*, Kegan and Lahey (2009) observe that resistance to change does not always reflect active opposition or passive inertia. Instead, even as people are sincerely committed to change, they are unwittingly investing energy towards a hidden competing commitment that blocks the change that they consciously aspire. The resulting equilibrium impedes further action as a kind of personal immunity to change. The authors give the example of a woman who receives new responsibilities in an organization which gives her more social power as she is placed in an equal position in relation to her earlier superiors. However, she feels unable to change her behaviour. After intense self-examination, she discovers that, although she truly wants the project to succeed, she has an accompanying unacknowledged commitment to maintaining a subordinate position in relation to her earlier superior. At a deep level, she is afraid to become more a peer than a subordinate with the consequence that she tends to shy away from actions needed to make the project successful. This means that, when it comes to change, people may have one or more *I*-positions which are in favour, but also one or more *I*-positions, at some deeper level of awareness, which are opposed to change. Therefore, a well-developed meta-position is required to become conscious of the dynamic relationship between *I*-positions that want change and those which are unwittingly blocking it. Moreover, effective promoter positions are in need of the support of a wider variety of *I*-positions which, each from their own specific point of view and specialization, contribute to the motivation to realize one's purposes 'wholeheartedly'. Both meta-positions and promoters have central leadership roles to play in the organization and reorganization of the self. [For the relevance of self-inquiry to change, including attention to moment to moment experiences in the self, see also Torbert et al.'s (2004) work on 'action inquiry.']

Content of Chapters: Nine Methods

The book contains nine chapters, each presenting an original method for assessing and stimulating a dialogical self. The chapters reflect different levels of functioning, that is, they are 'climbing' from a personal level to social and organizational levels (see Table 1). Whereas the first four chapters focus on the content and organization

Table 1 Authors, methods and content of chapters

Author	Method	Content
Ch. 1. Nir	Negotiational Self	Win-lose vs. win-win in decision making
Ch. 2. Visser	Self-Confrontation	Awareness of personal meanings in career
Ch. 3. Lengelle	Expressive Writing	Narratives of different inner voices in career
Ch. 4. Konopka & Van Beers	Composition work	Bringing together the verbal and non-verbal
Ch. 5. Van Loon & Van den Berg	Dialogical Leadership	Moving between different leadership positions
Ch. 6. Krotofil	*I*-positions and Focus Group	Personal positions and focus group discussion
Ch. 7. König & Clarke	Dialogical Culture	Dialogue between different cultural positions
Ch. 8. Zomer	Team Confrontation	Giving space to deviant voices in teams
Ch. 9. Van de Loo	Organization Confrontation	Dominant and hidden voices in organizations

of one's personal position repertoire, Chaps. 5, 6, 7 concentrate on the functioning of individuals in groups and cultures. Chapter 8 deals with processes on the team level, and Chap. 9 focuses on processes on the level of the organization. Altogether, the chapters examine the content and organization of *I*-positions in personal, social, cultural and organizational contexts.

Each chapter starts with a theoretical exposition which shows the conceptual relevance of the specific method and then proceeds with an extensive presentation of the method together with an illustrative case study. Finally, each chapter answers two questions: (a) for which problems is the method particularly suitable and (b) which practitioner qualities are needed to apply the method appropriately and successfully?

In Chap. 1, Dina Nir offers a *Negotiational Self Method* that guides people towards resolving inner conflicts and making every-day (major and minor) decisions that support personal happiness and well-being. The theory-driven method integrates the dialogical self with inter-personal negotiation principles and suggests that decisions people make are the result of an internal negotiation between *I*-positions that push and pull the self in different and opposing directions. Such internal negotiations lead to decisions that vary from low integration that satisfies some *I*-positions at the expense of other *I*-positions to high integration that is able to creatively satisfy opposing *I*-positions at the same time and therefore enhance well-being.

Chapter 2 presents a *Self-Confrontation Method* in the context of career counselling. Harmien Visser starts this chapter with the consideration that in today's complex world, with many job losses and reorganizations, people are forced to shape their own career over and over again. Such changes invite people to become engaged in processes of self-reflection, dialogue and meaning-making. The Self-Confrontation Method, a narrative method for assessing and stimulating the personal meaning system, is presented as a tool that provides an answer to these challenges in career counselling. After an introduction on the history and background of the method, Visser describes how the method can be used to study the content and organization of one's personal meaning system.

In Chap. 3, Reinekke Lengelle emphasizes the importance of narrative career counselling in a society where work is increasingly insecure and the diversity of work roles has proliferated. She argues that in a situation in which individuals have to navigate in a complex and multifaceted world, the awareness of their dialogical multiplicity is a potential asset. Her approach, *Expressive Writing*, includes creative and reflective writing exercises for career development and enables participants to uncover, construct and write stories about their own career. It involves a dialogical learning process – one in which internal as well as external conversations are stimulated through writing exercises. More precisely, it fosters the expression of *I*-positions, stimulates the expansion of those positions and leads to the development of meta- and promoter positions.

Chapter 4 is devoted to a procedure, *Compositionwork*, to study an organized position repertoire in both verbal and non-verbal ways. As Agnieszka Konopka and Wim van Beers explain, the method is based on Dialogical Self Theory and inspired by Japanese Zen gardens. In this method, participants are invited to create a composition with the use of stones of varying size, form, colour and texture, which represent relevant *I*-positions, externalized in the creation of a personal landscape of mind. In the overview of this landscape, a meta-position is taken which facilitates the understanding of the dynamic relationships between the different and opposite *I*-positions. By their abstract and sensory quality, stones help to evoke and symbolize non-verbal aspects of *I*-positions. The method combines two basic dimensions of the self, the verbal/reflexive and the nonverbal/sensory, as an optimal condition for the integration of conscious and non-conscious levels of the self.

Chapter 5 is devoted to a *Dialogical Leadership Methodology* presented by Rens van Loon and Tessa van den Berg. The authors pose that effective leadership requires a reflexive and dialogical mindset that makes them better prepared to deal with complexity, interconnectedness and continuous change as a response to problems in globalizing organizations. They see leadership as a way to open up and use different *I*-positions in the self (e.g., as entrepreneur, manager, coach, expert) as an effective response to complex environments in business. They show how dialogical leaders develop the capacity to move flexibly back and forth between such positions and how these positions can be combined into new adaptive patterns. They demonstrate how theoretical notions, like promoter position, internal versus external positions and centring versus decentring movements in the self, can be meaningfully applied in the practice of leadership.

In Chap. 6, Joanna Krotofil introduces a *Personal Position Repertoire* (PPR) method in combination with focus group discussion. This combination was designed with the aim of studying the content and organization of *I*-positions, not only internally within the self but also in social interaction with real others. This procedure allows us to study the process of positioning and repositioning and the construction of common meanings as emerging in a group context. The advantage of this approach is that participants have the opportunity to discuss and share their *I*-positions with other participants so that they have an opportunity to further refine, articulate and even change their original formulations. Krotofil examines the role of institutional power and collective voices in the process of renegotiation of the self in the 'in-between' space of voices of participants who migrated from one country to another.

In Chap. 7, Jutta König and Kate Clarke observe that increasingly in our globalizing world, people that have lived or grown up in different cultural contexts experience stress related to different cultural voices in their personal position repertoire. The authors show that power structures exist between cultural positions as related to dominant discourses in society and how these structures are mirrored in the dialogical self of migrants. On the basis of these considerations, they propose a method of Dialogical Culture Coaching that can be used to explore the personal cultural position repertoire on an emotional level and to facilitate acculturation processes through dialogues between personal cultural positions. They employ repositioning statements, in-between and meta-positions as stepping-stones to developing a dialogical culture coaching approach. This method enables migrants to become aware of subtle power relationships between personal cultural voices that are related to dominant discourses in society. This awareness makes it possible to address and transform institutionalized collective power structures.

In Chap. 8, Peter Zomer starts with the observation that in today's corporate environment teams take a central role in the production of goods and services and that their collective intelligence is capable of tackling complex challenges like innovation, crisis management or problem analysis. In this context, he presents a *Team Confrontation Method* devised to break counterproductive patterns of cooperation in teams. It draws on a blend of Dialogical Self Theory in combination with other approaches such as Weick's conceptualization of sense-making and Senge's method of systems thinking. Basic concepts underlying this method are collective and deviant voice, collective valuation and collective affect. Zomer demonstrates in detail how counterproductive patterns in teams can be broken with the aid of lever deviant voices that open up new experiences and behavioural possibilities.

Finally, Chap. 9 is devoted to a method of *Organizational Self-Confrontation*, presented by Richard van de Loo. He describes this method as suitable for assessing and revising organizational stories in the service of team- and organizational development. Van de Loo demonstrates that the method helps to clarify not only the main concerns, dilemmas, fears, hopes and ambitions within a team or organization, but also the dominant and more hidden voices of the members. His aim is to show how the acknowledgment of the less dominant voices stimulates the dialogue within the team or between different departments of an organization. Inspired by the multivoiced nature of the self, he presents the case of two different groups in a hospital unit, one group consisting of unit managers, the other one of medical specialists. He shows how the stimulation of dialogical relationships within and between the participants improved their cooperation and led to a more shared view on the organizational structure.

The present book includes a broad variety of theory-guided methods and each chapter presents a detailed protocol for the application of a specific technique. It should be emphasized that the protocols are not absolutes. This is a theory based on dialogue and the use of the protocols should be dialogical. Therefore, the protocols should not be sealed in amber. Instead, a good protocol should be adapted rather than adopted. Therefore, I would like to propose the reader to keep this message in mind while reading the different chapters.[1]

We may remember Kurt Lewin's famous statement that there is nothing more practical than a good theory. I would like to add that a theory needs good practice in order to add value to self and society. I hope that this book will embody the intimate interconnection of theory and practice as a contribution to an open relationship between self and society.

Radboud University of Nijmegen
Nijmegen, The Netherlands

Hubert Hermans

[1] With appreciation I quote one of the anonymous reviewers who strongly emphasized this point.

References

Bakhtin, M. (1984). *Problems of Dostoevsky's poetics.* (C. Emerson, Ed. and Trans), Minneapolis, MN: University of Minnesota Press.

Georgaca, E. (2001). Voices of the self in psychotherapy: A qualitative analysis. *British Journal of Medical Psychology, 74,* 223–236.

Goffman, E. (1959). *The presentation of self in everyday life*. London: Penguin Books.

Hermans, H. J. M., & Gieser, T. (2012) (Eds.). *Handbook of dialogical self theory*. Cambridge, UK: Cambridge University Press.

Hermans, H. J. M., & Hermans-Konopka, A. (2010). *Dialogical self theory: Positioning and counter-positioning in a globalizing society.* Cambridge, UK: Cambridge University Press.

James, W. (1890). *The principles of psychology* (Vol. 1). London: Macmillan.

Kegan, R., & Lahey, L.L. (2009). *Immunity to change: How to overcome it and unlock potential in yourself and your organization.* Boston: Harvard Business Press.

Leijen, A., & Kullasepp, K. (2013). All roads lead to Rome: Developmental trajectories of student teachers' professional and personal identity development. *Journal of Constructivist Psychology, 26*, 104–114.

Torbert, B., et al. (2004). *Action inquiry.* San Francisco: Berret-Koehler.

Valsiner, J. (2004, July 11–15). *The promoter sign: Developmental transformation within the structure of the dialogical self.* In XVIII biennial meeting of the International Society for the Study of Behavioral Development, Ghent.

Chapter 1
Becoming the Leader of Your Decisions

Dina Nir

> *The self is by definition always a complexio oppositorum [collection of opposites]* (Jung, 1970, p. 716)
>
> *Dumbeldoor: It is our choices, Harry, that show what we truly are, far more than our abilities.* (J.K. Rowling, Harry Potter and the Chamber of Secrets)

Humans are prewired to experience internal tension and conflict. Being the complex beings we are, we often find ourselves overtaken with emotions, thoughts, desires, and urges, each pulling and pushing us in different directions. To move from internal disarray to actionable behavior, and conduct our lives with some purpose and perhaps a flicker of grace, we need to make a never-ending stream of decisions. These decisions govern every aspect of our lives, whether small or large, mundane or life changing, at home or at work. In fact, one could say that the person you are at this very moment, and the precise circumstances of your life are the sum total of all the decisions you have made to date. In other words, we are the sum of our decisions. Therefore, how well we make these decisions, matters. How deeply we understand what we really want, how wisely we choose, and how astutely we expand our options, profoundly affects the quality of our lives and consequently the lives of those around us. In this chapter, I will offer a novel approach by which to better understand our dilemmas and inner conflicts, and present a four-step method that is designed to guide people towards a mindful decision making process that effectively resolves dilemmas in a way that supports well-being and flourishing.

Negotiational Self Theory

To gain an understanding of how we manage our inner conflicts we first need to understand how the *self* is structured. A fundamental tenet of the Dialogical Self (DS) theory (Hermans, 1996) maintains that the self is not a single unit, but is rather

D. Nir (✉)
Ono Academic College, Kiryat Ono, Israel
e-mail: dr.dinanir@gmail.com

H. Hermans (ed.), *Assessing and Stimulating a Dialogical Self in Groups, Teams, Cultures, and Organizations*, DOI 10.1007/978-3-319-32482-1_1

multifaceted and complex. More specifically, DS theory suggests the self is organized as a dynamic landscape of autonomous *I*-positions (i.e., positions of the self, or selves) that continually influence each other through dialogical interchanges. Each *I*-position is endowed with different memories, motives and feelings, and has a unique story to tell from its own experience and its own stance. Just as in any social system, the internal society of *I*-positions is diverse and political. Some *I*-positions are dominant and overpowering whereas others are more quiet and subdued. Some tend to be supportive, caring and confidant, while others tend to be fearful, derogative and criticizing (Hermans, 1996, 2001; Hermans & Dimaggio, 2007; Hermans & Hermans-Konopka, 2010; Hermans, Kempen, & Van Loon, 1992; Hermans, Rijks, & Kempen, 1993).

As our mind wonders from one position of the self to the next, from one thought to another, an endless array of emotions, urges, desires and needs are elicited and experienced. However, these different internal pulls and pushes rarely work in symphonic tandem. In fact, most often than not they move in different directions, clashing, colliding and conflicting with one another. Think of the first moment you wake up in the morning. Do you promptly align all your *I*-positions, put your legs on the floor and decisively begin your day? Or, do you deliberate, negotiate and plead with yourself, as some *I*-positions are ready to responsibly get out of bed and others prefer staying under the protective warmth of the covers. An overwhelming majority (95 %) of people I have taught and trained over the years (students and managers alike) describe this as the first inner conflict they encounter of the day, every day. The picture is just as clear when we look into the last inner conflict of the day. Almost all admit that they battle between going to sleep and watching a little more TV, reading or surfing the net, writing emails, etc. If we look at both these experiences as framing our waking hours, than it becomes apparent that from the moment we get up to the moment we go to sleep we encounter and need to resolve hundreds of inner conflicts and make as many decisions. It seems that our multifaceted and dialogical self functions and directs ongoing behavior through a continuous movement from chaos to order, from collision to action, from conflict to resolution.

The Internal Negotiation

Building on the dialogical nature of the self, Negotiational Self Theory (NST; Nir, 2009, 2012; Nir & Kluger, under review) suggests that just as between people, whenever conflict erupts within the self and a decision is called for, the dialogical interchange between *I*-positions takes the form of a negotiation process. As the internal negotiation unfolds, contrasting *I*-positions come to the foreground to promote their standpoint, and advocate their unique perspective with the aim of influencing the decision. As arguments and counter arguments are presented, internal clashes erupt within the self. Like self-absorbed actors zealously fighting over the limelight, so *I*-positions battle for their place in the internal landscape of the mind. As the first *I*-position opens the negotiation with a stand in one direction, a second

I-position quickly responds, always voicing the opposing concern. Then a third, a fourth, and a fifth *I*-position offers additional conflict-relevant information, supporting some *I*-positions and negating others. Being complex and multifaceted, many *I*-positions can take part in this negotiation, each bringing forward different 'for' and 'against' considerations, offering new information and countering the previous stands with additional details and autonomous concerns. Gradually, two opposing coalitions of *I*-positions are formed, each supporting a different pole of the conflict. One group supports one plan of action, while the other group collaboratively roots for the opposing alternative. Just like people in a complex negotiation, *I*-positions are able to join forces and form coalitions in order to exert more influence on the opposing side. This tense complexity is the reason why the experience of being of multiple minds is taxing emotionally. It evokes feelings of confusion, frustration, distress and even helplessness. In fact, the experience of multiple *I*-positions battling each other is so unnerving and distressful that at times people opt to make a decision, any decision, just to have the conflict over and the internal battle behind them.

The Modes of Internal Negotiation

If such a rich array of motivated *I*-positions takes part in the internal negotiation, how does the self arrive at a decision? How do the *I*-positions reach an agreement? To understand the different modes of internal negotiations it is important to first outline how scholars describe the different modes of interpersonal negotiation. Overall, negotiation researchers discern between two fundamental negotiation strategies, a distributive (i.e., coercive, win-lose) strategy, and an integrative (i.e., collaborative, win-win) strategy (Deutsch, 1973, 2000; Fisher & Ury, 1981; Follett, 1942). Negotiators applying a distributive strategy tend to view the negotiation as a competition or a zero sum game, in which gains of one party come at the direct expense of the other. To maximize their outcome, competitive negotiators use tactics such as threats, manipulation, intimidation and unilateral action to persuade the other party to yield. The outcome of such negotiations is either a win-lose agreement in which one party gains and the other party comes out losing, or at best it results in a compromise agreement in which both parties end up gaining some and losing some. These negotiations create low joint benefit for both parties and are often detrimental to their relationship. In contrast, integrative negotiators actively listen to one another, build trust and work together to find creative solutions. A process of co-construction takes place that leads to win–win solutions, yielding high joint benefit and 'expanding the pie' (Weingart, Thompson, Bazerman, & Carroll, 1990; Zubek, Pruitt, Peirce, McGillicuddy, & Syna, 1992).

While these negotiation strategies have been widely delineated and researched within the interpersonal domain, they have not been previously discussed in relation to the internal landscape. NST is the first theory to incorporate these negotiation strategies into the workings of the self. It specifically maintains that as in negotiations between people, internal negotiations can either adhere to coercive win-lose or integrative win-win negotiations (Nir, 2012). These strategies are reflected in the way different *I*-positions communicate and influence each other. When a distributive win-lose negotiation transpires within the self, dominating *I*-positions take over the negotiation space and direct the decision in their favor. As a result, the winning *I*-positions come out satisfied, pleased and strengthened, whereas losing *I*-positions come out lacking, discontent and unfulfilled. As long as the needs, aspirations, fears and concerns of any *I*-positions remain unmet, the self continues to suffer from incongruences and deficiencies. No matter how much satisfaction the winning *I*-positions bring to the self, unsatisfied *I*-positions will continually seek redemption and work toward fulfilling their wants and needs. In some situations, they may harass and haunt the self or even prevent carrying out the decision. Freud called this psychological process 'The return of the repressed' and believed that any discrepant or unsatisfied part of the self will eventually reappear in consciousness or in behavior to seek fulfillment (Freud, 1923, 1939; Westen, 1998).

In contrast, when a collaborative negotiation develops within the self, different and conflicting *I*-positions are equally acknowledged and considered, and an integrative solution is constructed that fully addresses and simultaneously satisfies the needs and interests of multiple *I*-positions. While integrative negotiations are clearly more beneficial for the self, recent research has shown that when trying to resolve their inner conflicts most people end up making coercive win-lose decisions (Nir, 2012).

Negotiational Self Method

Oscar Wild once said, "Hell is to drift, heaven is to steer". I find this quote accurately portrays the phenomenological experience of inner conflict as well as our need to move from automatic coercive win-lose patterns towards mindful decision-making that enhances well-being. To help manage and steer the inner conflict towards an integrative solution a four-step process was developed and empirically validated termed Negotiating Self Method (NSM). The method was tested in laboratory studies and shown to be effective in enhancing integrative solutions (Nir, 2012). More recent research has revealed that integrative decisions are associated with higher post-decision satisfaction, increased enthusiasm, and most importantly with higher general well-being (Nir & Kluger, under review). When applying NSM, a democratic negotiation process is facilitated, which makes room for opposite opinions to come forward and be equally heard. A creative win-win solution is actively constructed which acknowledges and satisfies the different and opposing concerns. This change in focus drives us beyond our automatic dichotomous coercive thinking. It takes us off the path of least resistance, and places us on the road towards richer more mindful options that are more likely to enhance our well-being.

In the following section, I will outline the four steps of the NSM and for each step I will present a rationale and guidelines. In addition, to make the process more tangible, I will accompany the guidelines with a case study of a young woman I have named Roni, who is facing a stressful inner conflict regarding her career.

Roni's Conflict

Roni is a lively, energetic and talented 28-year-old MA student who is currently writing her thesis while supporting herself with two jobs. Her main income comes from her work at an international airline company, while she also works as a part-time paramedic at the National Emergency Services. Feeling overworked and stressed by her multiple responsibilities at her different jobs Roni had made the difficult decision to give up her second job as a paramedic and subsequently submitted a letter of resignation to her boss. However, knowing her deep commitment and abilities in her field, Roni's boss persuaded her to rethink her decision and come back with a final answer within a couple of weeks. Roni approached me for counseling on this matter since she felt torn and conflicted about her decision. Her work as a paramedic was much more than just a job and it pained her to relinquish it. To help Roni resolve her inner conflict, I guided her through the NSM step-by-step.

Step One – Framing the Conflict

Rationale

Inner conflict is a stressful and chaotic experience that can be best described as a cacophony of battling voices that overwhelm the self. As alternative options are conjured, a pendulum effect takes place that throws the mind from one possible course of action to the opposite one. No matter how many voices support a specific option, counter voices keep coming forward to stress the grave cost associated with that alternative and convincingly promote the opposing alternative in its stead. This is the reason inner conflicts are cognitively confusing and emotionally taxing.

To begin a process of transforming the internal wrestling arena into an ordered negotiation space, the first step of the NSM aims to quieten the internal clash and to create a framework that will allow the different *I*-positions to voice their unique perspectives, aspirations and concerns in a calm and systematic manner. Therefore, NSM begins with first voicing the full story of the conflict, and then defining the conflict poles in simple and straightforward terms.[1]

[1] Note that NSM is designed to address and resolve conflicts that originate from tangible real-life situations, and not general or philosophical conflicts, such as a conflict between 'work and family', or between 'security and self-fulfillment'.

Guidelines

If you are working on your own, write down your 'conflict story' as you would if you were writing in a journal. If you are coaching or counseling, actively listen to the story and from time to time check your understanding, encourage your client to elaborate, and summarize. In any case, it is important to tell the 'full story' of the conflict and its background in detail. To start the process of managing the inner conflict, after describing the conflict story, take a moment to define the opposing poles of the conflict in 'for' and 'against' terms.

Example

Listening to Roni's story, I learnt that being a paramedic was much more than just a job for her. She first joined the emergency medical services as a teenager, and gradually became a professional part-time paramedic, tending to emergencies and saving lives. On the one hand, she gained much meaning and satisfaction from this work and found it empowering, vitalizing and character building. At the same time, the work was emotionally stressful, time consuming, and limited her social life. After sharing her conflict story with me, Roni defined the conflict poles as "for quitting my job as a paramedic" and "against quitting my job as a paramedic".[2] By the end of this first step, Roni felt I was 'with her' since now both of us were 'holding' her difficult situation, and she had a clearer understanding of her internal dispute. Next, I gave Roni a brief review of the coming NSM steps, and described the main aim of creating a win-win solution that will satisfy all her battling selves. This preview instilled hope within Roni and she was enthusiastic to proceed onwards.

Step Two – Mapping the Conflict Space

Rationale

Inner conflicts typically contain a wide array of *I-position*s, each representing a unique perception and assessment of the situation at hand. Therefore, the aim of the second NSM step is to create a map or chart of all the *I*-positions that are relevant to the conflict. The more *I*-positions we are able to elicit, the more self-knowledge we gain and the better our understanding of the conflict space. Therefore, the guiding principle here is "if it's about me – it's with me". I stress this aspect since in order to reach win-win solutions, each conflict-relevant *I*-position must be taken into account. Even those voices we tend to judge or label as negative, unworthy, or undesired (i.e. my childish, petty, mean, lazy or weak self) need to be heard and addressed

[2] It is also possible to define the conflict in "for" and "for" terms. For instance, "for quitting my job as paramedic" and "for continuing my job as a paramedic".

as they often represent underlying fears, frustrations and concerns. Regardless of the content voiced, it should not be repressed or ignored, but rather fairly acknowledged and empathetically accepted. By bringing the value of each *I*-position into clear view, and honoring it for its contribution to the self, we begin the process of creating a whole-system shift from internal conflict, hierarchy and dichotomy to democracy and cooperation.

Guidelines

An effective way to start the process of voice mapping is to first elicit the voices which support the 'for' pole of the conflict. This should be continued until all aspects, concerns and perspectives have been elicited. Then it is time to start eliciting the *I*-positions that support the opposing 'against' pole. A simple and effective technique for revealing more *I*-positions is to ask: "What else is relevant in this situation?" This usually prompts a broader search for relevant information and ensures comprehensive data collection. It is crucial to record every *I*-position in such a way that all information can be seen and appraised in a single glance. A simple and effective technique to record and manage the mapping process is by writing it on a paper divided into two columns under the two poles of the conflict (see Table 1.1 for an example).

Most people find this mapping process very helpful and encouraging, because they begin to gain some order and lucidity. The previously chaotic and emotional internal negotiation subsides, and clearly articulated understandings become present. It is no longer the limited space of the mind that holds the information but the page, and so different *I*-positions no longer need to fight for attention. Each has its space, each is affirmed, and each is fully and equally acknowledged. As a result, there is a clear shift from drifting to steering and the internal landscape moves from hierarchy to social equality, from anxiety to confidence.

Example

Overall, Roni and I spent a good 30 minutes working according to the guidelines, mapping the different 'for' and 'against' voices. As we finally concluded the mapping process, it was clear Roni felt lighter and more lucid. For the first time she was able to see the whole picture of her conflict and the feelings of chaos and distress were replaced with increased confidence and a touch of optimism.

Table 1.1 presents the map of Roni's conflict space (some details and names were changed for anonymity purposes). Note how many aspects and concerns Roni was able to voice. Significantly more than she was aware of in the first place. In fact, the Table became an exposé of who Roni is at this point in time. To gain an understanding of the internal split Roni was burdened with, I invite you to do the following exercise: Read the 'for quitting' column of the table without reading the 'against quitting' column. By exclusively reading the list of voices urging her to leave her

Table 1.1 The map of Roni's conflict space

For quitting my job as a paramedic	Against quitting my job as a paramedic
The work is very challenging physically.	I get so much satisfaction from this work. I save lives.
The work is also very challenging psychologically. The sights I see are often gruesome and distressing. We see people in very harsh life situations, and these sights stay with me for a long time afterwards.	Helping people is something that I really love to do, helping for the sake of helping. I feel I make a difference in the lives of people.
The responsibility is enormous. I have to make life and death decisions in seconds.	This work develops character. Aspects I'd like to strengthen within myself: quick decision making, quick thinking, finding good solutions for problems, working well under pressure, inner strength, organization skills and more.
The system doesn't support paramedics if something goes wrong. My friend was left out in the cold when he made a mistake.	My Master's advisor thinks I shouldn't quit. "It will be good for me in the long run," he said.
My shifts often include staying in the station and working at the call center answering emergency telephone calls. I really don't like this work at all. It's boring work and the shifts seem horribly long.	This job balances my other job because it gives me so much meaning.
I feel I've not reached the professional level I need to perform at.	I get to see and learn about extreme human conditions and situations that I would not encounter anywhere else.
Exams – I'm continually being tested and I need to study and pass exams. It's a lot of pressure.	The extra income helps a lot.
Someone I know (Jack) said this is no work for a woman.	I get a pension and benefits from my job as a paramedic.
I'm single and looking for a partner and this work may scare some men off.	I also get nice benefits during holidays (like very cheap airline tickets).
I don't feel like working so hard all the time. I'm tired.	Prestige – people are very impressed when I tell them what I do.
There is always a lot of pressure to finish up emergency situations quickly and move on to the next person in need, so I don't get to connect with the people I help.	My mom wants me to continue because I have control over my schedule and do something that is very interesting.
I'm only 28 and I already feel burnt out.	When I work I'm on a continual "high", I feel vitalized and full of life. It is empowering work!
The pay is terrible; I work long hours and get paid very little.	I love the buzz I get when we are on our way in the ambulance. It's cool to run red lights with the siren on.
There is always some problem with my paycheck so I often feel I'm working for nothing.	I will miss the action if I leave.
The general environment is cold and harsh. People are not friendly at all.	I enjoy working with Tom. He is lots of fun and I always learn from him.

job you will probably find yourself utterly convinced Roni must quit being a paramedic at once. At the same time if you only read the 'against quitting' column, you will most likely find yourself unable to fathom how Roni could ever do anything else but be a paramedic. This pendulum effect reflects the essence of being in conflict, and allows us some insight into how Roni felt being in such a bind.

The Table also reveals the rich array of *I*-positions that underlie the conflict. Each voice Roni elicited and mapped in the Table comes from an *I*-position that has its own perspective on reality and its own agendas, memories, and feelings concerning working as a paramedic. While some *I*-positions are more elaborately portrayed in the Table and voice two or even three sentences, most of Roni's *I*-positions are more modestly voiced, and are represented by a singular sentence. For instance, "I as responsible" is voiced by the sentence: "The responsibility is enormous. I have to make life and death decisions in seconds.", and "I as Tom's friend" is voiced by the sentence: "I enjoy working with Tom. He is lots of fun and I always learn for him." However, the *I*-position "I as burned out" is voiced by two sentences: (1) "I don't feel like working so hard all the time. I'm tired." and (2) "I'm only 28 and I already feel burnt out." And the *I*-position "I who loves the action" is voiced by three sentences: (1) "When I work I'm on a continual "high", I feel vitalized and full of life…" (2) "I love the buzz I get when we are on our way in the ambulance…" And (3) "I will miss the action if I leave."

Although there is an evident association between the different sentences in each column, and some *I*-positions are more elaborately portrayed than others are, note that the Negotiational Self Method has reduced the hierarchy among the *I*-positions. There are no 'important' or 'less important' voices, all *I*-positions are equally heard and valued. The voice "I save lives – this is very satisfying." is as valued, honored and acknowledged as the voice "I get nice perks during holidays".

Step Three – Revealing Underlying Interests and Needs

Rationale

A well-known principle in interpersonal negotiation suggests that to promote collaboration negotiating parties need to reveal the deep-seated interests that underlie the initial positions they state. Positions are the tangible concrete demands or specific solutions people put forward. For example, an employee asking for a raise in salary and stating her demand in monetary terms, is voicing her position. Interests on the other hand are the underlying concerns, desires, and fears that spring from deep human needs that continually seek fulfillment (Burton, 1984; Lewicki, Saunders, & Minton, 1999; Nierenberg, 1968). The multiple interests underlying the employee's position may include a desire to improve her standard of living, to feel her work is appreciated, to be paid equally to her peers, to save towards her children's' education, etc. By focusing on interests rather than on positions, seemingly resolution-resistant conflicts often become solvable. The reason is that interests are intangible, and therefore can be addressed and satisfied in many creative ways. In contrast, a position is a specific demand, and so can either be accepted or rejected. Therefore, focusing on interests in interpersonal negotiations enables the parties to expand their understanding and learn what is important, and then use this information to build creative solutions and construct mutually beneficial win-win agreements (Fisher & Ury, 1981; Thompson, 2001).

As in interpersonal negotiations, the Third Step of NSM encourages the inquiry into the concerns, fears, dreams and aspirations that reside at the base of the inner conflict via specifically designed questions. The purpose of these questions is to bring to mind extensive self-knowledge regarding the conflict. In doing so, the internal space becomes clarified and what was once obscured and shadowed is out in the open, clearly articulated – and finally illuminated.

Guidelines

To gain an understanding of the different interests underlying the inner conflict, the following questions should be addressed regarding each of the two alternatives that frame the conflict (i.e., the 'for' and 'against' conflict poles): "Why do I really want this alternative? How will choosing this alternative deeply benefit me? What are my deepest concerns and fears regarding this alternative? What are my deepest aspirations and dreams regarding this alternative? What else is important to me in this situation?" The answers to these questions should be added under the relevant 'for' and 'against' poles, in continuation of the content mapped in the second step.

Example

Table 1.2 describes the deep-seated interests, concerns and fears Roni mapped in the third step.

Table 1.2 Roni's underlying interests and needs

For quitting my job as a paramedic	Against quitting my job as a paramedic
What worries me most is that that I may not be a good enough paramedic.	If I quit this job, I will always feel a quitter and be ashamed of myself.
Deep down I don't really feel confident that I'll always be capable of saving lives.	I'm really worried that if I stop being a paramedic I'll miss it and then if I want to come back I'll be out of practice and have a problem returning to this work.
I'm actually worried that someday I might make a grave mistake with a patient in need.	Being a paramedic makes me a better person and more professional at everything else I do. I'm worried that if I leave, I might become less effective in all other areas of my life.

Notice how these interests tap upon insecurities and worries that are at the base of Roni's *I*-position as a paramedic. It seems that in addition to all the voices mapped in the previous step, Roni questions her level of professionalism on one hand, and on the other hand she feels she will never forgive herself for quitting and giving up on the opportunity to become more professional at her work and at everything else she does.

Step Four – Building an Integrative Win-Win Solution

Rationale

After gaining a deep and broad understanding of the conflict space and its underlying interests, Step Four of the Negotiational Self Method focuses on transforming what was previously experienced as an internal clash into a mindful collaborative (i.e., win-win) process that tends to all the selves. Therefore, the final NSM step guides towards building a comprehensive resolution that follows a singular distinct principle: The solution must address, acknowledge and honor each and every *I*-position that was elicited and mapped in the previous stages. This principle aims to override the automatic tendency to use traditional heuristics that emphasize the weight (i.e., importance) or political station (i.e., dominance) of *I*-positions and make dichotomous decisions. Furthermore, it makes room for internal leadership to emerge that intentionally steers the self towards integration and collaboration where all aspects of the self are equally addressed and none are left unacknowledged or unmet.

Guidelines

To offer a means of evaluating and leading the self towards an internal win-win agreement, I offer a key variable termed Decision Integration (DI) level (Nir & Kluger, under review). DI measures the extent to which different and opposing *I*-positions are satisfied in any given decision. A low DI outcome refers to a coercive 'zero-sum' decision, in which *I*-positions grouped at one pole of the conflict come out victorious and satisfied, whereas *I*-positions grouped at the opposing pole remain lacking and unmet. A high DI outcome refers to a mutually satisfying decision in which the needs of all conflicting *I*-positions expressed and listed in the 'for and 'against' table are addressed and met. The more *I*-positions satisfied in a given decision the more integrative it is and the higher the Decision Integration (DI) level. Note that while some *I*-positions can be soothed and appeased by gaining insights and new perspectives on old stories, other *I*-positions can only be fulfilled by creating new outcomes in the real world. Therefore, reaching high DI mandates becoming the leaders of our life circumstances and proactively taking action in areas we did not tend to previously.

Example

As described earlier, Roni approached me for counseling after she had already decided to resign, to leave her job and career as a paramedic. Her decision clearly reflects low DI since all those aspects she rejoiced in, which vitalized and empowered her and gave her life meaning and purpose, were on the chopping block. Like many of us, she was imprisoned in the belief that the conflicted parts within herself are irreconcilable and that to end her internal battle painful decisions must be made.

So how did Roni conclude her NSM process? How integrative was the solution she reached? Once Roni could literally see the map of who she was in her conflicted situation, and once she understood that she is the leader not the follower of her circumstances, she was able to create a high DI solution. After just a few moments of contemplation, she came up with a rather detailed plan of action. Her plan included the following components: First, she decided to renegotiate her terms with her boss. She would ask to reduce the amount of shifts she does per month, and no longer work at the emergency call center. The idea of negotiating with her boss was new to her. She previously thought she could either reject her situation or accept it. Now she realized she could change it. Regarding her professional level, Roni decided to continue her training as a paramedic and to become even more proficient and independent. At the same time she realized that she has nothing to be ashamed of and that if she looks at the facts, she already was a very good paramedic. She recognized that if she is professional enough to be sent out to treat a person in need, then she is probably the right person for the job and that she can allow herself to feel confident and happy. In addition, instead of seeing the frequent exams she needs to take as something negative, she realized that this is the path to her becoming more and more professional at her job. Concerning her pay, she decided to go to the Salary Department and finally clear up all the problems she was having. She also realized that the 'right man', when he comes along, would be proud of her being a paramedic, and that since she already has many friends at the National Emergency Services, it's ok if not all the people there are warm and friendly.

Note that once Roni had decided to stay, she had automatically satisfied all the *I*-positions under the 'against quitting my job as a paramedic' pole. To reach high DI she also came to take active responsibility over the all *I*-positions that were listed under the 'for quitting' pole. In doing so, Roni ended up caring for all her *I*-positions, for herself as a paramedic, as a professional, as a woman, and as a person. She faced her inner conflict, bravely delved into it, and came out the other side brighter, lighter, wiser, and resourceful. She came out winning.

Discussion

Who Should Use This Method and When?

The Negotiational Self Method (NSM) was specifically designed to address any type of real life inner conflict in which a decision is called for, whether personal, financial or professional. Moreover, it is just as effective for resolving mundane or recurring life conflicts as it is for arriving at major life changing decisions. NSM can either be applied to resolve a dilemma you yourself are facing or it could be used as a professionally guided process within organizations or in a consulting session. In any case, the key to being successful in applying NSM is to fully adhere to the precise guidelines and directions described in each step. If you decide to apply this method to guide someone else in their quest towards optimal decision-making, it is important to apply active listening and unconditional support for your client as they go through the process. In addition, make sure you have attained enough experience resolving your own dilemmas before you begin working with others. Once you have gained enough hands on experience with the four stages, you will find that you have acquired a deeper understanding of the method and a greater belief and confidence in its effectiveness. You will also discover that as you guide others to attain their win-win solutions, your own trust in the potential of reaching such integrative solutions to different life conflicts will enhance, and you will become more optimistic and empowered to boldly take on more of life's conflicts and challenges.

In my own experience working in organizations, I have found that NSM also offers a powerful tool for managers. As organizations function and grow through ongoing decision making processes, how these decisions are made highly effects the bottom line of the organization. A manager that learns to create high DI win-win decisions will be able to better address the multiple demands of the different stakeholders and come up with proactive and creative solutions that can lead the organization forward towards achieving its full potential.

A Good Dialogue

Conceptualizing the workings of the self in the state of inner-conflict as negotiational, was inspired by the theoretical advancements put forward by DS theory. NST draws heavily on the notion of *I*-positions that advocate unique perspectives, cognitions and emotions, as well as deep interests and motivations. Like different people in a society, they maintain a degree of autonomy and at the same time have the ability to function as part of a larger collective. NST also gains from the idea that different *I*-positions are able to communicate and influence each other through a dialogical interchange that resembles how people interact and converse with one another.

The method presented here, supports a self developmental process, described by Hermans and Hermans-Konopka (2010) as a 'good dialogue'. By systematically directing the internal dialogue towards integrative win-win solutions, the guidelines outlined in the four-step methodology adhere to the principle criteria of a good dialogue. Specifically, the process of framing and mapping the inner conflict as created in steps one-to-three organizes a 'space' in which new self-knowledge may be obtained. By this, the method promotes an active and unconditional process of internal listening, one that is in coherence with Rogers (1951) humanistic practice of active listening and unconditional positive regard. NSM promotes a democratic acceptance of all *I*-positions relevant to the conflict space regardless of their station in the internal hierarchy. The process also aims to elicit deep-seated interests thus promoting self-knowledge, and reducing biases and misunderstandings within the self. Finally, by persistently directing the inner conflict towards a mutually beneficial win-win solution that simultaneously addresses the needs of opposing *I*-positions, NSM creates a fertile ground for innovative thinking, and most importantly sets into motion the movement from relations of power and dominance among *I*-positions to unconditional acceptance and honoring of the other within the self.

Mindful Decision Making

I have recently begun describing the Negotiational Self Method as Mindful Decision Making. As outlined in this chapter, NSM offers an alternative to our automatic tendency to be caught up in the emotional pulls and pushes of the inner conflict, and mindlessly succumbed to one position or another. Yet, the question is can NSM lead to mindful decision-making? Mindfulness is an ancient practice rooted in Buddhism and in other contemplative traditions that actively cultivate conscious attention and awareness. Mindfulness is described in the West as "the awareness that emerges through paying attention on purpose, in the present moment, and non-judgmentally to the unfolding of experience moment by moment" (Kabat-Zinn, 2003). A recent metacognitive model of mindfulness (Jankowski & Holas, 2014) suggests mindfulness is a state of consciousness that is itself aware of continuous changes in the content of consciousness – an awareness of one's perceptions, emotions, images and thoughts. In other words, the witnessing of current experiences without being entirely immersed in them, so that events are seen as occurring in the mind, rather than as direct reflections of reality (Teasdale, 1999). Because mindfulness promotes continual non-judging contact with experience there is opportunity for insight. Moreover, maintaining clear and open awareness over time leads to knowing one's true nature. Being mindful is consistent with Hermans' notion of eliciting a Meta *I*-Position – a higher order *I*-position that impartially witnesses or observes the interchange among other *I*-positions, also inferring a degree of separation and non-attachment between Meta position and other positions (Hermans, 2003). Mindful practice also emphasizes the role of unconditional and compassionate acceptance of the self and of others. Compassion arises automatically with mindfulness and teaches the ameliorating effect of self-understanding, patience and balance during difficult experiences. The benefits of being mindful for well-being are manifold. A growing body of research has demonstrated that practicing mindfulness can bring improvements in both physical and psychological symptoms as well as positive changes in health, attitudes and behavior.

I liken the process of NSM to Mindful Decision Making for several reasons. First, the process assists in creating some detachment from the emotional experience of the conflict. Specifically Step Two, which facilitates a process of cognitively forming and wording the different 'for' and 'against' concerns, enables to attend to the conflict space as an observer, with a somewhat detached view. Looking from above at the internal power plays at the different concerns and voiced *I*-positions without taking part in them. Second, NSM advocates being patient and taking the time to systematically elicit as many perspectives as possible to gain a deep understanding and a broad view of the conflict space. Both steps two and three assist in becoming open to new conflict relevant information and to insightful new perspectives, and deep seated aspirations and fears that otherwise may have remained unseen. Often clients gain new insights during these steps and pensively conclude with "I didn't realize until now that my conflict was also about X and Y."

To meditate is also about allowing 'whatever is' to surface, and accepting any content with tenderness and compassion. NSM likewise advocates a democratic unconditional acceptance of whatever aspects of the self emerge, equally valuing all. The outcome of such an inclusive mapping process in steps two and three is an encompassing holistic view of self and a detailed psychological map of the person experiencing the inner conflict. Moreover, the final step of NSM prescribes befriending, attending, and taking responsibility over all aspects of the self. Most people are taught and eventually come to believe that they need to choose between the different 'for' and 'against' perspectives. That is, to choose between *I*-positions, and so automatically creating hierarchy and division within the self. The self becomes split between the so called 'more important', 'better' perhaps even 'morally superior' aspects of the self and the 'the weaker' 'less important' or 'undesired' selves. However, NSM predicates a shift in perspective towards a more inclusive, democratic, humanistic and companionate view of the society within the mind. Instead of feeling obligated and predestined to choose between *I*-positions, the method slows down the process, and services the belief that what first seemed chaotic, polarized and irreconcilable, can become better understood, accepted and reconnected. When this shift in perspective is adopted, new ways of thinking emerge, and multiple creative, novel and applicable courses of action come to mind. As we steer our internal negotiation from battle and coercion to acceptance and collaboration, we become the mindful leaders of our own decisions and the wise navigators of our well-being.

References

Burton, J. W. (1984). *Global conflict: The domestic sources of international crisis*. Brighton, UK: Wheatsheaf Books.

Deutsch, M. (1973). *The resolution of conflict*. New Haven, CT: Yale University Press.

Deutsch, M. (2000). Justice and conflict. In M. Deutch & P. Coleman (Eds.), *The handbook of conflict resolution: Theory and practice* (pp. 41–64). San Francisco: Jossey-Bass.

Fisher, R., & Ury, W. (1981). *Getting to yes: Negotiating agreement without giving in*. Boston: Houghton Mifflin.

Follett, M. P. (1942). Constructive conflict. In H. C. Metcalf & L. Urwick (Eds.), *Dynamic administration: The collected papers of Mary Parker Follett*. New York: Harper.

Freud, S. (1923). *The ego and the id – The standard edition of the complete psychological works of Sigmund Freud* (Vol. 19). London: Hogarth.

Freud, S. (1939). *Moses and monotheism*. New York: Vintage Books.

Hermans, H. J. M. (1996). Voicing the self: From information processing to dialogical interchange. *Psychological Bulletin, 119*(1), 31–50.

Hermans, H. J. M. (2001). The dialogical self: Toward a theory of personal and cultural positioning. *Culture & Psychology, 7*(3), 243.

Hermans, H. J. M. (2003). The construction and reconstruction of a dialogical self. *Journal of Constructivist Psychology, 16*(2), 89–130.

Hermans, H. J. M., & Dimaggio, G. (2007). Self, identity, and globalization in times of uncertainty: A dialogical analysis. *Review of General Psychology, 11*(1), 31–61.

Hermans, H. J. M., & Hermans-Konopka, A. (2010). *Dialogical self theory: Positioning and counter-positioning in a globalizing society*. New York: Cambridge University Press.

Hermans, H. J. M., Kempen, H. J. G., & Van Loon, R. J. P. (1992). The dialogical self: Beyond individualism and rationalism. *American Psychologist, 47*(1), 23–33.

Hermans, H. J. M., Rijks, T. I., & Kempen, H. J. G. (1993). Imaginal dialogues in the self: Theory and method. *Journal of Personality, 61*(2), 207–236.

Jankowski, T., & Holas, P. (2014). Metacognitive model of mindfulness. *Consciousness and cognition, 28*, 64–80.

Jung, C. G. (1970). *Collected works of CG Jung: Psychology and religion: West and East* (Vol. 11). Princeton, NJ: Princeton University Press.

Kabat-Zinn, J. (2003). Mindfulness based interventions in context: past, present, and future. *Clinical Psychology: Science and Practice, 10*(2), 144–156.

Lewicki, R. J., Saunders, D. M., & Minton, J. W. (1999). *Negotiation* (3rd ed.). Boston: Irwin/McGraw-Hill.

Nierenberg, G. I. (1968). *The art of negotiating: Psychological strategies for gaining advantageous bargains*. New York: Hawthorn.

Nir, D. (2009). *The negotiational self: Identifying and transforming negotiation outcomes within the self*. Ph.D. thesis, The Hebrew University of Jerusalem, Jerusalem.

Nir, D. (2012). *Voicing inner conflict: From a dialogical to a negotiational self. Handbook of dialogical self theory*. Cambridge, UK: Cambridge University Press.

Nir, D. & Kluger, A. N. (under review). Making decisions that make us happy.

Rogers, C. (1951). *Client-centered therapy: Its current practice, implications and theory*. London: Constable.

Teasdale, J. D. (1999). Emotional processing, three modes of mind and the prevention of relapse in depression. *Behavior Research and Therapy, 37*, 53–77.

Thompson, L. L. (2001). *The mind and heart of the negotiator* (2nd ed.). Upper Saddle River, NJ: Prentice Hall.

Weingart, L. R., Thompson, L. L., Bazerman, M. H., & Carroll, J. S. (1990). Tactical behavior and negotiation outcomes. *International Journal of Conflict Management, 1*(1), 7–31.
Westen, D. (1998). The scientific legacy of Sigmund Freud: Toward a psychodynamically informed psychological science. *Psychology Bulletin, 124*(3), 333–371.
Zubek, J. M., Pruitt, D. G., Peirce, R. S., McGillicuddy, N. B., & Syna, H. (1992). Disputant and mediator behaviors affecting short-term success in mediation. *Journal of Conflict Resolution, 36*, 546.

Chapter 2
Self-Confrontation Method: Assessment and Process-Promotion in Career Counselling

Harmien Visser

In recent decades a lot has changed in vocational and career guidance. Former vocational psychologists made a match between the individual and suitable occupations by comparing personality traits to the requirements of a job. Later on, career guides translated someone's answers on interest inventories and aptitude tests to occupational possibilities. Those objective techniques are rooted in the assumption of stable personal characteristics and secure jobs in bounded organizations.

However, in today's globalized, complex world, with many reorganizations and redundancies, this approach neglects the subjective perspective of clients, living in a continuously changing and uncertain world. Career counsellors are confronted with existential questions about life issues from, for example, clients in the so-called 'mid-life crisis', long-term unemployed adults and elder people that want to phase out their career. People are forced to shape their own career over and over again. Many are required to change their routinized behavior, are forced to choose a (subsequent) study or to take substantial steps in their career, like choosing a quite different profession.

Such changes invite people to become engaged in processes of self-reflection and meaning-making. In addition to hard data as intelligence and skills, soft factors such as motivation, needs and values, have become important ingredients for good career (self) management. Concepts as locus of control, (labour-) identity and emotional intelligence were introduced. Therefore, the current objectifying approaches have become insufficient (Cochran, 1997; Savickas et al., 2009). The role of the career guide is changing from the role of the expert who gives advice, to a counsellor: a person who facilitates an awareness process. "People do not separate the rest of their lives from the career choices they make (…); decisions in a changing world are influenced by and grounded in prior experience. Allowing individuals to tell

H. Visser (✉)
Vis-à-Vis Agency for Career Guidance and Counselling, Leeuwarden, The Netherlands
e-mail: Hvisser@vis-a-vis.nl

H. Hermans (ed.), *Assessing and Stimulating a Dialogical Self in Groups, Teams, Cultures, and Organizations*, DOI 10.1007/978-3-319-32482-1_2

their stories can help us to understand their concept of career and what is possible." (Reid, p. 135).

A method that offers an answer to these challenges in career counselling, is the Self-Confrontation Method (further referred to as SCM). The SCM is based on the Valuation Theory (Hermans & Hermans-Jansen, 1995) and Dialogical Self Theory (Hermans & Hermans-Konopka, 2010). Both theories are based on narrative psychology, in which people are considered as story-tellers. In dialogue with a counsellor, clients examine how they value experiences in everyday life (the manifest level) and how basic motivations give direction to their behavior on a less visible (latent) level. The SCM is a systematic method, that enables individuals to an in-depth self-investigation, from which desired goals or changes can be determined. By composing their life story together with a counsellor, clients elaborate their pivot questions in a broader perspective. The SCM creates moments of reflections, from which people can survey themselves with all their strengths and weaknesses and thus can come to new insights. By analyzing the relations between various life experiences and interpreting the feelings underneath, clients can discover a unifying life theme, from where they are able to create a new, future narrative. The collaboration between counsellor and client, the use of a computer program (as discussed in paragraph 3) as well as the combination of objective and subjective data make this method a valuable resource for taking concrete steps in the direction of (career-) alternatives.

In this chapter I will discuss the Self-Confrontation Method in the context of career-counselling and outplacement. After an introduction to the history and background of the SCM and its place within literature about career counselling, the specific characteristics and the performance of the method are described. Next, the SCM is illustrated with a case study and finally, how it can be used effectively in everyday practice.

History and Background Behind the Self-Confrontation Method

Personality psychologist Hubert J.M. Hermans constructed in 1972, together with psychotherapist Els Hermans-Jansen, a quite unique approach. He designed a valuation theory and a self-confrontation method with the following characteristics: (1) a gradual and theory-guided *transition between assessment and change*; (2) people can express a great diversity of '*units of meaning*' (several concrete acts and events, related to each other, that play a significant role in their daily lives); and (3) a *cooperative relationship* between client and consultant in which clients are invited to act as the investigators of their own self-narratives and are challenged to take initiatives to change their situation (Hermans & Hermans-Jansen, 1995). During the next 30 years, theory and method were continuously modified and expanded, based on feedback from practice.

The Self-Confrontation Method is a narrative method. People experience the world around them in their own way. But by telling their experiences to another person, events become particularly meaningful. By asking people what they perceive as important and meaningful in their lives when they look at their past, present and expected future, clients are invited to start an in-depth process of reflection. While telling, arranging and rearranging their stories, people explore how they are functioning, where they find strength and challenges, from which perspective they look at the world and how they are involved with work, family, friends, colleagues etc. Looking back at the past from the present, they can interpret the past in another, potentially more meaningful, way. By doing so, people can integrate new and sometimes confusing experiences in their life story and discover the deeper motivations underneath their behavior. From there, they can re-create their self-narratives and develop life- and career perspectives in a more conscious way.

Theoretical Basis of the Self-Confrontation Method

Hermans' vision on the 'self' is, just like Cochran (1997), influenced by the theory of William James (1890): the 'self' is not seen as a whole, but consists of multiple 'selves' or '*I*-positions', depending on where people are or which role they are playing at some point in their life. Those can be internal positions (*I* as uncertain, *I* as mother, *I* as employee, etc.), and external positions (for example an inspiring teacher, a sibling or neighbor, even opponents or enemies may take a place in our minds as we utter – as part of imaginary interactions – imprecations to them). Also a coach or counsellor may enter the life of a client as an external position in the self and may give, in a particular period of the client's life, a valuable contribution to his or her internal dialogues and self-reflections.

Hermans and Hermans-Jansen (1995) were inspired by the polyphonic novel of Dostoyevsky, that is composed by a number of characters that are not subordinated to the author, but have their own voice, thoughts and behavior. Each of these characters can have independent viewpoints, sometimes disagreeing with the author, even rebelling against him. They can tell their own story and are involved in dialogical relationships. This idea led to the theory of 'The Dialogical Self' (Hermans and Hermans-Konopka, 2010). The central theme in his theory is that there is not only a dialogical relationship between the self and his (social) environment, but also between different positions in the self of one and the same person. For example: the '*I* as open' and the '*I* as closed'; the 'assertive one' and the 'wait-and-see' or the 'fighter' and the 'quiet one'. One has to know the parts, to understand the functioning of the self as a whole.

Two suppositions underlie Hermans' narrative and dialogical approach. First: space and time are basic components of storytelling ("in order to make a meaningful plot structure, it is necessary to move back and forth between 'plot' and 'events'"). Second: stories acknowledge both the perception of reality and the power of imagination ("stories are organized around actors who, as protagonist and antagonist, have opposite positions in a real or imaginary space") (Hermans & Hermans-Jansen, 1995, p. 11). Even when people are outwardly silent, they have, for example, imaginary dialogues with others (rehearsing an important debate or repeating parts of earlier conversations), with their own conscience or their reflection in the mirror (Watkins, 1986). In the SCM people have the chance to discover their '*I*-positions'. Clients are invited to tell their life story and formulate short sentences, so-called valuations, that are related to their different *I*-positions. By examining these valuations, clients are broadening their view and are able to develop a '*meta-position*': to look at different parts of themselves from a distance and see their interrelationships. So they can move to different and opposite sides in the landscape of the self and search for dominant or hidden *I*-positions. From there it is possible to develop a so-called '*promoter position*', which organizes and gives direction to a diversity of other positions in the self and functions as a catalyzer that enables persons to come into action (Hermans, 2014, pp. 148–149).

The importance of such a narrative approach can be derived from the latest insights about career counselling. Cochran (1997), Reid (2005), Savickas et al. (2009)) and several international research groups show the need for new ways of career guidance, placing clients in their context. They emphasize the importance of human flexibility, adaptability and life-long learning in today's rapidly changing globalized world. Narrative-based approaches are considered as useful to facilitate clients to construct their own life story, make meaning of their experiences and take an active role in designing their future life and career, in connection with their environment. Some examples (I place the similarities with Hermans' theories in Italics):

- Schein (1985) developed the concept of 'career anchors'. He discovered that in their career managers are guided by a fundamental pattern of motives. For this purpose he designed a model for a *dialogue* - the career anchor interview - to help clients understand what factors shape a career (and by which it is limited) by *exploring patterns and themes* in events during their education, work situations and free time.
- Reid (2005) mentions the (international) concerns about young people who leave education early, often being unskilled employed, combined with periods of unemployment (p. 126). She discusses how *narrative-based approaches* can be useful for helping them with educational and vocational decision-making. In particular the need to place emphasis on '*meaning*' by *profound listening*. A listening "that believes that the client's understanding of the meaning of events, and how they think, feel and construe the impact of them on their lives, is the important meaning" (p. 129) and that "allows the client to construct a career narrative that resonates significantly with their values and interests for life, not just for a job" (p. 132).
- Like Hermans, Savickas (2005) believes that due to the increasing uncertainty and turbulence of the present world, it is more and more important *to develop a flexible identity*. Work loses its central role in the life course of people. It is replaced by something new, that Savickas calls 'biographicity': the ability *to integrate new and confusing experiences in one's own life*. He considers a career

as an *active construction* of the own life story and not passively diagnosed by tests or questionnaires. Savickas (2011) developed his 'Career Story Interview' (CSI) from the idea that language and stories qualify themselves to provide the best *meaning*. In the CSI Savickas works together with the client towards a *'life portrait*', similar to Hermans' *life story*. In the space between client and counsellor unifying life themes from significant experiences emerge, in order to formulate career scenarios and to come to concrete steps.

- Savickas et al. (2009)) and eight representatives from various countries formed an international research group to formulate innovative approaches of career counselling. They developed a 'life-design intervention model', rooted in *contextualism*, focusing on *meaning making* "through intentional processes *in the ongoing construction of lives* (…). *Self and identity are constructs built by the person through continuing reflection and revision* (…). Career denotes a moving perspective that imposes *personal meaning* on *past* memories, *present* experiences and *future* aspirations by patterning them into a *life theme* (…). Today, it is the life story that holds the individual together and provides a biographical bridge with which to cross from one job to the next job" (p. 246).
- The Australian lecturer McMahon and three South African psychologists (2012) proved that a narrative approach was being successfully trialled in a developing country with a non-western population of disadvantaged clients. Facilitating the client's development by *reflection, connectedness, meaning making, learning and agency*. They believe that "*telling stories* assists clients to *make meaning* of their life experiences and to recognize the holistic, culturally embedded nature of careers" (p. 128). "*The identification of life themes, or the threads or patterns that connect life stories, is facilitated through meaning making*. Meaning making and interpretation help individuals make sense of what has happened in their past and present, and more importantly, project their future life career course" (p. 134).
- Cochran's (1997) narrative approach of career coaching also depicts the person as a motivated storyteller: "Narrating a story about oneself creates a distance between *a person as narrator and a person as an actor or participant in that story*" (p. 25). Cochran describes several narrative techniques that (in *a strong collaboration between client and counsellor*) can contribute to: elaborating the career problem – composing a life history – founding a future narrative – constructing reality – changing a life structure – enacting a role – crystallizing a decision. According to Cochran, the counsellor has to support the client in getting a *sense of agency*. "A person has a strong sense of agency if he or she has formed an authentic narrative of self as an agent taking meaningful and effective action toward major goals of life" (p. 30).

The SCM includes most of the foregoing elements; even goes a step further (see also the following paragraph). The use of open-ended questions can overcome the problem of one-sidedness or partial stories. Formulations of valuable experiences are put in the words of the clients themselves. Analyzing the outcomes of affect scores on previously phrased valuations, it is not the subjective perspective of the counsellor but the clients' own interpretation that matters. The SCM takes stock of subjective data (valuations and affect-scores), analyses these in an objective manner and offers methodic steps for the use of the results. This procedure, as well as the visual representation of all data that offers an overview of the clients' life story, make it an accessible and structured method that gives clients the feeling to be in charge.

The Self-Confrontation Method: How It Works

People are always situated in time, place and space (*contextualism*, Hermans, 1995, pp. 7–8). The meaning that people attach to their most important experiences, will change depending on the stages in their life and the context or environment in which they operate. Every recollection of an event, all circumstances that individuals have been going through, touched them more or less. This will influence their outlook on life and themselves. People and their valuation systems are therefore considered as a dynamic whole that is continuously evolving. Thus, the SCM has three functions:

- A *diagnostic* function: as an assessment of content and organization of the valuation system as a whole.
- *Process-promotion*: as a validation/invalidation process in which clients reorganize their life (or parts of it) through self-reflection and action.
- *Evaluation:* evaluating the changes when people retell their self-narrative, enabling them to investigate how actual experiences or actions contribute to their feelings of well-being.

In a cyclic process clients – as spectators – are telling about their past, present and future – as actors in their own life. By re-interpreting their past, they are better able to understand the present and to create a new future in a more conscious way. Thus, new vocational choices, life- or career perspectives are developing.

Reason and emotion alternate in identifying all facets that are meaningful in one's life. Facets that have shaped the person and that affected the person's functioning, motivation and sense of well-being. In an intensive process of self-reflection clients analyze their thoughts and feelings. This is supported by a computer program that produces insight in similarities among valuations by means of the Pearson's correlation coefficient. A high correlation between the affective similarity of several different life experiences is likely to reflect a common underlying pattern or a guiding life theme. The leading thread, the basic theme in the story, becomes perceptible. This way, clients' self-confrontation with their own actions and feelings create a process of growing awareness, in which they develop a better insight into the organization of their valuation system and the themes that govern it.

While telling and reflecting, clients discover which fundamental motives have a guiding influence on their behavior. In the many years of their research and practice, Hermans and Hermans-Jansen (1995) became aware of the importance of the duality of human motivation. On the one hand a person is an autonomous entity that attempts to maintain and enhance itself as an independent being. On the other hand one has the need to be part of some larger whole and feel love and contact with others. So in the valuation theory two main basic motives are distinguished:

- The S-motive: the pursuit of self-enhancement (for example by defending, to maintain or to develop oneself); to distinguish oneself from other persons.
- The O-motive: longing for contact and union with something or someone else (for instance a person, group, object or the surrounding world in general); the desire to be part of a larger whole.

These two basic motives can be conflicting (e.g., if someone consolidates him- or herself while opposing another person), but also mutually complementary (e.g., feeling self-esteem while being accepted and loved by family members). Both the S- and the O-motive can be experienced in positive as well as negative ways, depending on the satisfaction or frustration of the motive.

In the SCM clients analyze how the basic motives S and O occur in their life. Based on this, they design a plan, clearly showing which basic motives they want to accentuate in the future. Do they want to have a high degree of autonomy, being independent and standing out from others? Or would they prefer to make themselves serviceable, feeling connectedness, in a receptive attitude? Or do they wish those two motives being more in balance? Through this increased self-knowledge, desired personal changes, career directions or vocational goals become clear and measurable.

The Process of Self-Investigation

The self-investigation process follows five steps:

1. **Constructing a self-narrative: formulation of valuations**

In the first stage of a self-examination people are invited – based on a fixed set of open-ended questions (so-called 'triggers') – to tell their life story, referring to past, present and future. E.g.: "Has there been anything of major significance in your past life that still continues to exert a strong influence on you?" Depending on the setting, special sets of triggers are being used. For example career-triggers, triggers for delinquents, for adolescents and for chronically ill patients and triggers about bereavement. Special sets of questions have been developed for stress and burnout, vocational guidance, team management and personal leadership. Even a set of drawn pictures for children from 9 to12 years is being used.

Career-triggers focus on issues like:

- persons, circumstances and experiences from the past;
- the current function and tasks;
- one's strengths;

- one's weaknesses;
- leisure activities
- major changes in career;
- goals that one is trying to achieve in life and work
- persons against whom one is opposing;
- persons with whom one feels attachment.

By asking the questions, an association process starts, in which clients tell those experiences that have a particular meaning to them: events that may have touched them or affected them in some way. Those can also include a thought, a film they recently saw, a dream or a fantasy, even a picture or a drawing. Thus, in an intensive dialogue with themselves and with the counsellor, clients explore their own life like a voyage of discovery. At the end of each self-investigation two questions are added, concerning the General Feeling ('How do you feel in general recently?') and the Ideal Feeling ('How would you ideally like to feel?') both in work and private.

In about 3–4 h a complete overview of a person's situation is created, in which the main facets of the client's life emerge. These facets can include one's present career question, influential persons or role models, competencies, values and future fantasies, and issues in the person's social and private life. The wide variety of life experiences is becoming manifest in the formulation of 20–50 short sentences depicting a valuable event located in time and space, so-called 'valuations'. They should reflect the personal meaning that the '*I* as author' relates about the 'Me as actor', involved in the interactions with others. Clients write these valuations on little cards.

Of course, a complete life cannot be described in full. The intention of the triggers is to enlighten precisely those experiences which constitute the tip of the iceberg and which are typical for the life of the client. From this perspective looking at their own lives gives clients already order and structure.

Examples of valuations you will find in the following case study.

My client, let's call him Roger, has fulfilled various technical positions at the Foreign Office, but could not serve operational functions any more due to his weak physical condition. He was transferred several times against his will, resulting in conflicts with his executives. Besides, he was not happy with the content of those functions. The disappointing experiences affected him so much that he got overstrained. On his own initiative, he had himself retrained to ICT specialist, after which he was many years responsible as a manager for the automation of various departments. Because of the poor health of his son, he let himself transfer from abroad to the Netherlands. Later, he refused a new foreign appointment and therefore resigned.

At the time of the self-investigation Roger is interim manager at a temporary staffing agency. However, due to lack of jobs, the agency has no more application for him and requests counselling support aiming at outplacement. In the first interview I suggest to do a self-investigation using the Self Confrontation Method. This method appeals to him, because he gets the chance to investigate the deeper motivations in his life, so he can make a well-thought choice in which direction he wants

Table 2.1 Some of Roger's valuations

Till my 15th it was as if my father wasn't there. Either he was at work, or he was studying and then I had to be quiet.
Before my 27th I didn't have any urge to perform. If I only enjoyed the things I did.
The message that my son had a brain tumor made me feel paralyzed.
Despite of my weak ankles I keep running, though I should choose another way of exercising.
I think it's great to see my kids grow up. I am thankful to help them to develop into independent actors.

to develop in the next 5 years. Roger takes this opportunity to get answers on three specific questions:

- *Why have the conflicts with his executives had such a great impact on him?*
- *People in his surroundings find him hard to fathom because he does not show any feelings; what does this say about his emotional world?*
- *Which career options are possible to him?*

Some of Roger's valuations are provided in Table 2.1.

2. **Connecting valuations with affects**

The things people care about, are fed by deeper lying feelings. Hermans had the fundamental assumption that each valuation has an affective connotation, i.e. emotional value. Those feelings become visible by means of a computer-scoring program, using a list of affect terms. The affects are assigned to a number of categories:

- Self-enhancement (S), expressed in feelings as self-esteem, strength, self-confidence and pride.
- Contact and union with others (O), reflected by affects as caring, love, togetherness and intimacy.
- Positive (P), expressed by joy, happiness, safety or inner calmness.
- Negative (N), expressed by anxiety, loneliness, inferiority or anger.

In career counselling sometimes the following category is added:

- Stress (S), reflected by affects as nervousness, stress or agitation

Reading each valuation, the client is asked to indicate the affect intensity on a scale from 0 to 5. This results in a typical affect profile, the so-called 'affect modality', which is a quantified pattern of affects that is connected to the sentence.

Some other valuations, combined with their affective indices, are mentioned in Table 2.2.

3. **Analysing the results**

With the aid of a computer program, client and counsellor together are examining the valuations and their affective profiles: whether the S or the O-motive is dominating, whether both basic motives appear to be equally strong, and whether the profiles are positive or negative.

Table 2.2 Valuations with their affective indices

		S	O	P	N
1.	Due to my weak physical condition they assigned me to a job I did not want.	4	1	2	22
2.	The combination of reassignment, no appreciation and low working pressure made me overstrained when I was 28.	1	1	1	29
3.	Due to the brain tumor of my son I have not been able to enjoy life for at least a year.	4	13	2	19
4.	When I was young I had regularly fights with my sisters: I often lost my temper and stroked them a blow. I regularly got punished, sometimes unearned.	5	5	1	24
5.	The dentist pulled 8 teeth when I was 12. Because mom and dad weren't there, I went on my bicycle to our former neighbor to be comforted.	9	10	2	27
6.	I became angry when my boss addressed me on the bad functioning of the group. I thought that criticism was not justified.	14	1	4	20
7.	After the conflict with my executive, I burst in a fit of crying. The doctor arranged for me to be taken home and I spent three months being ill from stress.	0	4	0	29
8.	How did I recently feel in general?	23	24	19	11
9.	How would I ideally like to feel in general?	29	26	30	1
10.	How did I recently feel in general at work?	12	8	8	15
11.	How would I ideally like to feel in general at work?	29	18	26	1

Note. S: affect referring to self-enhancement; O: affect referring to contact and union with the other; P: positive affect; N: negative affect. All indices range from 0–30.

In the first analysis of the outcomes of Roger's self-narrative, we take a look at the General Feeling (nr. 8 in Table 2.2). It becomes clear that both feelings of self-enhancement and feelings of contact and union are rather high. However, in the General Feeling with respect to work (nr. 10) Roger feels less Self-enhancement and Contact with the Other, and there are less Positive and more Negative feelings. It is very unpleasant for him being put on the sideline, especially now that he's been unemployed for the last half year. There is a rather large discrepancy between his General Feeling at work (nr. 10) and his Ideal Feeling at work (nr. 11).

Subsequently, one of the valuations is taken as a starting point for further analysis. The choice of which is to the client. People often choose a valuation referring to the main issue they want to discuss. It also can be a sentence that strikes them, an affective rating that has surprised them or a sentence that shows an extremely high or low score on any of the affects. The computer program has calculated correlations between the affective profile of starting valuation and the profiles of all other valuations. The chosen valuation and the highest correlating valuations, each of them written on separate cards, are compared and explored. One by one clients place the relating cards next to the chosen valuation, being invited to explore what these experiences have in common. The counsellor supports this association process by asking specifically about the common meaning (the latent emotional level), accurately writing down the answers and at the end repeating them all. This way, clients can create a summary of the theme that emerges from the interdependence of this group of valuations and write it down on a colored card.

The very first valuation Roger selects for a modality analyses, is sentence 2:

"The combination of reassignment, no appreciation and low working pressure made me overstrained when I was 28." This valuation shows extremely low scores on the basic motives S and O, like on the positive feelings, together with a very high level of negative feelings. In the pattern of affective indices we find strong similarities to successively valuations 1, 7, 4, 5, 6, and 3 (see Table 2.2).

Comparing these sentences one by one with the chosen valuation nr. 2, Roger points to the similarities with the following keywords: "things I do not control; unhappy; lack of appreciation; feeling powerlessness; loneliness; anger and injustice; my lightheartedness was gone."

Looking back at this cluster of valuations, Roger tells me that in his youth he experienced his social world as unjust to him. He often responded as a hothead, resulting in much hassle (with sisters, parents or executives). Roger: "When I experienced injustice or powerlessness, there was a great risk of becoming angry. I tried to maintain myself, which was suppressed. At those moments feelings of loneliness and unhappiness laid in wait." The affective patterns in the sentences 1, 2, 3, 4, and 7 are showing that Roger has no grip on the situation. The valuations are highly loaded with negative affect, together with a low level of self-enhancement and contact and union with others.

I continue by asking him how he managed to survive in this threatening, unfair world. Roger replies: "If I can control situations I don't like, I am trying to change them. I am approaching people and looking for the confrontation." The emphasis on the negative feelings, together with a higher level of self-enhancement in the valuations 6 and 10 in Table 2.2, reflect this need for self-maintenance. Roger feels opposed to someone or a situation that is threatening his self-esteem and he is trying to defend his position. This movement is reflected by strength, energy and self-confidence.

After that, the opposite pole can be examined, based on the most negatively correlating valuation with the pivotal sentence.

When we examine the opposite pole of sentence 2, we discover sentence nr. 12 (see Table 2.3). A valuation with a completely opposite emotional pattern, with maximum scores on S, O and P and a score of zero on N.

Valuations 13 to 18 (Table 2.3) are highly correlating with sentence 12. Roger mentions the following keywords about this group of phrases: "happiness, connectedness, joy, being active, being in connection with my feelings, personal growth; pursuit of happiness for myself as well as for another."

By placing the summaries of the positive and the negative pole (typically, sources of energy and sources of frustration) next to each other, an important theme can emerge. For example, people may discover that they have never effectively used their S-motive, always gratuitous doing what others expected. Such a client could formulate as a theme:

Table 2.3 The opposite pole

		S	O	P	N
12.	S (wife) is my buddy. We share weal and woe and although sometimes we tell each other some hard truths, we always make up again and we love each other very much.	30	30	30	0
13.	My trip to the Caribbean made me very aware of the question: what is the meaning of life?	24	25	27	5
14.	I am dreaming about emigrating with my family to a developing country to do something in the domain of housing, education and income.	27	27	20	12
15.	I like to challenge people to look across borders, in order to get them thinking.	28	24	27	4
16.	I can enjoy a good glass of whiskey and good food with my family, with friends or just with the two of us.	30	30	30	0
17.	I love to perform on stage with my choir. I would like to have some more performances, to stay motivated to practice.	27	23	24	3
18.	I intend never to get overstrained again.	30	23	27	1

"I do have a lot of power, but I have used it only to keep up appearances. At important moments I often have exhibited escape behavior. I always easily pulled back and let other people make decisions, handed down to what is happening around me."

Frequently found themes are, for example, the dilemma between freedom and union, or between looking for challenges and the desire for safety/security.

Putting the two summaries side by side, the following conclusion, referring to basic themes in Roger's self-narrative, arise: "Without connectedness happiness cannot exist. In my surroundings I want to be leading and not following. But at the same time I want to do so in union."

The dialogical self is appearing from Roger's inner world: the position 'I as a leader' referring to the S-motive and 'I as longing for union' referring to the O-motive.

4. **The validation process: awareness and change**

The confrontation mentioned above stimulates an awareness process. A similarity in affective profile between two sentences that are very different in their formulated content, may hint at a connection on a deeper level. Individuals become aware of behavior or circumstances that are preventing them from functioning effectively or from being happy. A client may discover a repeating pattern of feeling useless or inferior that emerges in stress situations. It is even possible that this person develops a certain perfectionism through the years, to compensate these unpleasant feelings of inferiority, resulting in becoming stressed out or even burnout. Through this increased self-knowledge, the tension between inferiority and perfectionism can be recognized. Together with the counsellor clients formulate changes or goals for the future in specific and achievable steps.

Roger formulates a vision for the future. He seems to be a bit moved when he realizes: "One of the most important things is that I want to be significant for people that surround me. If I can be liable to service other people, I can be happy." Roger has reached a meta-position from which he becomes aware that the S-motive has been dominant in his life hitherto, suppressing the need of being devoted to other people. Now, in formulating this vision, the balance of the S- and the O-motive is becoming more central. Self-enhancement and contact and union coexist, creating a high level of well-being. In the periods of his life in which he experienced no connection with others, both the S- and the O-motive were declining to nearly zero. "I got lost", in Roger's words. This discovery is very important for him for the future: connectedness is essential, even a precondition for a new job.

After this, an action plan can be formulated to be realized in everyday life. This so-called period of validation includes three phases: attending – creating – anchoring (the ACA cycle).

- First, persons are paying attention to the disadvantageous behavior that they discovered in their self-investigation, with particular attention to behaviors which deviate from this pattern, as an exception to the rule.
- In the next creating phase they will explore alternative ways of behavior and step-by-step experiment with it, gradually rising the degree of difficulty.
- In the anchoring phase clients are focusing on the conditions that are necessary, in order to get used to this new behavior and being able to show it in different situations.

To make a gradual transition between the foregoing discussions and the validation period to come, Roger is invited to formulate a concrete plan for the next few weeks. As an assignment to himself he writes down: "Every day I'm going to observe myself, being alert on the emergence of feelings of injustice and powerlessness. If they occur, I try to make a connection with people that surround me and consider it as a challenge, instead of feeling powerless and unhappy." He agrees to make daily notes in a diary, writing down all specific details: e.g. when, where, and with whom it occurs. This procedure enables him to integrate his different I-positions and to develop a promoter-position, that organizes other positions in his self and helps him to create a future self.

In career counselling various valuations about work or study and vocational choices (possibly obtained through psychological tests) can be related to the self-narrative. Based on the intended direction in which the basic motives should go according to the client, these alternatives can be judged as more or less desirable. Besides, the highest affective correlation with the 'Ideal Feeling' can give direction to career choices. Through the increased self-knowledge and new stimulating experiences people get inspired to change the plot of their life-story and to re-shape their own life and career.

In our next meeting we look at Roger's future career options, from the perspective of his new vision on the future. In his self-investigation he has formulated three options (see Table 2.4) in such a way that he is able to connect them with the emotional impact. That is, as if it has been realized already.

Table 2.4 Roger's future career options

		S	O	P	N
19.	I'm going to immerse myself into the theory of change management, because then I can create a more focused contribution to changes in organizations.	25	17	24	6
20.	I'm going to study a Master in Management of Information so that I can further develop in professional knowledge, to be able to support the goals of the organization better on a theoretical level.	26	14	20	7
21.	It would be a challenge for me to be in the public service, coaching managers and team members. Also, I would like to improve the efficiency in the technical field.	29	22	28	6

In the hierarchy of correlations with the Ideal Feeling at work (valuation 11 in Table 2.2), we find sentence 21 (Table 2.4) at the top. The basic motives S and O, as well as the positive feelings, show higher ratings than options 19 and 20, and it shows a relatively low score on the negative feelings. Besides, valuation 21 is a realistic way to go, because there exists a vacancy for such a job. But at the same time there is still another option, which takes up Roger's thoughts. That is sentence nr. 14 (see Table 2.3): dreaming about emigrating to a developing country. However, this option has a lower rating, because Roger has associated it with more negative feelings. The thought of emigration, giving up everything he has, produces a lot of fear and uncertainty, we discover in the matrix of feelings. But the idea to do developmental work in a poor country, fits perfectly with his newly formulated vision to be at the service of others, as appears from the high level of self-enhancement and affects referring to connectedness with others.

In the final phase of the outplacement Roger decides to apply for the in option 21 listed public function, but at the same time to investigate the possibilities for developmental aid in a poor country. His contract with the temporary staffing agency will not be extended, but he rents himself as an entrepreneur to the agency, to get started as an interim manager at the civil service.

5. **The second investigation**

After a period ranging from several months to a year, a second self-investigation can be realized, if necessary or desired. The same steps 1–4 are repeated. This investigation has an evaluating function: it shows if progress has been made and to what extent the formulated goals have been achieved. Also the direction of the change from the perspective of the basic motives is assessed.

There is no need of a second investigation with Roger. Because a year after our last meeting he writes me that he has moved with his wife to a Caribbean island. He has found a position as responsible for the governmental ICT facility. This position represents a productive combination of his experience as a manager in automation, and contributing to the development of this island. He tells me he is enjoying this new challenge in a very different environment, climate and culture. It is an acknowledgement for the self-investigation that we performed together. With the insights he received, he went to work: now he is more stable and calmer, he writes. He is suffering less from conflict situations, trying to follow the strategy he mentioned in his validation plans. According to himself, he has better control of his temper and he has learned to have a more relaxed view of life.

In Summary

Referring to this client, the Self-Confrontation Method initiated a process of increasing awareness, in which the search for the basic motives has worked very enlightening and has provided an important orientation towards his future career options. In the conflicts with his executives, the focus was on self-defense and opposition: a defensive form of the S-motive. His self-investigation has resulted in the unveiling of a basic need for connectedness, which was already present on a latent level, but which has now become more manifest. As his emotional world has become more transparent for Roger, it has become clear that when his need for connection with other people was not fulfilled, he got so upset that he got overstrained. At those moments he was not able to move from negativism to positivism, nor to reach self-esteem and union with others, feeling himself imprisoned in those unpleasant experiences.

Roger discovered not only *I*-positions like '*I* as a hothead' and '*I* as a victim of conflicts,' but also '*I* as a caring father,' '*I* as a loving partner,' and an '*I* as a technical civil servant.' And finally he became aware of '*I* as connected with others,' '*I* as a development worker' and an '*I* as independent entrepreneur.' In dialogue with himself, he has created a 'self' as a more integrated whole. He is now able to move from one type of valuation to another. In Hermans' words: he has reached 'psychological flexibility' (1995, p.115-117). Of course his 'hothead' will still appear in his life, sometimes. But his need to be subservient to others and feeling connectedness, revealed a new '*I* as going for challenges'. Learning the impact of his basic motives, he has now the capacity to move flexible between these various '*I*-positions.'

The formulation of a guiding theme has changed Roger's self-narrative. The discovery that the O-motive is essential for him, gives direction to his future prospects. The SCM has been empowering and encouraging him to face uncertainties in life and work. He is prepared to consider future life events, both positive and negative ones, as new possibilities for his further development.

Application of the SCM in Everyday Practice

Despite of the fact that it uses figures, statistics and a computer program, the SCM is definitely not a test. Individual data are not compared to a standard norm and clients should not expect to get a cut and dried advice. On the contrary: data and ratings only get their value by interpreting them by the clients themselves. The personal meaning, in the language of the clients themselves, is the central element.

For Whom?

Career counselling with the Self-Confrontation Method gives clients their own responsibilities and is therefore meant for those who want to reflect on their work in the broader perspective of their whole life. Outcomes from vocational tests or psychological therapy can be part of the investigation. But clients always have to be willing to submerge themselves in a process of deep self-exploration, and therefore must be in a psychologically healthy condition. That is, they have to be able to communicate clearly and to take some distance from their own situation. The SCM should not be used with people who are severely depressed or addicted to alcohol or drugs. Besides, some problematic situations can prevent clients of thinking about career options or changes. Clients who are in a divorce, for instance, are often involved in legal cases that have to be solved first.

Under the preceding conditions, the next groups of clients, in particular, are expected to have advantage from the career-SCM:

- persons who have to make a choice for vocational education after finishing high school or after a few years of vocational training and who are uncertain as to their professional direction;
- clients who are questioning their chosen current career track to be the right one;
- persons who – after a period of illness or unemployment – want to participate again in the labour market;
- within the context of management development, a human resources officer can apply the SCM with people who want to reflect on a next career move. What skills and capacities must be strengthened?
- if a discrepancy arises between job requirements and person, one may search for solutions either within the organization, or through outplacement in order to gain an insight into new opportunities and challenges.

The Duration

If it concerns only a relatively simple choice between some career options, the counselling can be done within a few weeks. The minimum number of sessions is four (one for telling the life-story, two for discussing the results, and one for formulating goals). However, it is possible that personal or relational problems show up in the course of the SCM. Still, also for those clients the SCM can be valuable, as an instrument to discover which next step (e.g., a particular kind of psychotherapy) is necessary. In other situations, when it concerns outplacement, or when it is necessary to investigate personal pitfalls and drawbacks that prevent clients from being effective, it possibly leads to a radical reorganization of their valuation system and future career perspective. In such cases the SCM can result in long lasting counselling from several months till over a year.

Required Skills for the Counsellor

Of course, SCM counsellors have to be familiar with the most common interview techniques and have to be able to keep a professional distance, being aware of possible transference and counter transference problems. But they also have to acquire knowledge about the theoretical framework and the details of this special methodology, combined with getting experienced to apply it in practical situations.

In this method, the client has a very active role. This requires a specific attitude of the counsellor, playing the part of an (active) mirror. First of all, SCM counsellors have to be very empathic: opening themselves up to the story of the client, inviting, listening actively in silence, asking in-depth questions, recapitulating and summarizing, remaining faithful to the client's words and intentions. When necessary they seek clarification, asking for specific details. In this way, a safe atmosphere is created, at first supporting the client in formulating valuations and structuring the self-narrative, later on in discovering connections between valuations and affect.

Further, there is a precarious balance between a following and a leading attitude in the dialogue. At one hand, counsellors are responsible for gathering a variety of valuations, both positive and negative ones. At the other hand, they must prevent clients from repeating themselves or becoming sidetracked. It's very important that counsellors withdraw from making normative statements and offering solutions to the clients' problem. Besides, they have to be prudent when giving their own interpretations and opinions. In dialogue with a less assertive client, it is not desirable to do so. With more assertive clients, the advice can yet be given, if the role of an expert is needed. Sometimes it even can be necessary to confront the client with contradictions in his story. It happens often that people repeatedly stick to existing themes and plots, because they experience a certain advantage of their old behavior. At some point in their life this was helpful for some reason. For example to survive extremely traumatic events by neglecting their negative feelings. Such clients are avoiding any exploration of negative experiences. The counsellor may have the impression that the client is attached to instant happiness and comfort, but this attitude has a deeper cause. However, not going into their negative experiences is preventing them from listening to the message of these experiences as a valuable source of information (Hermans & Hermans-Konopka, 2010). Counsellors have the opportunity to support such clients either by a compassionate or a more confrontational approach.

References

Cochran, L. (1997). *Career counselling: A narrative approach*. London: Sage.

Hermans, H. J. M. (2014). Self as a society of *I*-positions: A dialogical approach to counseling. *Journal of Humanistic Counseling, 53*, 134–159.

Hermans, H. J. M., & Hermans-Jansen, E. (1995). *Self-narratives, the construction of meaning in psychotherapy*. New York: Guilford Press.

Hermans, H. J. M., & Hermans-Konopka, A. (2010). *Dialogical self theory: Positioning and counter-positioning in a globalizing society*. Cambridge, UK: Cambridge University Press.

James, W. (1890). *The principles of psychology* (Vol. I). London: Macmillan.

McMahon, M., & Watson, M. (2012). Story crafting: Strategies for facilitating narrative career counselling. *International Journal for Educational and Vocational Guidance, 3*(3), 211–224.

McMahon, M., Watson, M., Chetty, C., & Hoelson, C. N. (2012). Examining process constructs of narrative career counselling; An exploratory case study. *British Journal of Guidance & Counselling, 40*, 127–141.

Reid, H. L. (2005). Narrative and career guidance: Beyond small talk and towards useful dialogue for the 21st century. *International Journal for Educational and Vocational Guidance, 5*, 125–136.

Savickas, M. L. (2005). The theory and practice of career construction. In S. S. Brown & R. W. Lent (Eds.), *Career development and counselling: Putting theory and research to work* (pp. 42–70). Hoboken, NJ: Wiley.

Savickas, M. L. (2011). *Career counselling*. Washington, DC: American Psychological Association.

Savickas, M. L., Nota, L., Rossier, J., Dauwalder, J. P., Duarte, M. E., Guichard, J., et al. (2009). Life designing: A paradigm for career construction in the 21st century. *Journal of Vocational Behavior, 75*, 239–250.

Schein, E. H. (1985). *Career anchors – Discovering your real values*. San Francisco: Jossey-Bass/ Pfeiffer (A Wiley Company).

Watkins, M. (1986). *Invisible guests: The development of imaginal dialogues*. Hillsdale, NJ: Analytic Press.

Chapter 3
What a Career Coach Can Learn from a Playwright: Expressive Dialogues for Identity Development

Reinekke Lengelle

> *Society is inside of man and man is inside society, and you cannot even create a truthfully drawn psychological entity on the stage until you understand his social relations and their power to make him what he is and to prevent him from being what he is not. The fish is in the water and the water is in the fish.* (Arthur Miller)

Writing expressive dialogues can be used to assist individuals in developing their career identities – that is: stories that are needed to help people position themselves in relation to the current labour market. Writing expressive dialogues entails having written conversations with various parts of us – much like a playwright does with his characters – and making developmental gains in the process. In Dialogical Self Theory (DST) terms, it means talking to and with various *I*-positions on the page, perhaps forming coalitions, discovering counter positions, and innovating and integrating the self (Hermans & Hermans-Konopka, 2010, pp. 228–234). And as the playwright Miller suggests in the above quote, the creation of identity is an interactive process between self and others.

Expressive dialogues as a writing exercise, which primarily cultivates the dialogue within the self (i.e. the internal dialogue), is part of the "career-writing" method, a narrative and dialogical approach to career counselling (Lengelle, 2014). The method is based in narrative psychology and Dialogical Self Theory (DST) both in the way the nature of the self is perceived – as a dynamic multiplicity of *I*-positions in the landscape of the mind – and in the way that progress of a narrative can be promoted and identified (Hermans & Hermans-Konopka, 2010). In DST terms, a beneficial narrative (i.e. identity) develops when individuals begin to express what is important to them (articulate *I*-positions), expand those *I*-positions

R. Lengelle (✉)
Faculty of Humanities and Social Sciences, Athabasca University (Canada's Open University), Athabasca, AB, Canada
e-mail: reineke@tic.ab.ca

H. Hermans (ed.), *Assessing and Stimulating a Dialogical Self in Groups, Teams, Cultures, and Organizations*, DOI 10.1007/978-3-319-32482-1_3

and subsequently develop and express meta- and promoter positions (Winters, Meijers, Lengelle, & Baert, 2012). What these positions entail and how writing expressive dialogues might help in stimulating their development will be described below in greater detail.

In this chapter, I will explain the reasons narrative approaches are needed to assist people in surviving and thriving in the current employment climate. More specifically, the central goal of the chapter is to show how writing expressive dialogues can promote career identity development. It will become clear that doing so can augment or be used as a form of career guidance. Writing expressive dialogues will be placed in the context of DST where the development of particular *I*-positions promises particular developmental gains in the process of creating a beneficial career narrative. Metaphors from playwriting will be used to describe the *I*-positions (i.e. developmental stages) and two case studies will be featured that show how expressive dialogues might be written and how they can foster career development. One of the case studies is from a student and the other is a recent career story of my own. A discussion about who would benefit from using the exercises and what qualities a practitioner should have in order to work with groups or individuals will follow to conclude the chapter.

A Need for Narrative Guidance

The career-guidance methods we generally associate with career development and which focus on matching skills to jobs, no longer work (Jarvis, 2014; Pryor & Bright, 2011; Savickas, 2011). The so-called "trait and factor approach" which had career professionals making inventories of people's skills and aptitudes and trying to match those to available jobs (Holland, 1973) is out-dated. It served people well in the industrial age when manufacturing was central to economic growth and the world of work was not as complex, insecure, and individualized as it is now. Employers are no longer the main source of security and belonging for workers, nor is counting on one's traits and focusing on a possible match; the proliferation of types and forms of work is ubiquitous and we no longer have the grand narrative to inform us about occupational identity (Meijers, 2013).

A sense of continuity and congruence must be put together and found in co-created personal narratives – stories that also grow and change as circumstances shift and include details about how we can and wish to relate to others. Indeed, various researchers and practitioners have recognized the importance of this shift in career guidance in recent decades and this is, in part, the reason why narrative methods are increasingly considered central to career counselling in the twenty-first century (Cochran, 1997; Savickas, 2005; McMahon & Watson, 2012; Reid & West, 2011).

The adjectives that describe employment nowadays are: insecure, contingent, part-time, individualized, complex, and requiring increased emotional competence (Cherniss, 2000). The ground under our *employment* feet was once the work-floor of the companies and institutions we worked for, the clear do's and don'ts of internalized societal norms, and our skill base. Now the 'ground' under our *employability* is a kind of flying carpet, woven from the many strands of our personal histories, combined with a fragmented melange of multi-cultural values, and put together in a way that makes sense to us as individuals. In guidance terms, we call this flying carpet a career narrative or career identity: a story about ourselves that gives us a sense of meaning and direction, and tells us how the multi-voiced "self of yesterday became the self of today and will become the self of tomorrow" (Savickas, 2005, p. 58). It is "not factual truth but narrative truth; meaningful to the individual in terms of experience, understanding of the world and of future possibilities" (Reid & West, 2011).

However, before I continue to describe how such an individual narrative takes shape through expressive writing, it is important to note that the claims made here do not condone neoliberalism and the agenda it sets that has stripped away security, benefits, and continuity in society. What is described here merely sets the stage – a stage on which young and old, who would succeed in the current economy, will have to tap into more inner characters to survive and thrive than before. They will have to be able to tell a story about them*selves* (i.e. construct a career identity) that allows them to gain insight into what has meaning for them and how they would like to be useful to others (Meijers & Lengelle, 2012). In terms of Dialogical Self Theory, they will have to develop particular *I*-positions in order to develop a narrative that they can use in the world of work.

Dialogical Steps to (Career) Narratives

As described more fully in the introduction of this book, Dialogical Self Theory describes the self as a dynamic multiplicity of positions or voices in the landscape of the mind with a possibility of dialogical relationships between the positions (Hermans & Hermans-Konopka, 2010). This multiplicity of positions can be in conflict with itself, criticise itself, agree and consult with itself (p.127) just as we might do so with other individuals. Metaphorically speaking and in the words of a playwright, the "self" described here can be likened to the various characters on the stage of one's life. If that stage were the labour market, a successful career story could be worked towards if one character began by articulating what is important to him/herself (express an *I*-position) and if other characters then came forward to deepen and broaden those expressions (expanded *I*-positions). Subsequently, it would be important that a person would also be able to observe those positions as they enacted the conversation (i.e. develop a meta-position). A meta position, much like a play's narrator, observes from the side and articulates what (s)he sees. A meta position (1) "permits some distance from the other positions", (2) "provides an overarching view so that several positions can be seen simultaneously and their mutual relationships visible", (3) "makes it possible to see the linkages between positions as part of one's personal history or the collective history of the group or culture to which one belongs" and (4) "facilitates the creation of a dialogical space (in contact with others or oneself) in which positions and counter-positions engage in dialogical relationships" (p.147). In career terms this might be the combined position that says, "I became aware of both the part of me that wants to serve, but also the part that wants to invest more in learning before I do so" or "I realized that because of my upbringing that I actually see my own gender (woman) as less able to stand up to authority. The me that is a small-town girl from the fifties and the me that is a feminist are still not really talking to each other."

The (final) developmental step in identity formation in a career-narrative learning process – in addition to expressing an initial *I*-position, expanding that *I*-position, and meta-position – is the formation of a promoter position. This position most closely resembles the role of the play's director who guides, overseas, connects, and can act as an innovator to the characters on stage and can be seen as "the one who is able to take action". A promoter position implies openness towards the future and the ability to integrate the positions that appear and which were identified by the meta-position. The promoter position, like the play's director, can 'reorganize the self towards a higher level of development' and provides room for both continuity and discontinuity in the self (Hermans & Hermans-Konopka, 2010, p.228). In a career context, the promoter position may, for instance, be the voice of unconditional acceptance that allows the stalemate between "self as ashamed of being unemployed and therefore paralyzed" and "the hero self who is waiting to take a new action, but doesn't know how" to be resolved.

By extension and in the context of the expressive-dialogue writing exercise that I will be describing, the individual facing a career dilemma is encouraged to take on the role of the playwright. The playwright is the one who can – with the help of a writing mentor and inner characters waiting to speak and be born – co-author a new story about work or work struggles. In the sections below, I will refer to a 'first story' as a narrative that doesn't work and is characterized by flight, fight, or freeze responses and a 'second story' as a narrative where meta and promoter positions have been developed and are at the heart of a story that is life giving and allows an individual to move forward (Meijers & Lengelle, 2012).

The Method

Years ago, I discovered that writing about my life brought me insights and allowed me to solve problems. Researcher James Pennebaker discovered the same thing and began to study this phenomenon on a wide scale with a variety of populations (for an overview see Pennebaker, 2011). In one of his research projects, he and colleagues found that engineers who had been laid off found work more easily if they wrote about their deepest pain associated with the layoff (Spera, Buhrfeind, & Pennebaker, 1994). This as well as experiences with students and their personal-development-through-writing led me to develop and subsequently research the career-writing process (Lengelle, 2014).

Expressive-dialogue writing is one exercise or approach that can be used to foster career-identity development and involves writing from different 'voices' or positions in the self. This is done with prompts from a writing mentor who understands that to get from a 'first' to 'second' story requires the expression and feeling of emotions and a movement towards a more cognitive, structured narrative. In this exercise, that movement is stimulated by beginning with the expression of 'I positions', where one may for instance be asked to "write from the voice that is loudest and wants to be heard".

The reader can imagine: a person struggling with a particular career dilemma (e.g. being laid off) may write a conversation between the position "I as suffering" and a wise-self-position. In such an exchange, a discovery might be made that "I as suffering" is not suffering from the fact of unemployment, but from the societal shame perceived as a result. The future wise-self position – acting in this case as a meta-position – who is able to see things from a bit of a distance, might unearth this assumption and point out that what is holding a person back is not the fact of their unemployment but their perception of the stigma. When this insight is gained, another position, for instance of an accepting self, can be brought into the dialogue as well – this promoter position can subsequently soothe the 'shamed self' and allow a process of grieving to begin. The old identity (I-as employee or *I*-as capable and acceptable) and "I as ashamed" is then acknowledged and new space appears for positions such as "I as hopeful" and "I as an eager new beginner" for instance. Where this process in DST would ordinarily be done with a counsellor, it can also be done on paper and this will be illustrated with the following case studies.

Elaboration of the Method

Case Study 1

One of the exercises I have used in my writing practice with students is the following: "Take a piece of paper and tear it so that you have six separate strips. On each strip write one of the following words: Unemployed, Employed, Observer/ Witness, Victim, Wisdom, and the Labour Market (in which case, the 'labour market' is not a thing, but a position that is also a voice in the dialogue) . Fold the pieces of paper so you cannot see what is written on them. Choose two of the pieces of paper randomly and start a written conversation between the two 'roles', much like you would if you were writing the first lines of a play."

The idea here is that both an *I*-position can be expressed (e.g. role on first piece of paper), but also expanded *I*-positions that emerge in the dynamic of the dialogue where the 'voices' begin to explain themselves to each other. An *I*-position might for instancc be when the voice of employed says, "I want to be included" (i.e. this is important to me) while a conversation with "unemployed" starts to show expanded positions, who says, "...but I don't want to be employed at all costs. I want to be included in a way that shows my skills and talents. And travelling as far as before takes me away from my family too much" (i.e. who I am personally also matters, and that includes my skills, talents, and family. Frequently initial meta-positions also begin to show up, for instance, "I realize now that I have made parts of me disappear in order to do the job I did; being unemployed now is showing me how much I have compromised myself". Promoter positions make use of those insights and demonstrate an ability to act on them in the service of stimulating other positions, "when I go to the employment office, I will add what I have discovered to my file. The conflict that plagued me feels lifted now that I know what I will say."

Using the strips of paper and choosing the 'roles' randomly gives the writer a chance to surprise him or herself and get curious about what this new 'character' is about to say, instead of automatically defaulting to common scripts a person has about one's life or struggles.

In response to this exercise, Carla, a middle-aged woman and graduate student with a well-paying but uninspiring job wrote the following dialogue (her written dialogue is in italics):

Employed	*I'm busy.*
Victim	*You're always busy.*
Employed	*I am being useful and used. My skills are needed by someone. That is what is honourable and acceptable.*
Victim	*I really do not want to be like you. You're selling out for money.*
Employed	*I need to make a lot of money so I can do the things I really want to do.*
Victim	*Yeah, when you're dead because you do not have time to do what you want to do, and here I sit looking at all the tools to play the music, and I have to wait for you because you're busy. When you're not busy you're tired. When you're not tired you're doing something for someone else. When are you ever going to smell the roses and spend time with me?*
Employed	*I'm busy making good money. I am helping people. I'm helping you and the rest of the family.*
Victim	*That's just an excuse. You're as bitter about this stuff as I am. If you were really doing what you wanted to do, you would be happy. You're just copping out and being like everyone else. You left me behind and you're not getting any younger.*

What is interesting in this initial exchange is that although 'victim' and 'employed' seem at the outset to be two rather polarized *I*-positions, but their dialogue already creates space for initial insights like "You're as a bitter about this stuff as I am." If "victim" or even the voice of "wisdom" were to write alone – which frequently happens in the case of people merely journaling about their problems – there is less chance of variations and new viewpoints emerging. A monologue tends to strengthen or solidify positions, just as our own viewpoints tend to become more static if we not in conversation or challenged by others. Certainly in writing in non-dialogical ways, an *I*-position will be expressed, (e.g. "I as bitter"), but it is the introduction of a second voice (a potential of an expanded *I*-position) that the conversations starts to lead to the dialogical development of narrative identity (e.g. "I as wanting to do work that fits better" or "To work with people that make me feel valued").

The instruction after letting the first two voices speak is to add a third or fourth. It is important that one does so in an unhurried way so that each voice gets to offer its gripes, issues, responses and insights. In the course, Carla was asked to invite the 'witness/observer' and 'wisdom' to the table as she reported that she was currently employed. It became an expanded dialogue where meta-positions slowly emerged and eventually even a promoter position developed. Here are several pieces to illustrate:

Witness (speaking to 'victim' and 'employed'): *You know you both are on the same page from different perspectives. Why do you not learn from each other? Try out each other's suggestions. (...) It sounds that you both have excuses to fail: one appearing like a legitimate, positive reason, and the other in a negative, self-defeating way.*

It is noteworthy that Carla, by quite literally introducing a 'meta position' in the form of "witness" started to ask completely different questions, much more focused on the coming together of viewpoints: *I*-positions working together with respect for the differing points of view. The next position that was introduced (wisdom), served as a meta, but also as the beginning of a promoter position, where solutions grew in seed form and referred not only to what was observed by what could be done.

Wisdom: *Is it beneficial? Or are you just allowing yourself to be like victim only on the other extreme. Victim doesn't want to make choices that she will have to pay for, but you seem to want to control everything. Neither is fruitful. Both lead to pain and regret.*

At the end of the dialogue, Carla let each voice speak again. Although the pieces have been shortened for this chapter, it is apparent that the atmosphere of the exchanges had completely changed. The polarised *I*-positions shifted and a crystallising metaphor of a tree appeared – a tree that could stretch out and grow and also 'touch other trees'. Notice also how all the *I*-positions began to interact constructively. Each began to speak with its own purpose and contribute insight.

Employed (I positions and first expanded I position): *I believe in being helpful to others. If I have power, influence, network, and money, it gives me the capabilities to influence the direction of my life.*

Here, Carla expressed several *I*-positions, like serving others and having power, influence, a network and financial resources so that, she could (expanded *I*-position) "have influence over her life".

Victim (another expanded *I*-position)): *I do not believe in that imbalance.*

Here Carla specifies that "balance" is also important in addition to the work of being helpful to others and gaining power etc. She may even be saying that a balance is one way in which she has influence over her own life.

Witness (meta-position, noticing and expressing insights): *You two are really not that different. You're just at different places of knowledge and self-revelation. I see you as balancing each other out. The tender and the strong, like a tree.*

Carla's meta-position brings together the positions I-as-employed and I-as-victim and notes they are not really polarized at all. Here, like a play's narrator, she observes that each character has something to say and offer: I-as-employed brings the knowledge and revelation of wanting to be helpful and gain power to influence one's life and I-as-victim brings the knowledge of a need for balance (from the earlier part of the dialogue, 'balance' likely refers to getting enough rest and also investing in activities that were more personally meaningful to Carla). She brings these positions together in the tree metaphor, which she perceives as both "tender and strong". Wisdom (beginning of a promoter position in metaphorical form – an integration of insights and hint about action that involves investing in one's other interests "new heights" and "connecting with others meaningfully" – not just serving or earning money): *Tenderness is necessary in order to allow flexibility for the energy to run through the tree uninhibited, resulting in the birthing of leaves and fruit... It is focused energy reaching for heights and spreading itself out to meet other trees.*

Several days after the writing, Carla wrote more directly about her career interests in an online message. It was noteworthy that after doing the written dialogue the urgency to take action of some kind erupted (i.e. in her case asking new questions and networking).

Writing expressive dialogues in this case looks like the learning process from *I*-positions, to expanded *I*-position, to meta and promoter positions happened too as a result of happenstance, as the strips of paper Carla began with "I-as-employed" and "I-as-victim" were more likely positions for a 'first story' and witness and wisdom suited for the emergence of meta- and promoter positions. However, in my experience, a student can start with witness or wisdom and these will serve as initial *I*-positions. If 'victim' emerges at a later stage for instance, it will bring insight (meta) or suggest creative solutions or more dynamic views of how a particular issue can be addressed (promoter). What I mean is that there is no order in which a student should or must work with the positions in order to move towards a beneficial (second) story. That said, the guidance of a writing facilitator is key in the process if for instance a particular *I*-position gets caught up in a circular internal dialogue (e.g. victim repeating poor-me narratives). A writing teacher may then prompt the writer, to bring in an additional *I*-position, one for instance that comes from the imagination of the student. A question like, "who or what, in your imagination can see new things or knows how to solve serious problems". Students may respond with archetypal positions like "the sage" or "Buddha" or "compassionate witness" or with other more life-giving positions than come from their personal lives (e.g. My aunt June who always knows what to say) and which work to stimulate the development of meta- and promoter positions.

In a workshop, for instance, participants were prompted to write down a "career question that has been following you around." One of the participants, a widower, wrote down for himself a more urgent, personal, question, which was: "is it time to begin to date women again?" He had been raised strictly Christian, but had become disillusioned by the faith and left it in his adult life. He had spoken about this during the workshop briefly, so when he randomly chose the card "God" from a set of 78 archetype cards (Myss, 2003), he was surprised and later shared this in with the group in a fashion that caused quite a bit of laughter in the room. He wrote a dialogue with *I*-position "God", who advised that he also write his deceased wife directly. He later confided in me, that this conversation had 'set him free' and had been deeply meaningful. In the following year, he happily reported that he had a new partner.

Case Study 2

The second case study, which I will present now, is a story from my own career history and begins with a reflection on an entry from my journal.

> … *I left home early and stopped in a café to write a short letter to my future self – I told her not to worry if this afternoon's news turned out to be bad. An hour later, I would need those words of reassurance* (Lengelle, 2014, p. 13).

A few years ago, there were financial cuts at my university, layoffs followed and my position too was on the chopping block. All those teaching in the graduate program who did not (yet) have their PhDs, would be let go a colleague had warned me. Shortly after this, I was invited by my program director for an appointment and on the way there, as described in the quote above, I wrote myself a short letter to comfort and give my future self hope in advance.

That afternoon, I was indeed told that my series of one-year contracts would come to an end after a decade of employment at my university. This bad news could have easily locked me into a first story – a narrative characterized by victimhood that often sounds something like: "I will no longer be employed, this is not fair, the university does not see my value, I am a victim of the economy, and there is nothing I can do. Poor me." This I-as-victim is powerful and archetypal and it is our human tendency to use this narrative (i.e. first story) as a way of explaining our circumstances and remaining in the safety of our 'innocence'. As I walked back to my car, my mind predictably offered up a series of scared, disillusioned, and victim-like voices, but I remembered too what I tell my students: a 'first story' is absolutely natural and understandable, but it is a stop along the way, not a good destination.

A first story is only one act in the play of our life unfolding. We tend to panic, but we need not anticipate that the script of our lives is destined for a tragic ending. Hence, I invite students – and myself in times of trouble – to invite other voices, characters (i.e. *I*-positions) on to the stage to speak. Again, *I*-positions should be expanded, deepening and widening our viewpoints in emotionally salient ways. In my situation, the voices I began to express sounded like this:

I-as-notetaker: *my boss said my work was of superior quality. He did say that.*

I-as-hopeful: *he also said that there might be a case to be made for my employment; he even said he might be able to write something up*

I-as-realist: *not that he is going to put that case forward on your behalf! He's too darn busy. He's just trying to ease your pain.*
I-as-hopeful: *I might be able to do something myself.*
Emerging meta: *I notice, I kind of feel like he has left me a trail of breadcrumbs to get home and I better do that before the crumbs are (i.e. all hope is) gone.*

In this stage of expanding *I*-positions, often the voices of others outside ourselves (i.e. the external dialogue) help expand our insights and move us towards meta-positions. Indeed, a new narrative is a co-creation that takes shape as a result of an internal and an external dialogue. An internal dialogue alone is often a vicious circle with limited *I*-positions emerging, while an external dialogue alone may sound helpful, but the insights and suggestions from others if not felt (i.e. affectively internalized) and integrated cannot be acted upon with conviction.

The first person I engaged in an 'external dialogue' with was my partner and colleague Frans, who asked me shortly after the meeting with my boss:

F: *Do you want to keep this job? Is the work meaningful to you?*
This evoked in me the *I*-position that I will call "devoted".
I-as-devoted: *Yes, I am deeply committed to my work. I am doing the work that is for me. I also notice a lot of gratitude for that.*
Meta-position (or play's narrator): *As we see: devoted shows us her commitment and connection to her work. That this is the right work for her and that she doesn't want to lose it. She is deeply devoted. And in I-as-devoted there is energy to build a case for her employment. She does not yet know how to do that, but she sees that she is committed to trying.*

The promoter position (i.e. play's director) grew in part from the realization articulated by the meta-position. I wanted to keep my job and I was willing to do something about it. The promoter position (i.e. "I as able to act") followed when I wrote the response to Frans's question: *why should the university keep you?* This question prompted me to shift positions and to step for a moment into the shoes of university administrators who were being pressured to make cuts.

I thought about the fact that my boss had told me a case could be made for my employment, so I wrote down two main reasons why the university should keep me: they had hired me as professional writer (and professional writers, artists, and musicians without PhDs could teach in graduate programs – there was precedent). Second, the courses I design and teach on writing and personal development require special skills: creativity, empathy, and knowledge of this specialized field. The final prompt that activated and allowed me to internalize the promoter position, "I as able to act" and direct the play of my life came when I examined the positions "I-lacking-with no PhD" and "I not-lacking without a PhD". During the holiday break in December, within two weeks of hearing the news, I wrote the case for my employment, using the two afore mentioned arguments as well as the argument that I was working at a PhD level and had the publications to prove it. Early January I emailed the written case to my boss and the union representative and with it in hand they were able to influence the administrator's decision. In March I heard my contract would be extended.

Summarizing the process in dialogical terms: I expressed the *I*-position of victim that let me know I had a problem and was in my first story, then expanded that *I*-position finding positions like, I-as-devoted, I as hopeful, I as realistic. A meta- and promoter position grew as I began to write down what I noticed, starting with "I-as devoted" and subsequently responded to prompts in the external conversations I had with my partner. Noticing (meta position) my devotion and other qualities, I moved towards being able to take action (promoter position) where I argued for my employment and shared the case I had built.

The first story of, "this is terrible" transformed step by step into the empowering narrative, "I am devoted, committed, worthy" and finally, "I will communicate this message with important others and see what happens." The outcome, of course, could have been different. I could have simply lost my job anyway, but the exercise of moving out of the victim role and becoming empowered through the development of meta- and promoter positions would still have stood me in good stead had that happened. This is because other action-able (promoter positions) emerged from this exercise as well, positions such as, "I as capable of finding work elsewhere if need be" and "I as going to do a PhD" which I subsequently did.

The self-pity that might have grown if I had remained in the initial *I*-position, may well have paralyzed my efforts to move forward. Another discovery in this process has been that the culture of my family says "if you fail it is your fault". This I-as-self-blame could also have found a friend in I-as-victim and together formed a dangerous coalition, which may have sabotaged my efforts. Instead "I as devotion" and "I as case writer" worked together to put forward an argument for my continued employment; regardless of the result, I had invested in proactivity and a sense of worthiness.

Table 3.1 below shows the 4 dialogical phases and the *I*-positions that I identified and named in each, the kind of writing one can do in each phase and what stimulated me in each stage and allowed me to the move to the next.

To stimulate this type of writing in others or with groups, it is important to note that in expressing I and expanded *I*-positions, room must be made for all types of 'voices' or shadow positions, including the 'messy' ones (e.g. rage, disappointment, fear). Then a facilitator should slowly help the writer to bring in voices that may shed insight and lead to more life-giving actions. It is frequently the mistake of those struggling with a life issue, to stay too much in the first story with corresponding disempowering *I*-positions, but likewise, it is frequently the mistake of teachers or guides to move people too quickly to 'wiser' *I*-positions that are therefore not felt or lived through. Stories are inherently about conflict, pain, and struggle and at the same time, the author or characters long to resolve the tensions; the same goes for personal narratives. There must be room for both the first story and the emergence of the second and below there are seven recommendations to help support this dialogical learning process.

Table 3.1 Overview of the dialogical writing process (using this case study as point of reference)

Dialogical stage or type of position	*I*-position named	Kind of writing per stage	Internal dialogue and influences	External dialogue (e.g. writing mentor, counsellor, or conversation partner)
I "Character"	I as victim	Venting on the page, letting the I-as-victim get feelings out Expression of emotions	Human tendencies to avoid pain and be innocent. Raw emotions. (Fear)	Encourages the person suffering to express painful feelings and put those on paper
Expanded I "Other characters"	I as hopeful I as realist I as note-taker	Writing down the other possible perspectives that seem to have something to say – recording the "other" voices	One's ability to let other voices be heard, even in the middle of difficult times. (Opening)	Encourages the expression of potential 'other voices' to also express perspectives and feelings on the page by asking questions or giving additional writing prompts
Meta "Narrator"	Realizing and noticing *I*-as-devoted and I-as-meaningfully employed and having the willingness to act on that	Letting the narrator make a summary of what it observes about the selves	One's ability to observe one's self and imagine other possibilities. (Noticing)	Acts as external witness by encouraging the sharing of written work – either in written or verbal form.
Promoter "Stage director"	I as able to act: articulate the three reasons the university should keep me and communicating that with influential others	Writing down a plan based on meta positions	Ability to take what is observed and noticed in the meta phase into some form of action and reassessment (Courage)	Explore and suggest potential steps that might be taken based on insights gained in earlier stages.

Practical Recommendations for Using the Method

In the following section, I make suggestions for facilitating this narrative and dialogical process; a description is given of what constitutes a strong workable and enjoyable stage for practice.

1. Create a safe space for writing. The space – whether it is a real or online classroom – should be like a place where it feels okay to share personal stories. This can be facilitated if an instructor gives a personal introduction and invites

participants to do so in a playful way. For instance, students can be invited to complete the following sentence stems: (1) The meaning or origin of my name is…or I got my name because…(2) A question that has been following me around is… (3) If I told you one true or untrue thing about me, it would be… Keeping the space safe means not criticizing work, advising in directive ways, or projecting that there is a 'right' way to write. The safe space stays safe by focusing on the text, noticing things together in what is written, and being clear and gentle with students.

2. Play with language and keep the drama on the page. It is vital that those writing find enjoyment in the process and get in touch with themselves as I-artist or I-playwright. As a facilitator one might for instance start by getting students to write a short scene of a play. A piece of an existing play may be read aloud first (or shared online) and a line might be borrowed from it, to start a fictitious script of one's own. This allows those writing to create something new and gain experience with 'feeling' the difference in voices. Likewise, if someone brings up or goes on about 'a problem' they are facing, invite them to put it on paper. I tell students that in suffering and an urge to complain, there is energy and they do well to keep that energy on the page to infuse their writing. This emphasis on making something refocuses energy away from rumination and entrenched perspectives. Frequently when asked to share work in class, youth and adults alike will read enthusiastically and proudly from their work; an innocence and excitement is often palpable in class – that applies to online settings as well.
3. Don't look for answers; go on a journey. In getting people to write expressive dialogues, it is best to see the work as an exploration from which insights can emerge. It is a process. And the way to enable writers to open up is often through 'the backdoor'. The 'front door' is saying something like, "it's sounds like you are troubled about being unemployed, so you should write with the voice of I-as-ashamed". The backdoor approach would be to say, "who is the 'character' on your stage of life who is saying 'it's bad that I have lost my job' – give this character a name and see what he/she has to say alongside the scared one. You can write that down. You don't have to share it with anyone. See what might happens."
4. Slow down to the speed of the body. When leading a group or individual, it's important to be in touch with our own bodies. This is important in determining the natural speed at which we might work with someone or a group. Our own sense of timing (felt through the body in subtle and not so subtle ways) will tell us if we are pushing someone too quickly or if it's time to tell a joke or introduce a more light-hearted exercise or to go deeper. Time for the learning process is important, in particular because emotions are involved and need time to become integrated.
5. Give feedback that is kind, notices, supports, and inspires. In pieces shared aloud in a face-to-face class or online, it is important that the facilitator and peers follow some guidelines for giving feedback. The human tendency is to 'move out of the process' by either (1) offering interpretations, analyses, or solutions to problems instead of letting people spend time with the questions first (2) telling one's

own story without it serving the other or (3) criticizing or minimizing another's story in some careless or suggestive way. Feedback using these sentence stems works well, "I like the sound of…" and "I want to hear more about…(Scarfe, E. University of Alberta, Faculty of Extension, Writing course, Personal communication, 1993) and stimulates the development of expanded *I*-positions and meta-positions.

6. Have a structure to the process that moves writers from a first to second story by allowing more 'free' expression at the beginning, and incrementally bringing in more structure towards the end. For instance, at the start or course or writing process, one might encourage writers to make a list of a whole range of voices and let them all speak (i.e. cacophony), but by the end of the process, the messages of a meta or promoter position that have emerged as a result of more structured exercises may be summed up in a metaphor or translated into a Haiku. Students or clients, like in other narrative career counselling methods (Cochran, 1997; Savickas, 2005) should leave with a 'life portrait' or second story that clearly summarizes the insights (meta) and actions (promoter) they might take, but that at the start allowed for all kinds of raw material to arise. (For more details on the order and types of exercises, see Lengelle & Meijers, 2014).
7. Focus on art making and the writing craft, not only on life making. This last point may seem to contradict some of the previous recommendations, but it is essential and goes beyond the importance of play and enjoyment. Those writing are not only engaged in beneficial (or even therapeutic practice) but they are working as real writers. They are making art. They are trying in earnest to reach the reader with the 'truth' of their experience using vivid and visceral detail and are thereby working seriously at the craft of writing. As a facilitator, it is useful to bring in the advice of actual writers (and not only writing teachers!). Let those with their pens hear what Ralph Ellison said about Hemingway, "When he describes the process of art in terms of baseball or boxing; he's been there" (McRorie, 1988, p. 29). Let them hear from Maya Angelou about why humans write and what she believes fiction writers are doing, "I look at some of the great novelists and I think the reason they are great is that they're telling the truth…the truth about the human being – what we are capable of, what makes us lose, laugh, weep, fall down and gnash our teeth and wring our hands and kill each other and love each other." (Angelou, 2015). If students and clients work like writers, with the inspiration of writers, they will learn the hard work and pleasure involved and rekindle what has often killed by "The English teacher who wrote fiercely on the margin of your theme in blue pencil: "Trite, rewrite," (Ueland, 2010, p.7). And to inspire courage, remind them as Brenda Ueland did in her original 1939 advice to writers "Mentally (at least three or four times a day) thumb your nose at all know-it-alls, jeerers, critics, doubters. (Ueland, 2010, p. 8).

Discussion

It should be clear from the above that writing expressive dialogues is a process intended to help people create life-giving stories so that they can move forward in life and that setting the stage for such work is important and requires specific acts and intentions. Below are some reflections on its implementation in career-development contexts and a final word on facilitator capabilities.

Part of a Career Professional's Toolkit

Expressive-dialogue writing can become a part of a career counsellor's toolkit: an approach to helping clients gain insights and co-create ways of taking action. Teachers and guidance professionals in schools and universities can also use this approach when helping young people orient themselves in life, education, and work. Currently it is used in several graduate courses as a way in which people can promote their personal development and work on strengthening a conscious conversation with themselves.

There are several advantages of this approach over conventional one-on-one counselling services. First it is more time and cost effective as it can be done with a group of people at a time, either face-to-face or online. Second, participants can each work on their own written dialogues, (and then be invited to share them out loud with the group or post their written pieces online if they wish), and receive feedback from both instructor and peers. Third, other voices in the room stimulate the much-needed external dialogue, while the expressive writing continually serves to 'reconnect' to the inside voices and feelings. Fourth, people can continue to write expressive dialogues once they leave the course and no longer have direct access to a facilitator. This is because participants learn how to allow *I*-positions to be voiced and worked with in constructive ways: in ways that help people move beyond first stories. Fifth, writing is dialogical in nature: the moment words are committed to paper, the 'I' who is writing, connects to the 'me' who is expressed there. The act of observing and noticing what is written is the beginning of the formation of meta-positions and the conflicts and issues that are written black on white ask for resolutions and new actions. Writing stimulates and strengthens the internal dialogue in particular and that is perhaps why what is confessed to a friend over coffee can evaporate again, but the discoveries we commit to the page are much harder to retreat from or unsay. Finally, and as argued earlier, this narrative and dialogical approach can capture the human responses to the complexity, insecurity, and individuality of the current labour market in a way that traditional career guidance approaches cannot.

The Compassionate Facilitator

Those helping others to write out their stories, their fears, their problems and their first attempts at new insights and actions, must be compassionate. Those writing frequently feel afraid of what they might reveal to others, but also to themselves. Shame and a sense of failure or coming up short are common feelings when we begin to write about our lives. That is why facilitators of the process must be gentle: they must know when to be silent and listen, when to encourage a next dialogical step or to suggest a new voice enter into the conversation, and when to bring in humour.

Those who would use writing also do well to have a solid basic understanding of human psychology but without stepping into a therapist's role (unless they are qualified to do so). Those encouraging others to write should also have written about their own trials and issues, so they know in an embodied way what happens and is felt during such a process. Lastly, facilitators of this method must 'have a thing' with writing: that is, they must love something about writing, whether that is editing poetry, scribbling notes in a journal about scenery that has moved them, or lovingly underlining passages in a book. In order to use or create variations on dialogical exercises, a facilitator must be playing with words and voice, like a playwright, evoking in themselves a host of dialogical possibilities.

References

Angelou, M. (2015, October 2). *Maya Angelou's legacy: Inspiring quotes for writers*. Retrieved from: http://writerswin.com/maya-angelous-inspiration-writers/

Cherniss, C. (2000). Social and emotional competence in the workplace. In B. Reuven & J. Parker (Eds.), *The handbook of emotional intelligence: Theory, development, assessment, and application at home, school, and in the workplace* (pp. 433–458). San Francisco: Jossey-Bass.

Cochran, L. (1997). *Career counseling: A narrative approach*. London: Sage.

Hermans, H. J. M., & Hermans-Konopka, A. (2010). *Dialogical self theory. Positioning and counter-positioning in a globalizing society*. Cambridge, UK: Cambridge University Press.

Holland, J. L. (1973). *Making vocational choices: A theory of careers*. Englewood Cliffs, NJ: Prentice Hall.

Jarvis, P. (2014). Career development: Key to economic development. In B. C. Shepard & P. S. Mani (Eds.), *Career development practice in Canada: Perspectives, principles, and professionalism* (pp. 55–75). Toronto, ON, Canada: CERIC.

Lengelle, R. (2014). *Career writing: Creative, expressive, and reflective approaches to narrative and dialogical career guidance*. Published doctoral dissertation. Tilburg, The Netherlands: Tilburg University.

Lengelle, R., & Meijers, F. (2014). Narrative identity: Writing the self in career learning. *British Journal of Guidance and Counselling, 42*, 52–72.

McMahon, M., & Watson, M. (2012). Story crafting: Strategies for facilitating narrative career counselling. *International Journal for Educational and Vocational Guidance, 12*(3), 211–224.

McRorie, K. (1988). *The I-search paper: Revised edition of searching writing*. Portsmouth, NH: Boynton/Cook Publishers.

Meijers, F. (2013). Monologue to dialogue: Education in the 21st century. *International Journal for Dialogical Science, 7*(1), 1–10. http://ijds.lemoyne.edu/index.html.

Meijers, F., & Lengelle, R. (2012). Narratives at work: the development of career identity. *British Journal of Guidance and Counselling, 40*(2), 157–177.

Myss, C. (2003). *Archetype cards: A 78-card deck and guidebook*. Carlsbad, CA: Hayhouse Publishing.

Pennebaker, J. (2011). *The secret life of pronouns*. New York: Bloomsbury Press.

Pryor, R. G. L., & Bright, J. E. H. (2011). *The chaos theory of careers*. New York/London: Routledge.

Reid, H., & West, L. (2011). Struggling for space: Narrative methods and the crisis of professionalism in career guidance in England. *British Journal of Guidance and Counselling, 39*, 397–410.

Savickas, M. (2005). The theory and practice of career construction. In S. D. Brown & R. W. Lent (Eds.), *Career development and counselling: Putting theory and research to work* (pp. 42–70). Hoboken, NJ: Wiley.

Savickas, M. (2011). New questions for vocational psychology: Premises, paradigms, and practices. *Journal of Career Assessment, 19*, 251–258.

Spera, S. P., Buhrfeind, R. D., & Pennebaker, J. W. (1994). Expressive writing and coping with job loss. *Academy of Management Journal, 37*, 722–733.

Ueland, B. (2010). *If you want to write: A book about art, independence and spirit*. Macmillan.

Winters, A., Meijers, F., Lengelle, R., & Baert, H. (2012). The self in career learning: An evolving dialogue. In H. J. M. Hermans & T. Gieser (Eds.), *Handbook of dialogical self theory* (pp. 454–469). Cambridge, UK: Cambridge University Press.

Chapter 4
Compositionwork: A Method for Self Exploration and Development

Agnieszka Konopka and Wim van Beers

Introduction

The multiplicity of the dialogical self (Hermans, 1999, 2002) is a developmental challenge and opportunity. Being stretched between opposites or conflicting *I*-positions may be painful and make one long for peace and unity. On the other hand, discovering one's inner multiplicity can be enriching and fulfilling when one learns to surrender to its totality, in which imperfection has its necessary place. Compositionwork is a method to discover and get in contact with the richness of one's self. By means of it the landscape of mind is externalized and composed in the form of an artistic, symbolic landscape, consisting of natural elements like sand and stones. It speaks back to its composer in the nonverbal language of shapes, colors, forms and patterns and invites to enter into a dialogue with it. This dialogue involves the two fundamental dimensions of the self: the sensory, affective, preverbal world of the right brain and the more reflective linear and linguistic world of the left hemisphere. In this way it offers optimal conditions for learning and transformation (Greenberg, 2002).

Compositionwork is used in coaching, counseling and psychological training. The method was created by Agnieszka Konopka and Hubert Hermans (2010) and has been further developed by the authors of this chapter (Konopka & Van Beers, 2014). It is based on the *Dialogical Self Theory* (DST) and inspired by the tradition of *Japanese Rock Gardens*. In perspective of these sources Compositionwork can also be seen as the art of representing, exploring and cultivating the landscape of mind. In the first part of this chapter we will present the theoretical basis of the method which guides the interventions and understanding of the self. We then will shortly explain how Japanese Gardens became a source of inspiration for the method

A. Konopka (✉) • W. van Beers
Compositionwork, The Hague, The Netherlands
e-mail: agnieszkakonopka@yahoo.com

H. Hermans (ed.), *Assessing and Stimulating a Dialogical Self in Groups, Teams, Cultures, and Organizations*, DOI 10.1007/978-3-319-32482-1_4

and then present its distinctive features. After that we describe the way of working with the method. The second part of the chapter is focused on a case study that illustrates Compositionwork and shows its capacity to explore the self and its potential to stimulate change towards more authenticity and openness. We conclude with some short indications about usage of the method and requirements for the practitioner.

Theoretical and Philosophical Basis

The theoretical basis for Compositionwork is offered by the Dialogical Self Theory (DST; Hermans & Hermans-Konopka, 2010). In the process of Compositionwork the variety of *I*-positions in the landscape of mind of a client are explored, differentiated and expressed.

A fundamental role in the exploration of a composition plays the *meta-position*, which is realized by externalizing the inner landscape of the mind (see Sect. 2.1). A vital role in the process of change is taken by the *promoter position* (for multiplicity of *I*-positions, meta-position and promoter position see the introduction of this book) . Special attention in Compositionwork may also be given to *shadow positions* (Hermans & Hermans-Konopka, 2010). These rejected parts of the self are potential sources of energy when allowed and included. They may add to the integration and sense of completeness of the self.

The *'voice'* of an *I*-position can also play an important role in the exploration of *I*-positions. Verbalizing and vocally expressing what is happening in an *I*-position adds to its understanding. Involving voices from different positions in an interaction stimulates the innovative and integrative potential of the dialogue. Positions can be in a conflict or in harmony or even in coalition with each other. The qualities of these relations allow to better understand the dynamic organization of the self. We often invite our clients to experiment with new relations between positions, like e.g. by creating a new coalition between them. Creating a new coalition between positions can be a very important step for self innovation (Hermans, 1999). Exploring the *distribution of power* (Hermans & Hermans-Konopka, 2010) in the self allows to get useful indications for the development of the self. In some cases, like when one position is very dominant, this may require the development of a new distribution of power in the self, one that allows for a variety of *I*-positions to express their qualities and leads to a more 'democratic' organization of the self . Reorganization of power in the self may incite significant changes. This can sometimes take a dramatic form: that of a *dominance reversal* (Hermans, 1996). This happens when underlying positions quite suddenly take over the dominance from others. This may be experienced as an 'inner revolution', from which a new direction in life or work can result. In our work we have seen that this happens when dormant, suppressed or neglected ('shadow') positions have been ignored. When they express their voice and full attention is given to their corresponding bodily feelings these positions can catalyze a dramatic process of change, as will be shown in the case we describe later.

The dialogical view on *emotions* (Hermans & Hermans-Konopka, 2010) also plays an important role in the practice of Compositionwork. Taking into account the fundamental importance of a bidirectional relation between emotion and the self we are not only concerned to understand the message of an emotion but also how a person relates to a particular emotion. This attitude is often already visible in the spatial positioning of the represented emotion in the composition, and even more clearly in the person's reaction or felt impulse towards it.

The Basis of Composition Work in Japanese Gardens

Compositionwork is inspired by the tradition of *Japanese Rock Gardens*, which corresponds well with Dialogical Self Theory and enriches it in a concrete and spiritual form. In DST the self is seen as a multiplicity of *I*-positions in the landscape of mind (Hermans & Hermans-Konopka, 2010). Japanese rock gardens are sometimes also called 'mindscapes' (Nitschke, 1999). They represent the inner landscape of mind and its dynamic development. The rocky islands appear against the white gravel background, like our *I*-positions and feelings against the space of awareness.

There are some gardens which represent the opposites in the self. Opposites are often symbolized by a rock triad (Slawson, 2008), in which the vertical rock represents the element of heaven, the horizontal rock stands for the element of earth and the oblique rock symbolizes the human being, connecting heaven and earth. It shows the basic human condition and its challenge: encompassing the opposites in life. Gardens like Ryoan-jin, Daisen-in and the "Garden of Eight phases" in the Tofuku-ji temple, symbolize the basic dimensions of the self, namely the multiplicity of *I*-positions and the unity of awareness itself.

Another garden, Daisen-in garden, pictures the multiplicity of *I* –positions in the self in a dynamic, developmental way. A 'Turtle Stone' represents sadness and suffering while a 'Crane Stone' expresses joy of life. Walking a bit further into the garden one will find the 'Treasure Boat Stone', in which the Turtle and the Crane are brought together in the further flow of life. During this journey they develop a bound of friendship which represents wisdom as the ability to bring together opposite experiences and to move on in one's development, which later on is supported by the 'Hermit' stone.

From the perspective of Dialogical Self Theory (Hermans & Hermans-Konopka, 2010) stones can be seen as important *I*-positions and the pattern of stones can be viewed as an organization of the position repertoire that often includes opposites, third positions (e.g. Treasure Boat stone) and promoter positions (e.g. Hermit stone). The metaphor of the Japanese Garden, including its concrete miniature form, is used in Compositionwork for the exploration of the self.

In the next sections, we will describe the specific methodology of the Compositionwork. When you like to see an example of a composition of a client as a first impression you can have a look at Figs. 4.1 and 4.2 presented later in this chapter.

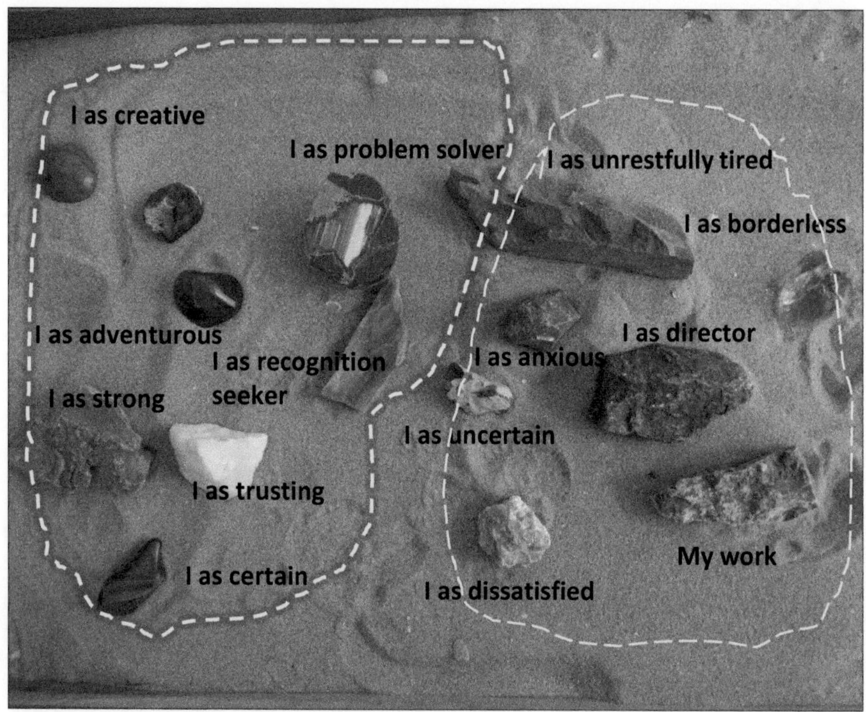

Fig. 4.1 Compositionwork first session

Fig. 4.2 Compositionwork second session

The Method and Its Features

In Compositionwork a person creates a symbolic landscape of his/her mind that represents his inner world. *I*-positions are represented with stones in a space with sand (usually a wooden box). The I-positions are identified by the client (this can be done in different ways, as will be explained further down). Clients symbolize *I*-positions by intuitively choosing stones from a heap of rocks, differing in size, color, shape and surface qualities (e.g. big, rough, smooth, edgy or rounded). The stones are meant to reflect the nonverbal qualities of the *I*-positions (e.g. a 'power *I*-position' can be represented by the size of a stone). The client allocates the chosen stones in the sandy space, according to their experienced relationships. Their spatial organization reflects the organization of the *I*-position repertoire including their relations and their overall pattern. The arising configuration is the 'composition'. The composition thus created looks somewhat like a Japanese Zen garden, in which the stones are seen as 'forms' in the formless space of awareness – the sand. This represents the landscape of mind as experienced by the client at this moment. A composition is created under the guidance of a coach who also helps to further explore and develop it (see also Sect. 6). We will now give an overview of the main features of Compositionwork.

Externalization and the Use of a Meta-position

A crucial process in Compositionwork is *externalization*. This process has been used as a technique in therapy and coaching and as a tool to enhance the accessibility of other levels of consciousness (cf. White and Epston, 1990), who use it in a verbal way in the context of family therapy). In Compositionwork externalization takes place on a highly *nonverbal* and *symbolic* level, since the inner world is represented by stones and sand. Translating one's inner world into an external form helps to relate to it in an easy and comprehensive way. Just like a picture can say more than a thousand words, a landscape can express feelings, emotions, tensions and issues that previously had no verbal language (Harris, 2012). Such a landscape 'speaks back' in the nonverbal 'presentative' language of space, colors, shapes and forms (Langer, 1979). These aspects give important information about qualities of *I*-positions, their relations as well the overall organization of the self as revealed in the created pattern. Thus, externalization of I positions in the form of a composition creates optimal conditions to take a meta-position, which renders a broader perspective. Any emotion a person feels or position he or she takes can only fully be understood in the broader context of other aspects of the self, not as an isolated element. The method creates such a context by composing and relating all elements simultaneously. Externalization helps to explore the meaning of an *I*-position or emotions in the broader context of the pattern formed by the position repertoire of the person. Externalization stimulates an optimal distance towards a position or emotion.

This distance enlarges one's space of freedom towards what is observed and supports one's agency towards problematic emotions and aspects of the self. Clients can experience that they do not coincide with their anger or professional role, but that they can relate to them from different perspectives (other positions) and make choices about how to proceed about it. This helps to make more balanced decisions about one's life, work and developmental direction.

Compositionwork Uses Natural Symbolism as a Source of Self-Insight and Innovation

Natural symbolism helps to reach and explore less reachable or hidden *I*-positions. Aspects of experience that are not directly accessible may become visible through a symbol (Tillich, 1960). An externalized landscape created in this way includes a broad spectrum of verbal and nonverbal information. By using natural symbols like stones and sand, not only information about well defined, verbalized and conceptualized positions is gathered (like in traditional verbal therapies and coaching) but also vague, undefined or partly unconscious material. This range of input allows for optimal expression and accessibility of what is going on in a person. Our own work and that of others (e.g. Harris, 2012) shows that using natural elements as symbols helps to access deeper thoughts and feelings. Tactile sensations and the symbolism of sand (e.g. ground, depth, unknown, discovery) enhance the process of exploration of the self and offer relevant metaphors.

According to Jaffe (1964) stones are often used as universal symbols of the psyche, representing the sacred and mysterious. They have symbolic meaning for ancient and primitive societies and they still speak to the psyche of the modern person. Sometimes stones are treated as symbols of transformation, connection and integration. Eliade (1958) argues that stones have been symbols of connection between different dimensions of life all through the history of humankind. Stones have spoken to the human mind through the ages and across continents, and play an important part in universal symbolism, as also described by Jung (1963). Stones can be useful in the exploration of the human mind, because of their appeal to the unconscious and to the affective, nonverbal dimension of the self by means of their nonverbal and nonfigurative properties and the combination of their naturalistic and abstract qualities (Konopka & Van Beers, 2014). By their abstract and sensory qualities stones can 'presentatively' symbolize and express experiences coming directly from the affective dimension of the self, unmediated by concepts (Langer, 1979). The language of stones is the language of colors, sensory experience, textures and space. The sand can be seen as the space of mind in which positions appear and relate to each other. Metaphorically speaking it is the background-space of awareness that allows us to contemplate what is there, what is happening and going on in this landscape.

Compositionwork Uses the Potential of Both Brain Hemispheres, Which Optimally Enhances Learning Processes

Human brain anatomy is seen as resulting in two important processes: the ability to have emotion and the ability to reflect on it (Greenberg, 2012). Emotions tell us whether things are good or bad for us and direct our behavior. Reflection helps us consider their impact and evaluates whether and how we should follow them up. However, these two can easily become conflicting: *The great complexity of being human is that, in essence, we are two 'selves' that do not necessarily get along* (Greenberg, 2002, p. IX.). The first self is rational, logical and cognitive. It is concerned with plans, goals and the future. It is the monitoring aspect that easily becomes an inner critic and maintains all the 'musts' and 'shoulds' we may stick to. The second self derives from the experiential, sensory stream of consciousness that is more passionate, sensitive and delicate. It is the basis for empathy and compassion. Many authors distinguish between these two basic levels of the self that correspond with the functions of the two brain hemispheres (Shore, 2012; Greenberg, 2004; McGilchrist, 2009; Klukhuhn, 2010; Hermans, in preparation). McGilchrist describes the world of the left brain as disembodied, related to language, abstraction and decontextualized knowledge. On the other hand the world of the right hemisphere is described as the realm of interconnection, implicit knowledge, embodiment, feelings and presence (McGilchrist, 2009; Taylor, 2006). In our Western culture there is a significant dominance of left hemisphere functions such as reason, cognition, verbalization, and rationality over right hemisphere ones such as emotional processing, creativity, aesthetic experience, empathy and direct present individual experience (Shore, 2012; McGilchrist, 2009). As a consequence the functions of the left hemisphere tend to get more power and influence in the self and the functions of the right hemisphere are easily restricted by this imbalance. According to Greenberg (2002) a *combination* of these two dimensions of the self is optimal for learning and development. In our work uncovering emotions and exploring conflicts between emotions and cognitions are often issues to address. The learning process in Compositionwork takes place in a dialogue between these two dimensions, or in other words in the dialogue between the heart and the head. Taking into account the dominance of the left brain functions in our culture and the importance of integration of the two levels of the self, we deliberately created conditions in the method for also expressing experiences derived from the affective, experiential dimension of the self. This is not only supported by using nonverbal materials like stones and sand, introducing the 'nonverbal language' of colors, textures, shapes and space, but also by focusing on the present moment, direct sensory and affective-embodied experience of the person. On the other hand, naming the elements of a composition (verbalizing them), voicing them and reflecting on them, as well as reflecting on the overall pattern, subsequently connects the activity of the right hemisphere with the left one. The 'co-operation' of the two hemispheres and their corresponding inputs and impact on the self add to the integration and development of the self (Hermans, in preparation).

Making a Composition: Process and Structure Oriented Approaches

Compositions can be made in two fundamentally different ways: process oriented and structure oriented. The process oriented approach addresses the dimension of the present moment, direct affective experience and is more related to the functions of the right hemisphere, while the structure oriented approach is more focused on the reflective and cognitive functions. The combination of these two approaches allows to create an optimal picture that includes aspects that derive from direct momentary experience as well as aspects of the self that a person can define via reflection.

The *process oriented* approach starts from a 'not-knowing mind' (a 'nowing mind') that allows to connect to the immediate ongoing affective experience. It opens the self to direct experience, to be in touch with feelings emerging in the present moment. We call a composition emerging on the basis of present moment experience a 'nowscape'. In the process oriented approach a participant is guided by a coach who helps to get in touch with one's ongoing affective experience. Forms (mind content) that appear in his or her direct experience: emotions, I positions or more subtle feelings and sensations, are symbolized and externalized.[1] The process oriented approach has two functions: it helps to open up to and connect with the ongoing process of affective embodied experience and it stimulates insights derived from the patterns and complexity of this experience. As Greenberg (2002) points: *"Trained in this scientific era to be reasonable and restrained, both in public and at work, people often neglect and lose touch with their internal stream of experience"*. Connecting with one's ongoing affective experience a person connects with a broad source of affective knowledge that includes information that helps to orient himself in the environment and in relations with others. Such a source can act as an 'inner compass' (Rogers, 1961,' inner evaluation center'). Since affective signals can be a complex mixture of old and new responses and adaptive and maladaptive feelings, it is necessary to articulate the direct experience with reflection about it. Such a dialogue between 'the heart and the head' is necessary to develop one's emotional wisdom further. In Compositionwork reflection finds its place in the second phase when the created composition is explored from the meta-position.

The *structure oriented* approach emphasizes reflection on different positions and addresses the larger time perspective from which these position are considered. In this approach, whether in an individual or in a group session, the person is invited to identify *I*-positions that are relevant in his or her life in general or in a particular context, and externalize them in the form of a composition. Elements of the composition can include both internal (e.g. I as dreamer, I as artist) and external *I*-positions

[1] Stern (2004) discovered that a broader self-organization can be revealed in the momentary experience and can be accessed by exploration of the pattern of the present moment. Micro experience can reveal a broader panorama: a pattern that a person functions in. In Compositionwork the organization of the momentary experience may show an important and sometimes unexpected organization of *I*-positions of the self

(my friend, my husband). The structure oriented approach helps to create a relevant overview on a broad spectrum of elements that are playing a role in one's self. It helps to see patterns that have appeared over a larger time period and to reevaluate them.

Exploration of a Composition

When a composition is created, it can be further explored, deepened and developed. This can be done in the same session but also be spread over more sessions, depending on the process the client gets involved in. For the exploration of a composition three methodological starting points for intervention are distinguished: (a) exploration of singular *I*-positions, (b) exploration of relations between *I*-positions, and (c) investigation of the pattern of the composition.

(a) Exploration and differentiation of singular I-positions

Exploration and differentiation of *I*-positions is guided by questions posed by a coach who can address various aspects, including the affective quality of *I*-positions, their energy, centrality, power, history, and their voices. The affective quality of *I*-positions can be related to the color, shape, texture, or size and weight of the stones that represent these *I*-positions. Looking at a stone and touching it may often lead to new insights into the qualities of the *I*-position. For example one client picked up a huge and edgy stone to represent his unrest. Exploring the sharp and edgy outlines of this stone he got in touch with the hardiness of demands coming from this feeling of unrest, which so harshly took away the peace and quiet he was so much longing for. The form of the stone symbolized the qualities of the feeling and the impact that it had on his self. Another client chose a heavy stone that had the shape of a thick wall for the position 'I as responsible', a position that took away his energy. Exploration of the quality of this stone led to a deeper exploration of his position of responsibility. The shape and the weight were expressing the quality of this position and led to the insight that this position was based on an underlying feeling of guilt. This was like a heavy and thick wall that obstructed his freedom and his free flow of energy.

Different positions are usually connected with different *voices* that often express varied or sometimes even contradictory stories, emotions, values, tendencies, and world views. Expressing these voices can be very relevant for the investigation. In Compositionwork people speak not only *about* their positions, but also *from* their positions. As Rowan (2010) argues, it is important to let the person experience a position from within, because it strongly connects the client with the affective quality of the *I*-position, helps to go into the experiential world of this position and see the world through its eyes. It can also be useful to enter into a direct dialogue with a position, by asking questions such as 'How old are you?' or 'When did you meet (name of the client) for the first time?' (Rowan, 2010). A client can give answers to these questions from a variety of other positions and in this way gets new insights.

The process of discovery and exploration of not fully conscious positions may also be stimulated by having a person choose a stone that somehow attracts him or her, or evokes some affective response without knowing 'why'. Exploring such a 'find' we often arrive at a new emerging *I*-position or a feeling that contains an important message. It can also connect a person to some energy that in the future can develop into a new *I*-position. An example of this was a green 'powerful' stone that a client called his 'sea position'. It represented new vital energy that became accessible when he let go of his need for control. Later on this energy became a new position that he called 'Being'. It represented a new way of relating to others that was open and accepting. The discovery of a relation between the qualities of stones and the emerging meaning of *I*-positions is a very personal and gradual process. As symbols, stones may reveal the enormous wealth of one's experiential world: a stone that represents a peacock may symbolize a feeling of pride; a stone that represented a green turtle symbolized the position that expressed the client's wish to slow down and reconnect with nature; a stone in the shape of a red egg symbolized excitement and new energy and became a new position: 'I as creative'; a yellow, 'sunny' stone symbolized a new relation towards oneself: 'I as taking care for myself'; a 'sky stone' represented one's 'Buddha nature'. Stones can be powerful symbols and help to differentiate and further explore the related experiences and give meaning to these new *I*-positions.

Differentiation and exploration of *I*-positions may show which positions give and which take energy, which dominate and which are suppressed, which are central and which are peripheral, which are close to one's core and enhance a centripetal movement in the self and which have a centrifugal influence on the self. It can lead to the discovery of vital positions that have a promoter function or of a shadow position which can potentially be integrated in the self. Differentiating *I*-positions and emotions enhances learning about and allowing one's inner richness.

(b) Exploring and developing relations between I-positions

In the society of mind, as in normal society, a variety of relations among positions is possible: tensions, alienation, dialogue, power struggles, or coalitions between positions that support each other (Hermans & Hermans-Konopka, 2010). Some positions have more power, or dominate in the self, and others can be suppressed or rejected. For example, a person who is always working hard and does not have time to enjoy life can realize that his self is dominated by the position 'I as hard worker'. Further exploration may show that this position is based on a hidden fear of failure. As a consequence, the underlying position 'I as afraid' can turn out to have much more power in the self than, for example 'I as enjoyer of life'. Compositionwork creates conditions for exploration of these relations.

In exploring relations between positions, we also pay attention to the space between them and to how they are positioned towards each other. Sometimes the distance between positions symbolizes the distance between them in real life. For one of our clients it was confronting to see the distance between the position 'I as authentic' and 'I as professional'. This distance in the composition led to the question how close, or rather how much apart these two positions were in his life.

The client confirmed that he could not feel 'being himself' in his job. At the same time the distance between the position 'I as authentic' and 'I as a playful child' was very small. This led to the question how they were connected and how the playful energy became totally excluded from his work.

(c) Exploration of the pattern of a composition

The essential quality of a composition is its overall pattern, which represents the organization of the self as a client experiences it. It shows the spatial organization of a variety of I positions the self may take. As parts of this pattern, singular positions and emotions receive additional meaning from their place in the larger whole. Not only the positions but also the space between them is an essential aspect of the pattern. The landscape can reveal a split, be overcrowded or empty; some positions can be concentrated in one corner, suggesting a coalition, whereas in other cases they may be spread out. A pattern can be chaotic, spread, concentrated, rigid or linear. The characteristics of the pattern are explored together with the client, which may lead to important insights in their meaning. The pattern of positions often reflects the power relations in the self (Hermans & Dimaggio, 2004), as will be illustrated in the case presented further down.

Broadening and Deepening of the Composition

A landscape of mind is not a static structure but a dynamic, developing landscape. Its organization can change and evolve. In the course of several sessions newly emerging positions and feelings can emerge and be incorporated in the composition. In this way ongoing experience is included in a process of deepening self-investigation, as new positions and feelings emerge and deeper layers are discovered, possibly down to the 'bedrocks of the psyche'. Expansion and differentiation of a composition also takes place when earlier avoided or suppressed positions and emotions ('shadow positions'; Hermans & Hermans-Konopka, 2010) are gradually accepted and included in the self. Taking into account that "*emotion is foundational in the construction of the self and is a key determinant of self organization*" (Greenberg, 2004, p. 3), allowing rejected emotions to be included can lead to a reorganization in the composition and the self.

Case Study

This case is about Steven, 53 years old, director in a large design company. Steven wanted to explore his situation at work because he had a feeling that something was missing. He often felt tired, a lack of enthusiasm or dissatisfaction. It was not very clear what was really missing, so he wanted to have a closer look on what was going on.

Session 1

Exploration and Differentiation of I-Positions

The first session took 3 h. We started with the process oriented approach in which feelings and experiences derived from the present moment were identified and symbolized. Then we moved on to the structure oriented approach and defined positions and emotions that played an important role in his work and life. First the positions and emotions were defined, differentiated and explored and after that we explored their relations and the pattern.

Dominant feelings were tiredness and unrest. Both feelings were represented by a heavy, edgy, big black stone, as 'I as unrestfully tired' (see Fig. 4.1). It was the biggest stone in his composition. He became aware that these feelings were so usual that he did not pay attention to them anymore; it had become 'normal'. He was also able to give voice to this stone. It said: *"You should take care for the things that are happening now in your company. Are you prepared for this afternoon meeting? It is not enough."* This statement was evoking a lot of 'tense readiness' in his body, as if he would have to be always ready, alert, mobilized to deal with a difficult or even critical situation. Under the stone of 'unrestful tiredness' lied the stone of 'anxiety'. It said: *"You will not manage it, all will collapse, you will lose the job, you must work harder"*. Very close to the position of unrestful tiredness was the position of 'director', that felt like a heavy load. From this position he said: *"It feels too big, too complex, too complex for me, with too much financial responsibility and load. Work is not fun here. There is no freedom nor creativity in this position. It is very attractive financially, but it is just like this stone. It is not like me. I am not myself here"*. At the same time this stone was the biggest of all his work positions, which for him reflected the situation that he invested most of his energy and time in this position, a position that he felt to be 'not really me'. Another position that was also problematic and very close to the director-position was 'I as borderless'. In this position he did not put limits. He tended to keep working endlessly, without breaks and also during the weekends. There would hardly be any time or mental space left for his family or to enjoy activities (sports, hobbies). Life was exhausting. He was afraid to lose recognition, appreciation, maybe even his job. 'Work' was included as an external position, giving a lot of pressure and stress, a heavy load of responsibility. It had similar qualities as the director position. 'Uncertainty' as an internal position was often blocking his spontaneity. It would become prominent when he thought about future possibilities. It easily turned into anxiety and tension.

The position of 'recognition seeker' played an important but ambivalent role. He wanted to be recognized and appreciated and could at the same time feel afraid to lose recognition. Striving for recognition gave fuel to the position 'I as borderless'. Another position that had ambivalent sides was 'I as problem solver'. He felt effective and strong when he solved issues but when he exaggerated this position he would take too much responsibility on himself which added to the heavy load of his job. He would try to solve things for other people including his team which made him often tired.

Exploring the Pattern

We also we explored how the energy was distributed among the positions. The pattern of the composition showed that the left side of the composition was colorful and consisted of energy giving positions. This part gave energy. He noticed that it was very limited in his life and work. The quality of these positions was also very different. He said: *"I feel somehow natural on this side, I do not have to make effort"*. But it was also very rare, which exactly reflected his situation in work and life: he did not have time and space for the positions that gave energy and joy. The right side, much bigger, was dark, took energy and felt 'not his own'. It was very clear that most of the *I*-positions related to his work just took energy and felt heavy. They also occupied most of the space in the composition and time and energy in his life. This 'energy-sucking' side of the composition was dark-colored, with the dominance of grey. The composition 'spoke back' to him through this ineluctable and forthright pattern. It was very confronting to see that the positions he invested in and gave attention and energy to were most of the time sources of fatigue, load and dissatisfaction. It was also confronting to realize that the positions in which he felt 'natural' and which were sources of joy, satisfaction and energy, got very limited space and time.

At the end of the first session we picked up the process oriented work again giving full attention to what was happening right now in his direct experience. The most important experience that appeared was a relief of tension and warm positive energy that he felt around his chest. He called it *"an experience of flow, when everything was opened and expressed. There is no heavy load at the moment. It is there, out there"*. We agreed that Steven would pay attention to and describe the experiences of unrest and the experience of peace/rest. A relevant exercise was supplied by the coach. Unrest was an important signal that showed him when he went beyond his borders, acted under the pressure of his anxiety or that he was not in peace with himself. Unrest was the very expression of his current situation in which he was overloaded by responsibility and driven by inner pressure. At the same time it was the signal that told him 'you are on the wrong track'. He had learned to ignore this 'red light' and the purpose of the exercise was to undo it by looking straight into it. If unrest was the red light, the opposite feeling of rest was the green one. The feeling of rest would become a relevant signal that he was transgressing his usual pattern. Another purpose of this exercise was to increase the connection with his embodied feelings as important feedback signals.

Session 2

Developing the Composition and Exploring New I-Positions

The second session started with a talk about what had happened in the period after the first session (4 weeks). After processing his experiences in the first session Steven had come to a far reaching conclusion: he had decided to share what he really felt and thought, as experienced in our first session, in a meeting of the board of directors. He had told them in which positions he felt being 'himself' and in which not, what gave him energy and what took his energy. And that he wanted to give more space to his creative side. And as a consequence that he wanted to work on other projects and try to make a combination between creativity and management. That he thought it would be better for him, but also for the company, because in this way he could more fully display and use his qualities. Being truthful to his intrinsic needs would give him more energy and enthusiasm. Without such a move he would lose his involvement and maybe end up with a burn-out. He commented: *"I took the risk of showing myself, just as I am. And I am proud of it"*. Telling all this, he had taken into account that he might lose his job, but being honest about it and improving the quality of his work *"was my aim and firm purpose"*. This was definitely a new way to relate to his colleagues. He concluded: *"It is very opposite to taking everything on my shoulders and suffering from that"*.

He was clearly taking a new position towards his colleagues and his team: 'I as open' (see Fig. 4.2). In this position he not only expressed his positive experiences like solidarity and involvement more explicitly, but also some negative feelings. Expressing 'all that there was' was a new step that made him more 'complete' and in that sense more authentic. It was the beginning of far reaching changes. 'I as open' was symbolized by a transparent stone, placed in the center of his composition. The transparency of the stone expressed that he now was transparent to himself and to others. A strong feeling of unrest and tiredness became an important signal that reminded Steven about the necessity of putting borders. Experiencing how much energy it cost him to work endlessly he decided limit the time he worked and to delegate more tasks to his team, rather than solving everything himself. He said: *"I told my colleagues how it is for me and realized: it is their problem how they will solve it, it is not always my problem: all that comes to me."* Several times he repeated: *"It is enough, this is what I can do but not more. I take care but it is often not my problem to deal with"*. Whenever he could be in this position he felt pride: *"I felt pride, big pride!"* Taking this attitude he took a new position: 'I as putting limits'. 'I as putting limits' led to another position: 'I as proud', that was represented by a big colorful stone which was put in the upper part of his composition. Another new position that was related to 'I as open' was 'I as decisive'. In this position he was clear about his expectations and he communicated not only what he wanted but also what he did not want related to the projects. Now, if things were not done he did not take over anymore but discussed it with his people. Again pride was the feeling related to this position. Pride was a crucial signal whenever he felt being on the new track.

In this second composition the position of 'uncertainty' had a new form: it was there but it did not block him any longer to express expectations and did not make him take over tasks that were not his. Nevertheless, uncertainty still appeared relatively often. The position 'I as certain' appeared now when he expressed concerns and expectations towards his team, like putting deadlines, talking to people in case there was something not done rather than doing it himself.

There was also an important development related to positions which in the first session appeared to be sources of energy but did not receive enough attention in his life. 'I as enjoyer of life' was going to get more space by picking up his hobby again, doing sport and planning some trips with his family. He said: *"It was so confronting to see and feel all this darkness in my first composition. I do not want to live like that anymore, I had to make serious decisions and steps."* Another new position that appeared was 'I as peaceful', also related to the new feeling of rest and opposite to the fatigue and unrest. *"I am feeling relief and peace. There is much to be done but I can feel peace. My body is at rest now"*. This position was symbolized by a green stone, the green color representing the nurturing quality of this feeling. A new position that still needed to be developed further was 'I as balanced'. He wanted to restructure his life in a way that would allow more balance between work and pleasure, between responsibility and fun.

'I as excited', represented by a green stone that had the shape of an egg, was a strong new feeling related to his new position in the company and his new profile in his other business. The shape and the color of the stone symbolized novelty, possibilities, vitality, something that is about to be born. 'Creatively managing' was a new position that he wanted to take. He had decided 'to go for it': *"It is me, it is so natural, and exiting. It is a new phase!"*. This new position appears to be a coalition between three *I*-positions from the first composition: solving problems, creative and trusting.

Relations Between Positions and the Pattern Explored in the Second Session

In this second session we noticed that 'I as putting limits' evoked 'I as proud' and led to the emergence of the new version of 'I as recognized'. There was also another path to 'I as recognized' namely via 'I as open'. He saw that there is another way to be appreciated or recognized: *"...by being open and honest and also taking myself into account, not only others"*. Putting limits also creates more space towards other positions which are important in his composition: 'I as enjoyer' and 'I as balanced'. It creates more time for himself, which allows him to do the things he likes and to access sources of positive energy and fulfillment. 'I as proud' is an emotional position. The feeling of pride functions as a very important signal: it tells him that he puts the right borders, within which he has found space to express his expectations and concerns and at the same time staying open to others. Feeling pride means 'well done, well done!'

There was a significant change in the pattern of this second composition. The colorful area of the composition became more central and bigger. Now there appeared new *I*-positions in this area, related to the new emotional qualities. This was reflected in the richness of the colors of the stones.

Observations and Evaluation

Dominance Reversal

A crucial moment in the process was Steven's fundamental choice to come out with his true feelings and thoughts about how things were for him – and his willingness to live up to this, despite all possible risks. Of course this moment in life must have been 'incubated' for quite a while: he had been feeling the burden of his position for a long time and it was beginning to cost him enough to come to see that he should not go on like this much longer. Still, he had to find an alternative and the courage to stand for what felt better. Through Compositionwork he was unexpectedly and uneluctably confronted with significant obstacles in his life situation and also came to see what really attracted him. The power of an externalized inner landscape is that it cannot be denied: he created it himself, identifying his feelings spontaneously via the processual approach. Then the composition speaks back, which can be heard in 'its own' (his) words: *"It is not like me. I am not myself here,... I do not want to live like that anymore, I have to make serious decisions and steps". "What are you going to do with this problem, how will you work on this issue? You cannot just sit and do nothing."* And he certainly did something about it! He surprised us tremendously with this immediate move and his 'coming out' in the meeting of directors. As said, he must have been ready for it, ready to make a fundamental change in the investment of life-energies in hitherto dormant positions. It was Soren Kierkegaard that said that the deepest form of despair is "to choose to be another than oneself". A 'dominance reversal' was required to move away from this towards a more fitting and more 'authentic' position.

Authentic Self

Steven's choice can be seen as a choice for a more authentic self, a self whose positions are more in accordance with his 'natural balance' and that also feels as natural and 'own'. Carl Rogers calls authenticity the deepest responsibility of a person (Rogers, 1961). The power of such a choice can be deeply transforming. It seems that in Steven's life the crucial moment had arrived: he could find the courage to choose to be himself, regardless of the consequences. It was a firm decision to choose for positions in which he felt natural and being himself and a willingness to let the positions go that were unnatural and draining his energy. His composition showed him undeniably how things were. He chose 'for himself' and that made him more authentic.

What is an authentic self? It is certainly not some kind of identity you build up by choosing the right positions. We agree with Rogers that the self is rather to be seen and experienced as a process than as a product (Rogers, 1961). We see authenticity as living in a moment to moment connection and openness to what is happening and evolving in one's self and in relation to others, rather than as an ideal self that would have found its 'best positions'. A self that is based only on conceptual knowledge about itself easily loses its vitality and aliveness, deadening the process of 'becoming' and any further development. In our view an authentic self is fluid, grounding itself in directly felt embodied experience.

Promoter Position

Discovering and cultivating a promoter position can be of great significance for a constructive developmental direction in oneself. In Stevens position repertoire 'I as open' seems to have a significant promoter function. It allows him to face things as they are (especially his feelings) and also communicate this with others. 'I as open' was invited and encouraged by considering all important aspects of himself and the corresponding feelings in his composition. It also encouraged him to communicate about them. This free and open position allows him to take into account what matters for himself and what is important for others, without trying to manipulate neither. This position has an integrative function by stimulating a dialogue with a variety of other *I*-positions and with other people. It allows his inner subjective truth to be heard by himself and others. This position is close to what we call an authentic self: openness towards one's real experience in – and even despite of – all its possible complexity. It includes both the courage to face, feel and confront what is happening in one's self and being open about it to the world. An authentic position usually has a lot of power because no energy is lost in covering up and manipulating things 'as they are'. This power could be called 'the power of truth'. This is not an outer 'objective' truth but rather truthfulness and openness to the reality of one's inner unfabricated world. Seeing and feeling one's inner subjective truth can be seen as an act of liberation from an I –prison that is created by blindly or unilaterally following social expectations: *"Then you will know the truth, and the truth will set you free"* (sermon of John in the bible). Such a position is truly dialogical, since it includes hearing and listening to one's own inner truth and letting others hear it as well. And it "feels good". Stevens' special signal for it was pride: 'I as proud'. It tells him he is on the right way.

Applications and the Role of the Coach

Compositionwork can be used in coaching, counseling, career counseling, psychological training or education. It is a helpful method for issues related to personal development, exploring inner conflicts, conflicts between cultural positions, dealing with multiplicity and transition. The method is also used in emotional coaching (Hermans & Hermans-Konopka, 2010), focusing on the development of emotional awareness and a constructive, growth promoting relation with one's emotions and feelings. The method is apt for individual and for group-work. It can be applied with people of different educational levels and verbal ability, with anybody who is interested in exploring the complexity of the self as a guide for personal growth.

To apply Compositionwork in a way that can bring reliable and valid results requires guidance from an experienced coach with sufficient knowledge of Dialogical Self Theory. The use of the method and intervention techniques is seen as enabling direct experience to occur. The coach enhances and supports the process of exploration and creation of meaning the client gets into and helps identify the needs for change. He does this mainly by asking questions, slowly guiding the client through his composition. The questions invite clients to elaborate and deepen the experience in order to become more aware of what is going on in themselves and stimulate them to further reflect on that. The coach may address feelings that seem to appear in the clients and if so invite them to bodily connect to these feelings. The coach hardly ever 'interprets' and holds the space for 'meanings' to be articulated. In this way the coach adopts a very supportive, non-directive but highly sensitive position towards the client from where he or she follows and stimulates the process of exploration and deepening that takes place. The purpose of Compositionwork is to deepen the awareness of what is going on in one's self[2].

References

Eliade, M. (1958). *Patterns in comparative religion*. London: Sheed and Ward.

Greenberg, L. S. (2002). *Emotion-focused therapy: Coaching clients to work through their feelings*. Washington, DC: American Psychological Association.

Greenberg, L. S. (2004). Emotion-focused therapy. *Clinical Psychology & Psychotherapy, 11*, 3–16.

Greenberg, L. S. (2012). Emotions, the great captains of our lives: Their role in the process of change in psychotherapy. *The American Psychologist, 67*, 697–707.

Harris, D. L. (2012). Techniques of grief therapy. In R. A. Neimeyer (Ed.), *Creative practices for counseling the bereaved* (pp. 61–66). New York: Routledge.

Hermans, H. J. M. (in preparation). *Society in the self: A theory of inner democracy.*

Hermans, H. J. M. (1996). Voicing the self: From information processing to dialogical interchange. *Psychological Bulletin, 119*, 31–50.

Hermans, H. J. M. (1999). Dialogical thinking and self-innovation. *Culture & Psychology, 5*, 67–87.

Hermans, H. J. M. (2002). The dialogical self as a society of mind: Introduction. *Theory and Psychology, 12*, 147–160.

Hermans, H. J. M. (2014). Self as a society of *I*-positions: A dialogical approach to counseling. *Journal of Humanistic Counseling, 53*, 134–159.

Hermans, H. J. M., & Hermans-Konopka, A. (2010). *Dialogical self theory: Positioning and counter-positioning in a globalizing society*. Cambridge, UK: Cambridge University Press.

Hermans, H. J. M., & Dimaggio, G. (Eds.). (2004). *The dialogical self in psychotherapy*. New York: Brunner & Routledge.

Jaffe, A. (1964).Symbolism in the visual arts. In C. G. Jung & M.L von Franz (Eds.), *Man and his symbols* (pp. 256–322). New York: Dell.

[2]Detailed information about our Practitionerstraining Compositionwork for coaches and counselors can be found on www.compositionwork.com

Jung, C. G. (1963). *Memories, dreams, reflections*. London: Collins and Routledge.
Klukhuhn, A. (2010). *Alle mensen heten Janus. Het verbond tussen filosofie, wetenschap, kunst en godsdienst* [All people are named Janus: The connection between philosophy, science, and religion]. Amsterdam: Uitgeverij Bert Bakker.
Konopka, A., & Van Beers, W. (2014). Compositionwork. Een methode voor zelfonderzoek [Compositionwork: A method for self-investigation]. In F. Meijers, M. Kuijpers, K. Mittendorf, & G. Wijers (Ed.), *Het Onzekere voor het Zekere* (pp. 185–204). Antwerpen, Belgium/Apeldoorn, The Netherlands: Garant.
Konopka, A., & Van Beers, W. (2014). Compositionwork: A method for self-investigation. *Journal of Constructivist Psychology, 27*(3), 194–210.
Langer, S. K. (1979). *Philosophy in a new key. A study in the symbolism of reason, rite and art* (3rd ed.). Boston: Harvard University Press.
McGilchrist, I. (2009). *The master and his emissary: The divided brain and the making of the western world*. New Haven, CT/London: Yale University Press.
Nitschke, G. (1999). *Japanese gardens. Right angle and natural form*. Tokyo: Taschen.
Rogers, C. (1961).*On becoming a person: A therapist's view of psychotherapy*. Boston: Houghton Mifflin Company.
Rowan, J. (2010). *Personification*. New York: Routledge.
Shore, A. (2012). *The science of the art of psychotherapy*. New York: Norton & Company.
Slawson, D. A. (2008). Sztuka ogrodow (Art of Gardens). In K. Wilkoszewska (Ed.), *Estetyka japonska*. Krakow: TAiWPN Universitas.
Stern, D. N. (2004). *The present moment in psychotherapy and everyday life*. New York: Norton & Company.
Taylor, B. J. (2006). *My stroke of insight: A brain scientist's personal journey*. London: Penguin.
Tillich, P. (1960). *Love, power, and justice: Ontological analyses and ethical applications*. Oxford, UK: Oxford University Press.
White, M., & Epston, D. (1990). *Narrative means to therapeutic ends*. Adelaide, SA, Australia: Dulwich Centre.

Chapter 5
Dialogical Leadership

The "Other" Way to Coach Leaders

Rens van Loon and Tessa van den Berg

In this chapter we take you on the journey of exploring the concept of Dialogical Leadership. Here we apply the concept of the 'dialogical self' to leadership. Leaders play an important role in our daily life, work, communication and society. Leaders are relationally connected with followers. We switch between these two roles, depending on the context, sometimes in the leading role, sometimes following. Dialogical aspects in the relation can be defined from an internal perspective and from an external perspective. You can reflect in an internal dialogue with yourself or in an external dialogue with another person.

In the first section of this chapter we explore aspects of Hermans' Dialogical Self Theory (Hermans, 2006; Hermans & Hermans-Konopka, 2010; Hermans & Gieser, 2012; Hermans, Kempen & Van Loon, 1992) and Leadership Theory (Grint, 2005, 2010; Hersted & Gergen, 2013; Hosking, 2011). In the second section we describe the outline of a methodology to develop Dialogical Leadership skills for those people who act as a professional coach. The third section contains a case study, where the core concepts we described in the theoretical part are illustrated. We conclude with some reflections on the case, when and for whom to apply this approach and the qualities needed for the Dialogical Leadership practitioner.

A gentle warning for the reader might be appropriate here. Leadership is a massive domain. We had to focus in this chapter. Without the ambition of being complete, we want to show you one particular path in the great wealth of leadership definitions. Our starting point is that a Dialogical Leadership approach will help people to better manage others by better managing themselves. This is a relational

R. van Loon (✉)
School of Humanities, Tilburg University, Tilburg, The Netherlands
e-mail: rvanloon@deloitte.nl

T. van den Berg
Deloitte Consulting, Amsterdam, The Netherlands
e-mail: TesvandenBerg@deloitte.nl

H. Hermans (ed.), *Assessing and Stimulating a Dialogical Self in Groups, Teams, Cultures, and Organizations*, DOI 10.1007/978-3-319-32482-1_5

approach to leadership development that creates a system of collaborative intelligence enabling leaders to tackle the complex problems they face. Let's have a look at the concept of Dialogical Leadership in more detail.

Self as a Society of Mind and Dialogical Leadership

Dialogical Self Theory describes self as a microcosm of society. Your "self" contains a collection of roles. Hermans uses the term "*I*-position" referring to you as a child, a parent, a partner, a professional, a worker, a leader, and so on, that relates to a wider society and network of others in which it functions (Hermans & Hermans-Konopka, 2010; Hermans & Gieser, 2012). This connects Dialogical Self Theory seamlessly with Leadership Development, as leaders have to show different roles which can be described as *I*-positions. To act as effective leaders, they have to form their own unique microcosm of *I*-positions. For leaders being able to flexibly move between *I*-positions (van Loon, 2010; Van Loon & Van Dijk, 2015) this is critical to be successful. If leaders get hooked too much and too long in one *I*-position their effectiveness might be affected. In contemporary organizations leaders differentiate between basic roles such as entrepreneur (setting direction for the organization), manager (getting things done), coach (developing people), expert (leading in your field of expertise, e.g. engineering, law, business, etc.) and change leader (leading processes of change and transformation in an organization's business process, culture and behavior). Leaders at times experience tension between these roles as they require different behaviors and mindsets. In the Dialogical Leadership approach we explore roles as *I*-positions, both the basic ones (entrepreneur, manager, coach, expert and change leader) and personal *I*-positions (e.g. I as inspiring, I as impulsive, I as intuitive, etc.) through internal and external dialogue. Let's have a closer look at the relational and generative character of leadership and dialogue.

We describe leadership as a *relational* process (Hersted & Gergen, 2013; Hosking, 2011) and dialogue as a practice designed to enable *emerging new meaning* (Bojer, Roehl, Knuth & Magner, 2008; Gergen, 2009). In a dialogue new meaning is relationally created (Gergen & Gergen, 2004; Gergen, McNamee & Barrett, 2001; Hersted & Gergen, 2013; Scharmer & Kaufer, 2013). In *Relational Being: Beyond self and community* (2009), Gergen puts relations at the heart of being human. His central thesis is that these mental processes are not so much in the head of individuals as in their mutual relationships. Being aware that both effective leadership and dialogue imply a *mutually reflexive, reciprocally implicated* (Hawes, 1999) mindset will make leaders better prepared to deal with complexity, interconnectedness and continuous change, in themselves, in relation to their organizations and the global context.

Dialogical Leadership can be described as "A dynamic *multiplicity* of *I-positions* in the *landscape* of the mind." (Hermans, Kempen & van Loon, 1992). At the individual level, a leader is faced with the challenge to reconcile/transform contradictions between various *I*-positions within him/herself. As an example: how to keep the relation intact between "I as an entrepreneur" who wants to grow his business and "I as a manager" who is required to cut costs in an economic crisis? At the level of teams or organizations, the leader is faced with the challenge to reconcile/transform the contradiction between the multiple voices of colleagues, stakeholders, competitors, etc., given the field of tension between the local and the global, unity and multiplicity, consistency and inconsistency and self and the other. Dialogical leaders create an environment where new perspectives, narratives and meanings are nourished and shared. *Dialogical Leadership* can be further elaborated as "flexible movements between a diversity of *I*-positions that are relevant to the functioning of the organization as a whole." (Hermans & Hermans-Konopka, 2010, p. 326). Leaders faced with the challenge of dealing with tensions and multiple voices have to develop an understanding in themselves as a "compass" for their thinking, feeling and acting. Dialogical Self Theory provides us with some concepts that are useful in developing this compass.

Theoretical Framework for Dialogical Leadership

Hermans describes some concepts in Dialogical Self Theory that also apply to leadership (Hermans & Gieser, 2012; Hermans & Hermans-Konopka, 2010). The "core position" is one of them. This is an *I*-position on which the functioning of other positions depends. As an example, "I as a finance director" is a leadership core position around which *being rational and analytic*, *being an expert* and *dominant over others* are grouped as related *I*-positions. We will later explore this one in the case study.

A second concept that is important for Dialogical Leadership is the "promoter position". This is described as an *I*-position which gives direction and order in the development of other positions in the position repertoire. For example "I as rational and dominant scientist" can be promoted/transformed by an *I*-position that is formulated as "I as an intuitive painter". By bringing the two positions in an internal dialogue with one another, a new direction might arise. Such an example is close to a "third position", where we describe the mechanism of mediating between two conflicting positions. The intuitive painter and rational scientist could be reconciled in a third position "I as an intuitive scientist". Although you might think this is "playing with words", our experience is that once leaders make a new connection/combination in words, the field of meaning might change radically.

Two more aspects of Dialogical Self Theory are important to mention here: centering and decentering. In the foregoing example, the third position is at the same time a centering movement. *Centering processes* can be described as movements that contribute to the organization and integration of the position repertoire. As an example, we worked with an IT leader who integrated two opposing *I*-positions with "I as a mountaineering guide". This new *I*-position reconciled "I as autocratic leader" and "I as motivated to develop people" in the "guide".[1] Here he is able to reconcile his direct behavior with his intention to develop others. In this role he was allowed to lead in a strict sense (commandeering), without upsetting his followers, as in hikes in the mountains clear instruction is needed. Through this new insight the IT leader was able to function more effective in his daily role, as he deeply understood how to redirect his more autocratic style of leading. *Decentering processes* are centrifugal movements that disorganize the existing position repertoire so that it opens up to innovation and change. Although this might be a positive tendency, leaders often experience this as odd and uncomfortable. In a decentering process you get temporarily out of balance and open up for new ways of thinking, feeling and acting. We worked with a technical engineer, who completely relied on his rational, controlling influencing style. In his private life he was a dancing teacher. When the *I*-position of the "rational engineer" was confronted (by himself in a dialogue) with that of the "dancing teacher", he was confused for a while. He lost balance in his job, and tried to restore it by bringing the way of leading of a dancing teacher into the rational engineering environment of his work. So the result of these processes is a more diversified way of leading. Both the technical engineer and the IT leader deeply understood and learned to apply more than their habitual leadership style. Later – in the case study – we will elaborate on these processes.

We close this section with three remarks, which might help you to better understand what we mean by Dialogical Leadership, before we dive into a more methodological description.

Firstly, a Dialogical Leader is able to facilitate a dialogue where new meaning emerges in the interaction between two or more people. Dialogical Leadership implies being able to create the conditions for new meaning to emerge in the interaction. As misunderstanding between people is inherent in relational influencing, there is a job for leaders to effectively deal with this phenomenon. Hermans (2006) describes as a task for a dialogical leader to recognize possible misunderstandings. In some cases, misunderstanding might be caused by power, another important factor in dialogue. Leaders have to be aware of the influence of power in conversations. Even if you feel being equal to all others in the meeting, the fact that you are the CEO might prevent other people from expressing what they really think or feel. Leadership coaching implies that you support them to create conditions and a mindset where sensitivity for misunderstanding and power is developed.

Secondly, there is a difference between dialogue and debate. While debate is about defending your assumptions, opposing and winning, dialogue is about questioning your assumptions, working together in a mutual space and trying to find common ground. Effective Dialogical Leadership implies that you are able to switch flexibly between these two modes of communication. You are also aware how others in the team/organization communicate, in which mode they speak and how they align/reconcile their differences, if relevant. As a dialogical leader you are – par

[1] The term guide, was brought up by the IT leader, not by the coach. In a process of reconciling the person has to come up with a word (metaphor or a real position) that brings two different *I*-positions together in a centering movement.

excellence – the one who shows that you are able to apply the principles of dialogue – respect, suspending judgments, listening, asking questions and voicing (Isaacs, 1993, 1999) – *and to break existing patterns*. You have the courage to *"put the fish on the table"* (Kohlrieser, 2006) at the moment it happens.[2] This entails you have the courage to break through a pattern of actions and words, which sometimes seems unstoppable. Leadership coaching implies to have the skill to listen silently, without any action or reaction, not interfering at any level.

Thirdly, for many leaders establishing a dialogue is not easy. The above description often differs from usual reality in organizations. Often there is no time, no awareness, and no willingness to slow down the process and to truly listen and explore the issue at hand. In our experience leaders need to be coached and trained how and when to apply the principles of dialogue. Keith Grint (2005, 2010) distinguishes types and issues that leaders in business, politics or society are faced with. Issues can be classified as crisis, tame or wicked based on two criteria: knowledge of the solution, and the leadership style required to tackle them. Each of these issues requires a different form of leadership. *Crises* require forceful action. *Tame issues* can be handled with routine and proper management, because we know how to tackle them. If we are faced with a tame problem, usually something we have seen before, the solution is known (e.g. heart surgery). Finding the solution is a matter of applying existing information or finding experts who have dealt with similar issues. *Wicked problems* are in a category where the solution is still shrouded in mystery. Wicked issues are those for which no known solution exists. Examples are climate change, peak oil and resource constraints and information and communication technologies that "disrupt" business models. For wicked, complex issues leaders cannot not assume to have the answers. They must empower people/their team to deliver solutions, and should accept the recurrent review and refinement of "clumsy" solutions as a valid way of tackling wicked issues. Many options and opinions are possible. In the category of wicked issues a dialogical approach is the most effective in Grint's view. Although CEO's are paid to have answers for the issues they are confronted with, their greatest contributions to organizations may be – in this line of thinking – asking the right questions and by doing so, directing the collective energy of the employees into what they feel as the most appropriate direction. Of course, dialogue is not a remedy for all situations we come across. The critical issue here is that leaders throughout their career are generally selected for situations where debate and rational argumentation are the primary methods to get things done, rather than getting things done through dialogue. As a leader you have to be able to deliberately switch between styles depending on the issue at hand. That is the reason why we propose to embed "dialogue experiments" in leadership development initiatives, allowing leaders to explore "the art of dialogue" in a setting where they receive feedback and which allows for reflection, that is, to sense what it means to

[2] Kohlrieser describes fishermen in Sicily, cleaning fish for the market. "Suddenly I realized this was what good conflict management is all about: "putting the fish on the table" and going through the bloody mess of cleaning the fish to prepare for the great fish dinner at the end of the day." (p. 108).

respect and be *respect*ed, to truly *listen*, to *suspend* your judgment and to *voice* what comes to your mind. A good dialogue might transform your meaning system, it opens up your thinking, feeling and acting in a way more appropriate to the *present, the now.* "Re-setting" of our way of perceiving could be one of the outcomes of a successful dialogue process. For leaders to transform their own "society of mind" is a first step, before they can transform (in other words, act as a promoter for) a collective "society of minds" in a culture or organization. It starts with consciously leading their own patterns of thinking, feeling and acting. Enabling these capabilities in leaders is therefore also the first step that coaches apply in a Dialogical Leadership framework.

In the next section we discuss a methodology that you can use as a coach to develop Dialogical Leadership with leaders in organizations.

Dialogical Leadership Methodology

Developing coaching capabilities in line with the concept of Dialogical Leadership is a continuous and long-term process. It takes you as a practitioner through a series of iterations that consist of exploring concepts of 'dialogical self', leadership, organization and change to form both a theoretical and a methodological foundation. Encouraging practitioners to apply these concepts in your practice of coaching leaders[3]; reflecting on what happens in the relation between coach and leader, between *I*-positions within leaders, and how these relate to issues, they are facing.

In this section we describe four iterations of exploring, applying and reflecting (see Fig. 5.1.), that in our view allow coaches to develop a foundational skill set, expertise and experience to support leaders in conducting meaningful dialogues with their teams. The four iterations are a starting point of a continuous learning process. Of course, what you do depends on your background. If you are a certified coach and psychologist, you go through a different type of learning process compared to a novice, having no experience. The first iteration focuses on theoretical concepts, the second on your *I*-positions as a coach, the third iteration practicing with clients/other people, the fourth on being a promoter for others.

Theoretical Concepts

In the first iteration you familiarize yourself with the basic concepts. This list could be the starting point of your exploration: Dialogical Self Theory: Hermans, 2006; Hermans & Gieser, 2012; Hermans & Hermans-Konopka, 2010; Hermans, Kempen &

[3] In defining coaching we follow the International Coach Federation's definition: "coaching is partnering with clients in a thought-provoking and creative process that inspires them to maximize their personal and professional potential". (Rogers & Van Dam, 2015, p. 117).

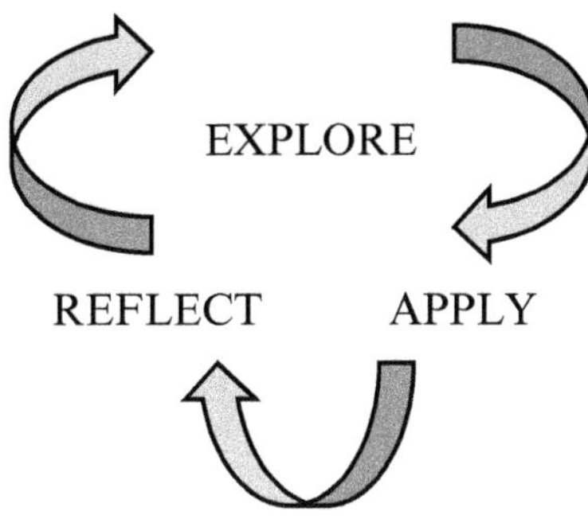

1. Theoretical concepts
2. Your own I-Positions
3. Practicing with others
4. Being a promoter for others
5. …….
6. …….

Fig. 5.1 Explore – apply – reflect

Van Loon, 1992. Leadership Theory: Grint, 2005, 2010; Hersted & Gergen, 2013; Hosking, 2011; Van Loon & Van Dijk, 2015; Coaching Theory and Practice: Orem, Binkert & Clancy, 2007; Whitmore, 2002.

By reading and understanding the concepts described above you build your first foundation.[4] This involves reading, digesting the information, applying it to your life and reflecting on it. By understanding the concepts you might start looking at "your" reality in a different manner. It might "open your mind". We recommend practitioners to regularly reflect on the concepts they are using in their daily practice.

Your Own I-*Positions*

After you have studied the theoretical concepts, you go through the second cycle of 'explore, apply and reflect' by applying this cycle on your own *I*-positions. What do these concepts imply for you? Here you think about the role leadership plays in your life, and what kind of *I*-positions are most meaningful to you in your life. Where are you in terms of coaching skills and insights? Here are some questions that might help you in applying the theoretical concepts.

"How many *I*-positions do I have?"

[4] You can find a complete overview of Hubert Hermans books, articles and conferences on his website: www.huberthermans.com

You could write down relevant aspects of yourself in relation to people that were/are important in your life and what position they take in your own position repertoire. For example, your mother telling you not to waste your time as an *I*-position "I as always being efficient".

"Exploring moments of change and transformation in my professional and personal life." Try to describe these moments in terms of *I*-positions. For example, "I am a mountain climber. You always need extra lung capacity. Once I applied this to my working life, I understood the importance of this *I*-position". Don't always work on maximum speed and energy.

"What does the multiplicity of *I*-positions look like for me?"

Try to make a picture. Try to visualize where the tensions are? Where are the moments of reconciling? Apply here the core concepts of Dialogical Self Theory, described before.

- What are my core positions?
- What are my promoter positions?
- Where are the centering or decentering movements in my *I*-position repertoire?

See Fig. 5.2. for an example of a position repertoire.

All these questions might help you to build experience in how to be in a dialogue with yourself. To become a strong coach for leaders you have to conscientiously build your experience around all these topics. Foundation for successful coaching is that you know yourself, that you are an effective, authentic and honest partner in dialogue. In our view this is a "journey" where you are free to explore basic concepts of leadership, dialogue, change and Dialogical Self Theory as you like.

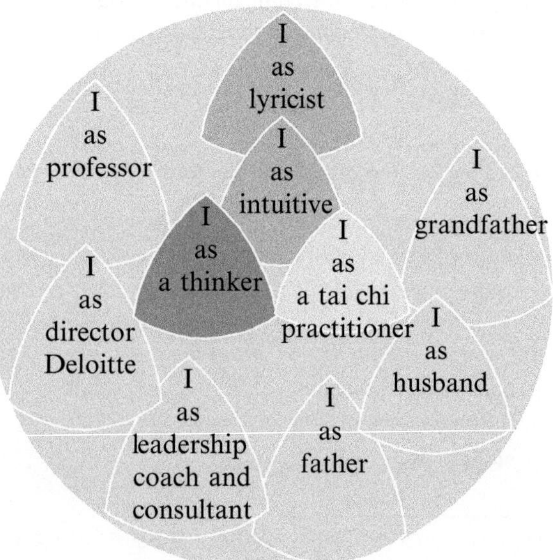

Fig. 5.2 Example of a position repertoire

Practicing with Others

After you have explored your own personal *I*-position repertoire, you start practicing with others. Here you enable others to explore and transform their personal *I*-position repertoire. Where you start this process is predominantly dependent on your skills as a coach/psychologist. Let us have a closer look at the core of Dialogical Leadership coaching by applying the dialogue. Remember that in a dialogue new meaning emerges in a natural way. Some questions and topics that might help you in this third iteration are the following:

> "What is your relation to the topic of leadership? When are you a natural leader? When, with whom, how, et cetera?"
>
> "What happens if you resist taking the lead?"
>
> "What does followership mean to you? When you are more like a follower? With whom, how, et cetera?"
>
> "What happens when you resist following?"

"If you are working as a formal leader in an organization, what type of leader are you (entrepreneur, manager, coach, change leader, professional)?" Reflect on the leadership style you choose.

> "What about your superior? Can you describe him/her for me? How do you influence your boss?"
>
> "What type of *I*-positions are relevant for you outside your professional and organizational life?"

Sometimes religion, values and personal beliefs are subjects for conversation. In general we recommend listening carefully to *I*-positions that are communicated explicitly and – very often – implicitly. Work with a flip chart and write down results in keywords. Experiment with a way of working that fits you best. We invite people to formulate "insights" when we change subject, before breaks and at the end of a session. An example is: "I realize that I have to speak more openly about my career plans and with more stakeholders."

How the conversation unfolds itself in practice depends on the dialogical process of building a relation of trustworthiness (Isaacs, 1999). A dialogue is not an interview, so what question you ask depends on the answer given by your partner in dialogue. The examples of the questions above are merely illustrative, you can't use this as a standard list. What we have in mind when we practice Dialogical Leadership is a conceptual framework: flexibly moving on the time axis "past – present – future", with different levels of depth and intensity in professional and personal domains. Where you are in the framework determines which questions you ask. All kind of topics might be brought to the table in a Dialogical Leadership process. You follow the flow in the conversation, not ticking off boxes.

Being a Promoter for Others

The fourth iteration is about creating conditions for opening transformational space in the dialogue and to stimulate the development of others. This is the essential critical skill for Dialogical Leadership coaches, as change takes places here. As a coach you enable the conversation to move in different directions, following your partner in dialogue. One of the main challenges for leaders – and coaches of the leader – is to suspend a judgment, automatically coming to mind. Authors use different terminology: The moment of freeing energy (Libbrecht, 2007), suspending judgment (Bohm, 1996; Isaacs, 1993; 1999), and creating space (Morioka, 2008; 2012). To give an example. You as a coach create space – in a relation of trustworthiness – when resistance occurs. In such a relation you can do a "here and now" timeout and make your partner in dialogue aware of *what is going on, while it is going on.* As a coach you must have free energy to be able to do a timeout on the right moment, *and* the trust in the relation – for both partners in dialogue – must be so high that your intervention is accepted. See also the case study in this chapter, where we describe this moment. Are participants in dialogue able to suspend their non-verbal/rational/emotional reactions or are they becoming aware of them and expressing them? This is where you support people in the process by making them aware from *a bird's eye view* of what is happening. By slowing down the process real time: what is happening in the present, now? What do you hear, what do you see, and what do you think, what is the difference between what you see and what you hear? Here the implicit is made explicit, the "I" of the participant, eyes and ears opened for *another* perspective. Emerging new meaning, new perspectives, new behaviors and intuitions in the *present* – that's the ultimate goal of the dialogue.

A final remark on all four iterations. All we described here has to be learned in a combination of experiencing, practicing, reflecting, reading and intentionally experimenting with new ways of thinking, feeling and acting in your role as a coach. A critical factor for success in applying the Dialogical Leadership approach as a coach is your capability to reflect on your practice in an open and realistic way. In the process of reflection your own performance and mindset are object for further reflecting. We propose to keep a diary and regularly write down self-observations and feedback you get from your dialogue partners. Ask what you could have done differently, after you have completed the session. Also intentionally think about different *I*-positions you take during the conversations with your client. Take your time regularly to sit down and reflect. We like to work with poetry, with pictures, photos and rational reflections. Make it a habit. Find your own formula for it. The quest to know yourself is a journey without an end.

Once you enjoy the process of living with a mindset of continuous learning, continuously going through iterations "explore, apply and reflect" you further deepen skills and build experience. Let's now have a look at a coaching case study, where these aspects are illustrated.

Case Study

In working with leaders over years we have many examples that could help the reader understanding and applying the principles of 'dialogical self' and Dialogical Leadership. We have chosen the case of a finance director for two reasons. He is a mature leader in his mid-forties, looking for new perspectives, both in his role as director and in his personal life. The second reason is that in his position repertoire different relations appear, illustrating processes of centering and promoting.

In applying Dialogical Leadership principles in coaching and leadership development, some people want to focus solely on business, but most of them realize that the leader as one whole person has to be involved in development. This is illustrated evidently in this case.[5] We describe four core *I*-positions, which were formulated in our conversations. *I as finance director* and *I as willing to help other people* are discussed in the first section. *I as an entrepreneur* and *I as a hobby farmer* in the second. These four are characterized as core positions, because a large variety of other positions are dependent on its functioning. E.g. *being rational and analytic, being an expert* and *dominant over others* are related to *I as finance director*. When Peter sensed his *willingness to help other people* was destabilized, he felt his entire repertoire was being disorganized. He used the expression '*I feel frustrated*'.

The process of Peter's development might be characterized by two phases, the first reconciling the tension between the *I*-positions of the finance director and his willingness to help other people. The second phase in reconciling the *I*-position of the entrepreneur with that of the hobby farmer. The conditions for dialogue must be fulfilled. By listening, showing respect, suspending judgements and voicing the coach facilitates the partner in dialogue in a process of reconciling. Let's have a more detailed look.

Peter is in his mid-forties when we meet. He is a successful finance director with a strong track record in business development. He pre-selected and bought many companies all over Europe. He describes himself as being impatient and sometimes impulsive. Over a period of two-and-a-half years we had seven one-on-one conversations[6] plus two team sessions with his team at peer level. His colleagues describe Peter as confident and sometimes arrogant as they often get the impression that he always knows better. He has a habit of overruling others, instead of developing them to a higher level of performance.

---

[5] This case has been disguised. Peter is not his real name.

[6] The first one was a one-and-a-half day in-depth dialogue, supported by additional tools such as 360° behavioral feedback and personality assessment based on Big5 theory. This is not described here. Follow-up conversations were two hour dialogues. Team sessions normally take one-and-a-half days with the entire team in an off-site location.

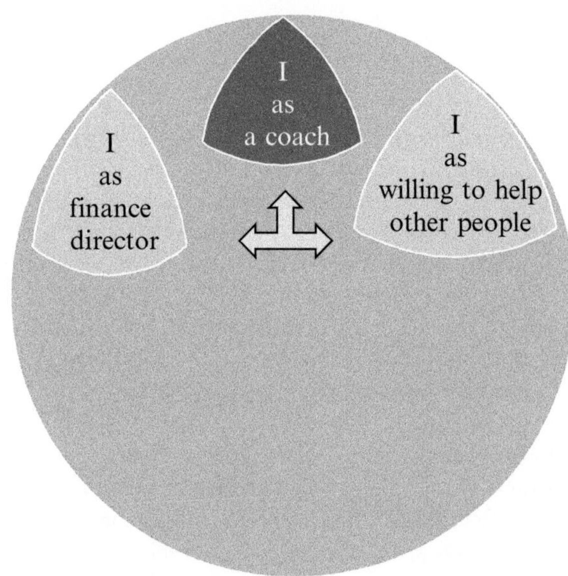

Fig. 5.3 I-Positions in Peter's position repertoire

I as Finance Director Versus I as Willing to Help Other People

In Fig. 5.3. Peter's *I*-positions are represented by triangles. On the top left, *I as finance director:* Peter is a brilliant thinker; he knows this is one of his truest talents. In his role as a finance director, he is able to use his rationality to the utmost. His successes in the organization are mainly dependent on this strongly developed *I*-position. Many of his technical competencies are interrelated. In this *I*-position Peter is described by his peers as a "know-it-all", indicating that he tends to over-articulate that competency. He is inclined to overrule people as they do not describe reality "as it is": the truth. In that case, this *I*-position is dominant and sometimes with a strong negative impact.

On the right (top) of Fig. 5.3. we have drawn the position *I as willing to help other people*. This *I*-position is described as "I as reliable and supportive". Peter feels happy in helping people, supporting them in understanding the case at hand. For him this is a vital *I*-position, primarily present in his private life, but also in the workplace, be it in a lesser degree. He loves working as a mentor with young people, looking for professional support.

In the conversations Peter expressed that he likes to teach young people, to use his knowledge and experience to support others in developing their business insights and skills. Occasionally he is invited to teach financial courses at a business university. He became aware that his tendency to act as a wiseacre hindered him from being perceived as a true supportive boss/colleague. Sometimes he felt as if these

I-positions of the finance director and 'his willingness to help other people' were unrelated and conflicting. It felt for him as a "confusing cacophony of voices, lacking any insightful organization" (Hermans & Hermans-Konopka, 2010, p. 228). Peter wanted to align his core competencies – being rational and being supportive – in a more consistent way. While talking about this tension, he also reflected about situations where these two *I*-positions were *not* conflicting. First, he spoke about a situation where he acted as a *coach*. Thinking about himself as a coach he used the expression "sharing knowledge by asking questions", instead of knowing better and correcting. A second situation was related to being a *teacher*. In front of students he was open and willing to support them in developing their insights themselves, instead of rectifying them. Consciously thinking about acting as a teacher and/or coach, he deliberately choose for the coach. He felt he wanted to develop his capabilities as a coach. This could create more order and give direction. He explored what he needed to do (in terms of training and courses) to become a professional coach. Although the coach role was not yet clearly visible in his behavior, in Peter's mind this *I*-position created a strong sense of direction and order in this conflicting set of *I*-positions. *I as a coach* can therefore be labeled as a promoter position. We added this in the middle of Fig. 5.3. (dark triangle), reconciling the other two *I*-positions.

I as a coach creates the openness to integrate different aspects of Peter's self. "By integration we mean that positions are reorganized in such a way that they result in a more adaptive self" (Hermans & Hermans-Konopka, 2010, p. 228). Peter felt that this newly voiced *I*-position had the potential to bring him to a higher level of performance in his working and private life. Let us have a look at the second pair of *I*-positons, functioning as core positions in Peter's personal repertoire.

I as an Entrepreneur and I as a Hobby Farmer

In Fig. 5.4. we add two core *I*-positions to Peter's repertoire. On the left (bottom) *I as an entrepreneur.* Peter describes a significant part of his working life in terms of expanding businesses. He truly acts as an entrepreneur, by pre-selecting, analyzing and buying companies in the market to create a stronger portfolio of businesses for the company. Viewed from this *I*-position, his rational and dominant behaviors are described as strengths (both by himself, his boss, his peers and the people he leads). Peter is a strong entrepreneur with well-developed commercial and analytical skills. Shadow-side of this strength is that he is stressed, unable to find relaxation, almost always travelling.

On the right (bottom) *I as a hobby farmer.* For Peter this reinforces his need for freedom and space (physical and mental), his feeling of being connected with his family and the animals on the farm. This is a strong counterweight for his *I*-position as an entrepreneur. In his own words: "I need space and I want to be connected

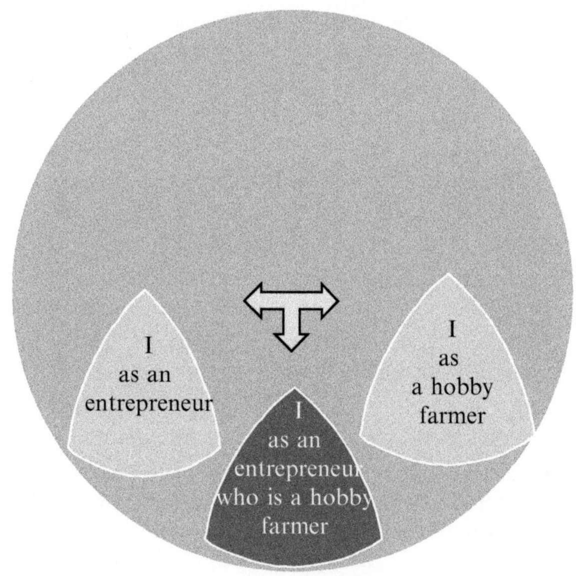

Fig. 5.4 Additional I-Positions in Peter's position repertoire

with nature". When he is at home he strongly recognizes what he misses when he is traveling and what he needs to be more healthy and happy. These two *I*-positions were tense opposites for Peter. He often felt frustrated as he seemed unable to solve this tension.

In our conversations we spent much time talking about the two *I*-positions. In this process Peter was asked to think about a possible connection between the entrepreneur and the hobby farmer, sketched on a sheet of paper. Looking at the two *I*-positions, generated an association immediately: *I as an entrepreneur who is a hobby farmer.* Through voicing in this manner, he re-organized and re-centered his position repertoire by integrating two elements conceptually in one *I*-position. The two positions are formulated in a dynamic balance, instead of being experienced as opposites, as Peter felt before the conversation.

Peter repositioned *I as an entrepreneur who is a hobby farmer* in his personal repertoire. He got the feeling that this way of viewing himself integrated the entrepreneur with his strong personal wish to be "in nature" and to develop more towards a coach. The series of dialogues had a deep transforming impact on Peter's professional functioning and personal life.

Summarizing the two aspects of his personal repertoire. At the end of our conversations he formulated: "*the gate of frustration is closed*". Peter has become less impatient and looked at the future with trust, although many threats were still present for him. We positioned all elements in Fig. 5.5.

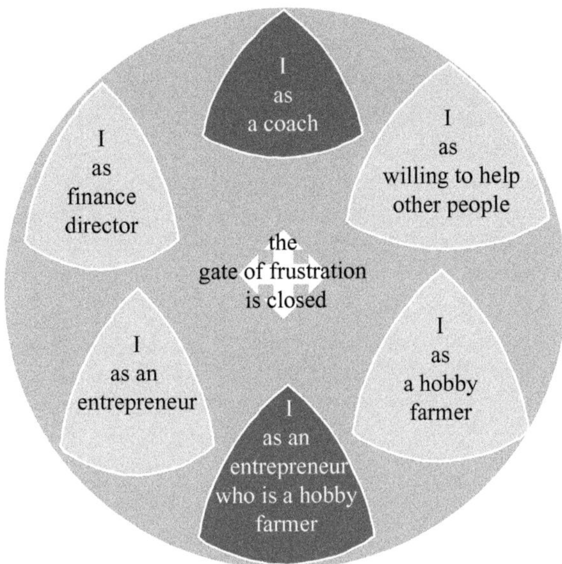

Fig. 5.5 Peter's entire I-position repertoire

Reflections

Applying some of the 'dialogical self' concepts on this case, leads to the following considerations:

Peter's position repertoire is characterized by a number of core-positions: *I as a finance director, I as willing to help other people, I as an entrepreneur, I as a hobby farmer.* These are connecting in different ways with one another, as we have seen above. As a partner in dialogue with leaders you develop the art of hearing words referring to core positions. Your role as coach is to consciously circle them back. Instead of interpreting a possible meaning, we prefer giving it back with a question: "You used the expression a few minutes ago: *I as a hobby farmer.* What do you mean? Could you tell more about you as a farmer?" Theoretically relevant is how you enable your partner in dialogue to integrate new *I*-positions into their position repertoire that formerly were on the edge. As we have seen above by connecting *I*-positions that were separated or even conflicting, the position repertoire can be centered and re-organized towards a higher level of development.

In Peter's case we can observe the 'dialogical self' concept of centering. The first one is in Fig. 5.3., where we see how a third-position emerges in the reflexive process of the two opposing/conflicting *I*-positions: I as finance director versus I as willing to help other people. The third-position *I as a coach* emerges from these two, as demonstrated above. By formulating the *I*-position of the coach, Peter truly connects two opposing aspects within himself. This is not playing with words. The field of meaning changed fundamentally for Peter by explicitly making this connection. Although as a reader you might think this is evident, for the individual *in* the narrative it is not. By intentionally, mentally connecting two opposites a new insight emerged in Peter in a combined internal and external dialogue process, as this is used by Bohm, Isaacs, Gergen and Hermans. Peter was able to integrate his development by formulating the third position of the coach. This is a form of *reconciling* the tension in his personal repertoire, between Peter as *finance director* and Peter as *willing to help other people*. As a finance director Peter is aware of being a rational pusher, while as supportive he is not. When he was asked: "What could be the "word/concept" that brings these two opposite elements together?" this *I*-position of the coach spontaneously emerged in the dialogue. We conclude that the third-position of the coach functions as a promoter position. *I as a coach* gives new order and direction to Peter's developmental process. The *I*-position of the coach functions as an innovator of Peter's self, one of the characteristics of a promoter position (Hermans & Hermans-Konopka, 2010, p. 228).

The concept of centering can be perceived in Fig. 5.4., where Peter formulated two *I-positions*: *I as an entrepreneur* as opposed to *I as a hobby farmer.* In his position repertoire these are contrasting and give Peter a feeling of disturbance. When Peter perceived the opposites positioned next to one another in space on a flip chart, he connected the two: "*I as an entrepreneur who is hobby farmer"*. This (third, promoter) *I*-position structurally has an ambiguous meaning, and simultaneously centers Peter's repertoire of *I*-positions. Before our conversations, the two *I*-positions caused a decentering movement in Peter's self. He did not feel completely comfortable in either of them. Originally grown up at a farm he loves nature, but as a finance director and business developer his focus was on rational competencies.

Two more reflections could be of importance for the practitioner who wants to apply the Dialogical Leader approach. Firstly, the role of visualizing; secondly, the importance of creating space.

In this process the role of visualizing opposites becomes clear. By writing opposites on a flip chart and asking how the two are connected, Peter's perception was re-set. He became more fully aware of a possible connection. What it shows you as partner in dialogue and coach in the process is not to think for the other person. Instead of interpreting, create the atmosphere for the other person to go through the process of associating himself. This is an illustration of Sampson's (2008) *Celebrating the Other.* The "Other" person as the coach in dialogue, enables Peter to actually make that connection of opposing and emotionally conflicting positions here and now. What might be clear for you as a coach, can be a puzzling Gordian knot for the individual.

A second reflection is related to Morioka's concept of "ma" (2008, 2012), in the sense of creating space. The case clearly illustrates in what manner *space* is vital in the dialogue. Firstly, by visually creating space on the flip chart and positioning different aspects of his personal position repertoire in it. Secondly, in the double meaning Peter gives to space: *physical* space at home, the farm embedded in nature, and *mental* space created by reconciling opposing *I*-positions. Both the entrepreneur and the farmer are both externally physical realities, and internal mind states. By reconciling the entrepreneur with the farmer Peter's conflicting emotions were reconciled as well.

If we take a look at this case from a distance, another reflection comes to mind: the importance of exteriorizing, of making words visible in space. This can be done by drawing, and by using other methods. In one of the chapters in this book Agnieszka Konopka describes "Composition work", a method inspired by Japanese rock gardens. These are called "mindscapes", representing the inner landscape of the mind and its dynamic development (Konopka & van Beers, 2013). The landscape metaphor accelerates working with spatial relations between *I*-positions and in this way potentially stimulates insights in the (re-)organization of the self. In our view this is a very promising way of exploring and transforming different *I*-positions.

A final remark about the process of change in our case. We focused the description on the process of reconciling *I*-positions. Peter also used other tools to gather feedback. He did a 360° behavioral feedback with his boss, peers and direct reports, where he got much information about how people perceived his behavior. The impact of his change process was also triggered by these tools. He also participated in workshops with the management team. Here he learned by trial and error to change his actual behavior into more exploring. In workshops with a team participants are invited to experiment with new behavior.

When and for Whom?

A Dialogical Leadership approach is not the panacea that solves all leadership issues you are confronted with as a coach. If you look at the framework of Grint (2005, 2010), it indicates when to apply this approach. It works most effectively in the case of wicked issues; issues that you cannot solve by technical training and teaching, nor by relying on earlier experiences to resolve issues. This entails that you cannot formulate the answer exclusively by thinking and analyzing. You need to ask questions, being invited to look for answers. For leaders who are confronted with volatile, urgent, complex and ambiguous issues, this skill set is a requirement in their competency framework.

We use the approach primarily with senior and executive leaders, individually (and in their teams[7]). If leaders need primarily technical and behavioral training, don't apply this approach. Once leaders are trained and technically equipped for their role, this approach might contribute to more effective and authentic leadership.

A second application is with leaders at an intersection in their personal life and/or career. In all phases of their career, you can apply this method to clarify, structure and promote a process of choosing between alternatives. By elaborating *I*-positions related to different options, people get more insight in what fits them best, and what they genuinely would like to do. In the case study, we showed this aspect of the application.

[7] How you apply this approach with teams and organizations was out of scope in this chapter.

Qualities Needed for the Practitioner

As a practitioner of Dialogical Self Theory and Dialogical Leadership you – next to knowing theories of personality psychology, organizational psychology, change and leadership – apply the principles of dialogue actively and consistently: listening, respecting, suspending judgment and voicing. Competencies that make you a robust practitioner: being flexible in your behavior and thinking, being able to create conditions and a trustful atmosphere for emerging new meaning, dealing with conflicts. As a coach you act as a promoter for others. By consistently applying the principles of dialogue, you create openness towards the future and enable integration of a potential variety of *I*-positions in the "Other". Essentially you contribute to the innovation of the self of your client, in the same way as a promoter *I*-position might do this in the personal position repertoire. As you work with leaders at the executive level, you also need to be a strong character that loves to have dialogue *and* debate, with long-lasting impact. You have a high level of presence. Presence as the level of "being" of the practitioner is critical for the effect. It is not simply a technique, but is applied through concentrated training and experience. The best practitioners in dialogue are those people, whose life is an expression of lifelong – practical and reflective – learning: reflective practitioners.

Acknowledgement We would like to thank Pom Somkabcharti for her help on this article.

References

Bohm, D. (1996). *On dialogue*. New York: Routledge.

Bojer, M., Roehl, H., Knuth, M., & Magner, C. (2008). *Mapping dialogue. Essential tools for social change*. Chagrin Falls/Ohio: TAOS Institute Publications.

Gergen, K. J. (2009). *Relational being: Beyond self and community*. New York: Oxford University Press.

Gergen, K. J., & Gergen, M. (2004). *Social construction. Entering the dialogue*. Chagrin Falls, Ohio: TAOS Institute Publications.

Gergen, K. J., McNamee, S., & Barrett, F. (2001). Toward transformative dialogue. *International Journal of Public Administration, 24*, 679–707.

Grint, K. (2005). Problems, problems, problems: The social construction of "leadership". *Human Relations, 58*, 1467–1494.

Grint, K. (2010). Wicked problems and clumsy solutions: The role of leadership. In S. Brookes & K. Grint (Eds.), *The public new leadership challenge* (pp. 169–186). New York: Palgrave Macmillan.

Hawes, L. C. (1999). The dialogics of conversation: Power, control, vulnerability. *Communication Theory, 9*(3), 229–264.

Hermans, H. J. M. (2006). *Dialoog en misverstand. Leven met de toenemende bevolking van onze innerlijke ruimte* [Dialogue and misunderstanding. Living with the increasing population of our internal space]. Soest: Nelissen.

Hermans, H. J. M., & Gieser, T. (Eds.). (2012). *Handbook of Dialogical Self Theory*. Cambridge, UK: Cambridge University Press.

Hermans, H. J. M., & Hermans-Konopka, A. (2010). *Dialogical self theory: Positioning and counter-positioning in a globalizing society*. Cambridge, UK: Cambridge University.

Hermans, H. J. M., Kempen, H. J. G., & Van Loon, R. J. P. (1992). The dialogical self: Beyond individualism and rationalism. *American Psychologist, 47*, 23–33.

Hersted, L., & Gergen, K. J. (2013). *Relational leading. Practices for dialogically based collaboration*. Chagrin Falls, Ohio: TAOS Institute Publications.

Hosking, D. M. (2011). Moving relationality: Meditations on a relational approach to leadership. In A. Bryman, D. Collinson, K. Grint, B. Jackson, & M. Uhl-Bien (Eds.), *The SAGE handbook of leadership* (pp. 455–467). London: Sage.

Isaacs, W. N. (1993). Taking flight: Dialogue, collective thinking and organizational learning. *Organizational Dynamics, 22*, 24–39.

Isaacs, W. N. (1999). *Dialogue and the art of thinking together. A pioneering approach to communicating in business and in life*. New York: Doubleday.

Kohlrieser, G. (2006). *Hostage at the table. How leaders can overcome conflict, influence others, and raise performance*. San Francisco: Jossey-Bass.

Konopka, A., & van Beers, W. (2013). Composition work: A method for self-investigation. *Journal of Constructivist Psychology, 27*, 194–210.

Libbrecht, U. (2007). *Within the four seas: Introduction to comparative philosophy*. Leuven, Belgium: Peeters.

Morioka, M. (2008). Voices of the self in the therapeutic chronotype: Utuschi and ma. *International Journal for Dialogical Science, 3*, 93–108.

Morioka, M. (2012). Creating dialogical space in psychotherapy: Meaning generating chronotype of *Ma*. In H. J. M. Hermans & T. Gieser (Eds.), *Handbook of dialogical self theory* (pp. 390–404). Cambridge, UK: Cambridge University Press.

Orem, S., Binkert, J., & Clancy, A. (2007). *Appreciative coaching: A positive process for change*. Hoboken, NJ: Wiley.

Rogers, E., & van Dam, N. (2015). *You! The positive force in change. Leveraging insights from neuroscience and positive psychology*. Raleigh, NC: Lulu Press Inc.

Sampson, E. (2008). *Celebrating the other: A dialogic account of human Nature*. Chagrin Falls, Ohio: TAOS Institute Publications.

Scharmer, O., & Kaufer, K. (2013). *Leading from the emerging future: From ego-system to eco-system economy*. San Francisco: Berrett-Koehler.

van Loon, R. (2010). *The dialogical leader. Developing leaders for the future*. Rotterdam, The Netherlands: Deloitte University.

van Loon, R., & van Dijk, G. (2015). Dialogical leadership: Dialogue as condition zero. *Journal of Leadership, Accountability and Ethics, 12*, 62–75.

Whitmore, J. (2002). *Coaching for performance: Growing people, performance, and purpose*. Boston: Nicholas Brealey Publishing.

Chapter 6
The Personal Position Repertoire method and Focus Group Discussion

Joanna Krotofil

Introduction

The advancement of the Dialogiacal Self Theory (DST) in the last two decades has been stimulated by vigorous developments in DST-based research methods recognizing dialogicality as a salient characteristic of the self. This chapter will present the combination of the Personal Position Repertoire (PPR), a method for studying the content and organization of the self, conceived as a dynamic multiplicity of *I*-positions, with a focus group. This integrated method gives insight into the construction and negotiation of meaning in the dialogue with others and sheds some light on interpersonal processes shaping the content and structure of the self. The chapter is divided into four parts focusing on: (a) the theoretical basis of the PPR method in Dialogical Self Theory, (b) description of the method, including an overview of different possible ways to analyse personal repertoires, (c) two case studies illustrating the application of the PPR method in combination with a focus group discussion, and (d) conclusions discussing the advantages and limitations of the integrated PPR Focus Group method (PPR-FG).

The multiplicity of preferred ways of understanding the world and building knowledge in the field of psychology is considered strength of the discipline. However this apparent diversity is undermined by the dominant Cartesian paradigm which asserts that the self and the outside world are, by definition, separate. Drawing on this dichotomy, traditional psychology endeavoured to study individuals independently of their sociocultural environments and many contemporary researchers continue to proceed in this way. By emphasising the dialogical, extended and multivoiced nature of the self, the Dialogical Self Theory attempts to overcome the gap between the world and the self. The theory brings together the concepts of dialogue

J. Krotofil (✉)
Division of Psychiatry, University College London, London, UK
e-mail: j.krotofil@ucl.ac.uk

H. Hermans (ed.), *Assessing and Stimulating a Dialogical Self in Groups, Teams, Cultures, and Organizations*, DOI 10.1007/978-3-319-32482-1_6

and self, and rejects the notion of the self as exclusively separated, bounded and relating to a separately existing other, residing in the external world. DST has proven to be particularly productive "as a conceptual system for analysing a variety of phenomena in divergent fields of thought" (Hermans, 2008, p. 186), and is strongly supported and balanced by a wealth of empirical studies. Jasper and colleagues argue however, that many empirical applications of DST have problems with reaching beyond the "self within its skin" and that methods of a more interpersonal nature, capable of capturing the self as socially situated, still need to be developed (Jasper, Moore, Whittaker, & Gillespie, 2011). In their view, the main shortcoming of existing methods is that they are limited to studying internally represented "society within self", and not "self in society", observed during actual social interactions (Jasper et al., 2011; Mascolo & Bhatia, 2002). The PPR-FG method I present in this chapter attempts to place greater emphasis on the dialogue with actual others thus enabling researchers to explore "the mutual complementing nature of intra and interpersonal dialogues in Dialogical Self" (Jasper et al., 2011).

Theoretical Framework

A comprehensive review of the DST is beyond the scope of this chapter (for a summary of the theory, see the introduction of this book). As such, in the following section, I will focus on elements of the theory which shift the attention of researchers from the inner world of the individual to the social word, and introduce the concepts of dialogue and power struggles to thinking about the self. These features of self – the notion of self as other-inclusive, extended, and multivoiced, – are central to the proposed method.

The dialogical self is defined as "a dynamic multiplicity of *I*-positions in the landscape of the mind, intertwined as this mind is with the minds of other people" (Hermans, 2002, p. 147; see also Hermans & Dimaggio, 2007; Hermans, Kempen, & Van Loon, 1992). Each position in the self structure is unique with its own meaning, significance and priority in relation to other positions. Using literature as a metaphor, the concept of position can be best explained as a character in a novel expressing his or her world views and capable of agreeing or disagreeing with other characters, questioning and challenging them and forming coalitions with them. The story of the self therefore is not told by one, central and omnipotent narrator; it is multivoiced, told from many different positions, and dialogically engaged with past, present and future audiences.

The term *I*-position is not reserved to the characters occupying internal domain of the self. The self is extended to the outside world, intertwined with selves of others and populated by their voices; it is not confined within the boundaries of person's mind and body (Hermans, 2003, p.103). "I" always emerges with reference to the "other" (Salgado & Hermans, 2005). When a person tells a story he or she incorporates the words and voices of others. The complex narrative structure of the self emerges as multivoiced utterances that originate from the author's internalization of past and imagined dialogues and encounters in the social world (Skinner, Valsiner, & Holland, 2001). The conceptualisation of the self-other relationship in the DST is based on a "soft" self-other differentiation (Hosking, 2011) and, as such it overcomes the separation of self and social context without collapsing these two concepts into one another (Valsiner, 2007). The other is not outside, or separate in relation to the self, it is rather an internal part of the self, strongly embedded within it and intrinsic to its nature. The other has a separate, independent existence outside of the self, but is also at the same time part of self, not in its objective, generalised form, but as the "other-in-me" occupying a particular position. In the theoretical model of the dialogical self, the other can be constructed on varying levels of abstraction and generalisation. The presence of the other in the self can take the form of a real person engaging in some form of interaction with an individual or it can be a personal construction of real or imaginary others in an individual's intra-psychological domain. Differently located *I*-positions create relationships across structural boundaries postulated to exist within the self structure (Valsiner, 2007). This implies that the self is a complex entity shaped by group membership, social structure, and multiple social forces, such as globalization, dissolution of hierarchies, and "production of locality" (Hermans & Hermans-Konopka, 2010). As Hermans notes, "individual voices are deeply penetrated by the culture of institutions, groups, and communities in which they participate, including their power differences" (2008, p. 192).

The dynamic structure of the self implies not only the diversity of perspective, but also hierarchy. Some of the *I*-positions in a given moment can occupy a central place in the self and be endowed with a voice, while others remain peripheral, subdued and silenced (Hermans & Hermans-Konopka, 2008). In this heterogeneous "society of mind" agreement, disagreement, conflict, contradiction and power struggle are constantly present, thus reflecting society at large. DST highlights the interplay between power relations in the social world and dominance relations in the "min*I*-society" of the self. Power differences between the collective voices representing groups or institutions in a particular community are reflected as power differences or power struggles between positions within the self. The dialogical self reflects society and therefore social interaction is at the core of this "mini society of mind".

The self, conceptualised as multivoiced, other-inclusive and embedded in social relations of power, is both relatively stable and constantly changed through the process of dialogue. The application of the PPR method I present in the following section focuses on dialogue itself, in an attempt to better understand the dynamic relational nature of the self and link these central parts of DST with empirical findings.

The PPR Focus Group

The method presented here combines the Personal Position Repertoire (PPR), a tool developed by Hermans (2001), with a focus group approach. It was designed with the aim of studying the dialogical self in social interaction, in the dialogue with real others, with a focus on the processes of meaning construction and repositioning. While the original PPR method was devised as a tool allowing the exploration of the content of the self and the organization and reorganization of the multiple positions within it (Hermans, 2001), the modification presented here builds on this and seeks to answer additional questions related to the relationship between positions and voices within the self and the perspective of actual others encountered in everyday life.

Procedure

At the beginning of the research procedure participants are presented with a list of internal and external *I*- positions. They are instructed to select those which they recognize as their own and which they perceive as aspects, or parts of their selves. All relevant positions are entered into a grid; internal positions are placed along the vertical axis (rows in the table) and external positions on the horizontal axis (columns in the table). In the next step participants are asked to complement their selection by additional *I*-positions not included in the list provided by the researcher, but identified and named by them. Participants then estimate how prominent each internal *I*-position is in relation to each external *I*-position, using a six point Likert scale (0 = not at all, 1 = very little, 2 = to some extent, 3 = quite a lot, 4 = considerably, 5 = very considerably). This process produces a unique matrix of internal and external positions depicting how the prominence of internal positions is distributed in relation to the range of external positions, as illustrated in Table 6.1. The method can be used in both research and in clinical practice; similar to the theory it is based on, it has strong face validity and is closely connected with the everyday experience of internal dialogue, conflict and indecision. This familiarity of experience encourages research participants' engagement in the matrix construction exercise (Jasper et al., 2011).

The personal matrix gives a concise overview of self-organization, but does not provide sufficient data in itself. In order to analyse and interpret the information contained in the matrix, in the original PPR procedure, the person who constructed it is interviewed by the practitioner or researcher. As Hermans notes, "the position matrix enables the researcher or practitioner to study the organization of internal and external positions, it doesn't help identify which stories are told and which meanings are expressed from the perspective of a particular position" (Hermans, 2001, p. 335). In order to examine the latter, he proposes to complement the construction of the matrices with an interview designed to elicit personal valuations

Table 6.1 Personal Position Repertoire constructed by David

	My mother	My Wife	My Father	My brother	My Friend	My Sister	God	My Grandmother	Somebody I love	Somebody I admire	Overall prominence
1. I as optimist	5	5	5	5	5	5	5	5	5	5	50
2. I as I am	5	5	5	5	5	5	5	5	5	5	50
3. I as Pole	5	5	5	5	5	5	5	5	5	0	45
4. I as father	4	5	4	3	4	3	5	5	0	0	33
5. I as resourceful	5	5	5	4	4	3	0	2	4	0	32
6. I as husband	4	5	4	3	3	3	4	4	0	0	30
7. I as man	4	5	5	5	5	5	0	0	0	0	29
8. I as catholic	4	4	4	2	0	3	5	5	0	0	27
9. I as adventure seeking	5	2	4	4	4	2	3	0	2	0	26
10. I independent	5	5	4	4	0	0	0	0	0	0	18
11. I dominant	5	1	0	4	3	2	0	0	2	0	17
12. I jealous	5	5	0	0	5	0	0	0	0	0	15
13. I fighting for myself	4	5	2	3	0	0	0	0	0	0	14
Overall prominence	60	57	47	47	43	36	32	31	23	10	386

Note: From Krotofil (2012) (Copyright 2013 by Copyright Holder. Reprinted with permission)

(for the description of valuation theory and self-confrontation method see Hermans & Hermans-Jansen, 1995). Exploration of personal repertoire through individual interviews has been applied in both research and therapeutic settings (Hermans, 2001, 2003). In the method described in this chapter, in order to gain more insight into the dialogical processes shaping the self, I propose to modify this procedure by inviting participants to take part in a group discussion after constructing the matrix. This modification draws on benefits of focus group method which gives researchers the clear advantage of being able to observe interactive process among participants in group interview (Madriz, 2000). Placing an individual face to face with others creates an opportunity to gain some insight in how the perspectives encountered in the social world can become an internal part of the dialogical self. Researcher observes participants engaging in dialogue with others from their own particular positions reflected in the PPR matrices they construct at the beginning of the procedure. It is assumed, that even if some of the positions included into the personal repertoire by different participants are given the same name, their memories, emotions and expectations associated with them are different (Hermans & Hermans-Konopka, 2010, p. 183). The individual meaning of these positions and changes in position structure are revealed in personal and collective stories told by individuals during the interaction with other participants.

The focus group discussion is informed by the specific research question and the content of matrices constructed in the first part of the procedure. The researcher takes the role of moderator and opens the discussion by asking participants which *I*-positions they included in their repertoires, what each of included positions means to them, how it is present in their life, and which relationships between *I*-positions they rated as the strongest. Other questions can be used to focus the discussion on the research topic of interest, for example, 'What is it like to be a migrant and a catholic?', or 'Is there a relationship between being a Pole and being a migrant?' Participants might also be encouraged to take a meta-position and reflect on the process of matrix construction (e.g. 'Was it difficult to choose the positions to be included in your matrix?', 'How do you feel looking at your matrix now?'). As participants engage in the discussion, they start asking additional questions addressed to each other, voicing their agreement or disagreement and challenging some of the positions.

Using PPR with focus group interviews has a number of implications. The aim of the method is still to examine the organisation of the self repertoire, but greater emphasis is placed on capturing and analysing individual's emergent narratives, and changes within the self structure occurring as a result of external dialogue with others. When engaging in dialogue, different *I*-positions convey messages to real and assumed audiences (Salgado & Hermans, 2005). As Lucius-Hoene and Deppermann argue, "along with the different voices and identity constructions, the narrator also constructs different recipients in his or her discursive positioning of the listener" (2000, p.199). People engaging in dialogue always have some assumptions about beliefs, values and expectations of the person they are addressing. These assumptions are rarely explicit, but they shape dialogue processes in different contexts of life, and perhaps most strongly in situations where the distribution of power is uneven.

Although different qualitative research traditions strive to minimize the distance between researcher and participant, this is not easily achievable when the interviewer determines the topics to be discussed, controls the agenda and decides when the conversation is terminated. Such dialogue is prone to become a stage for the exercise of power (KarnielI-Miller, Strier, & Pessach, 2009). One way to overcome this problem is for the researcher to transform the one-person audience by stepping into the background, becoming a part of a polyphonic audience and allowing research participants to set their own agenda. By forsaking the privileged position of the only addressee and sole dialogue partner, the researcher encourages participants to challenge their own assumptions, ask questions of one another, swap anecdotes and comment on others' experiences, opinions and ideas.

As a result of changing the audience from a single researcher or psychotherapist to a group of fellow participants, the repertoire of voices with which the participant is confronted becomes much broader. Focus groups have been successfully applied to research on identity in the past and one of the most recognized advantages of this method is the fact that a wide range of viewpoints, perspectives and behaviours associated with particular roles can be explored in a relatively short time (Dahl, 2009). By inviting participants to join the group, the researcher creates an environment with actual others who can introduce a variety of new elements to the self, thus prompting the correction, adjustment and revision of existing positions. Other focus group participants give immediate feedback to the speaker, and confront him or her with new views and positions. By encountering the voices of others, participants analyse their starting positions and engage in an exchange which, in some cases, leads to changes of their self structure. The use of focus group methodology also liberates the dialogue from psychological jargon, allows the researcher's voice "to intermingle with other voices" (Bandlamudi, 1999) and makes it more likely for the voices of participants to be "heard as they want to be heard" (Hermans, 2001, p. 324). The voices of people talking about their life and experiences relevant to them are the most important products of the procedure and they should not become lost in scientific concepts or covered by psychological interpretations. Another implication of using a focus group interview is the fact that shifting the attention from internal dialogues to the real dialogue happening in the outside word, the researcher is able to capture the more physical features of the dialogue, such as the flavour of the interaction, emotional register of the exchange, the intonation of the language. These characteristics of the dialogue bring in a new dimension into the interpretation of narratives produced during the session. Finally, as the primary exchange and most intensive dialogue happens between fellow participants, rather than the researcher and the respondent, focus groups can be considered less intrusive than individual interviews (Jarrett, 1993). Each focus group can be adapted to provide the most desirable level of focus and structure (Stewart & Shamdasani, 1990). Participants can be drawn into the process through the use of generic questions which create a space for them to focus the discussion on aspects of their self they are ready to discuss and slowly warm up to talking about the most salient parts of the self. This makes the method particularly useful for research dealing with sensitive topics, for example the exploration of stigmatised identities.

Analysis of PPR Focus Group Data

The Personal Position Repertoire (PPR) method has been conceived as both quantitative and qualitative tool (Hermans, 2001). It is innovative in distinguishing between internal and external *I*-positions. This distinction enables individuals to identify positions which are "functionally equivalent" and explore complex dialogical relationship between different positions (Hermans, 2001, p.325). Comparing the profiles of prominence ratings can unravel multiple relationships between positions and reveal how different positions complement each other. Different statistical procedures can be used to identify these relationships, such as product-moment correlations, or bi-clustering using Principal Component Analysis (PCA) to plot the graphical representation of positions structure form bird's eye perspective (Kluger, Nir, & Kluger, 2008). The overall prominence of external and internal positions can be assessed by adding the ratings within each column and within each row of the matrix. The organization of self constantly changes, as various aspects of the repertoire become more or less dominant. It is however possible to identify the dominant positions in personal repertoires, which are likely to be the positions from which "I" makes sense of the world and itself.

Another level of interpretation is facilitated by the distinction between social and personal positions within the structure of internal positions. Social positions (e.g. I as a mother, I as a teacher) represent roles and are to great extent formed by social prescriptions and expectations while personal positions (e.g. I as an achiever, I as responsible) represent qualities shaping individual experiences. As stated by Hermans and Hermans-Konopka:

> Whereas social positions reflect the way the self is subjected to social expectations and role –prescriptions, personal positons leave room for many ways in which individual responds to such expectations from his own point of view and for the various ways in which the individual fashions, stylizes and personalizes them. (Hermans & Hermans-Konopka, 2010, p. 76)

Particular relationships between social and personal positions might reflect the influence of collective voices of social groups and institutions expressing prescriptive rules on how social positions can be complemented by desired and undesired personal positions. In most socio-cultural contexts collective norms reinforce, for example, a close association between social position of 'I as a parent' and internal positions such as 'I as responsible', 'I as caring'. These relationships are represented by distance and proximity in the PCA plot, as illustrated in Fig. 6.1. Quantitative analysis enables practitioners and researchers to compare positions' structure both within and between individuals. The complexity and multivoicedness of the self is reflected in the idiosyncratic nature of the personal positions repertoire and therefore requires caution when making these comparisons. The relationships between different positions revealed in quantitative analysis can be examined in more depth by an analysis of the narratives produced by participants, in this case, in the focus group discussion.

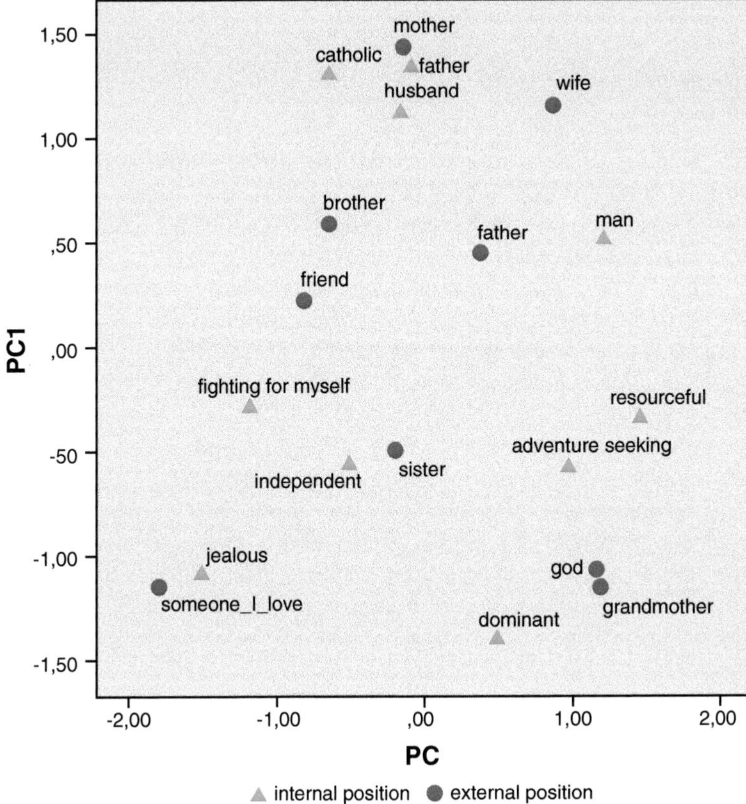

Fig. 6.1 David's Personal Position Repertoire from a bird's eye perspective
This figure is a result of principal component analysis used to explore the structure of the columns and the rows simultaneously, from a bird's eye perspective, as proposed by Kluger et al. (2008). This method correlates not only rows of the PPR matrix (internal positions) with each other and columns (external positions) with each other, but also rows with columns. Close proximity of different positions implies that there are significant commonalities among them
Note: From Krotofil (2012) (Copyright 2013 by Copyright Holder. Reprinted with permission)

Focus group data allows for the use of a broad range of data analysis methods. The choice of the methodological approach should reflect the study purpose and specific aims (Duggleby, 2005). Researchers can draw on methods such as Narrative Analysis (Polkinghorne, 1995; Ricoeur, 1984), Content Analysis (Krippendorff, 1980), Discourse Analysis (Van Dijk, 2001), or Meaning Construction Analysis (Sages & Lundsten, 2015) to guide the analysis of focus group data. The PPR Focus Group method can be applied to the study of many diverse subjects. In the case study presented below, I will illustrate how the method can be used as means for developing a rich and nuanced account of group identity of migrants settling in a new country.

Case Study

Background of the Study

The material presented here was collected as part of a research project exploring the relationship between religion and self in the context of migration, specifically the role of religion in self-construction processes of recent Polish migrants in the United Kingdom (Krotofil, 2012). The participants were young Polish couples settling in United Kingdom and attending a marriage preparation course run by their local catholic parish. When designing this study I was interested in the process of dialogical engagement with actual others and the role institutional power and collective voices play in the process of renegotiation of the self in the "in-between" space of migration (Hermans, 1999). The aim was to use DST as a framework to explore both global and local changes in the field of religion experienced by migrants and their consequences for the place of religion in the landscape of self. I chose the context of institutional religion to observe how the dominant positions of religious institution can be challenged and negotiated. Previous research demonstrated that although formal Catholic Church membership remains relatively high amongst young Poles, their relationship with Catholicism is ambivalent (Marianski, 2003). The prominence of religion among contemporary young Catholics changes from one situation to another. Based on this assertion, I postulated that in some contexts the collective voice of religious communities and institutions in the self becomes more audible, while in other contexts it is silenced. The fragmented and privatized religion can become significant in some situations in a migration context and, with a carefully designed method, it is possible to examine its influence on the self. In attempting to capture the voices of participants talking about their religion and responding to the voice of a religious institution, I chose an educational religious setting as a situational frame in which the research procedure was applied. I was hoping to identify groupings of personal positions around social and external positions in participants' repertoires which would reflect Church discourse on marriage and family roles and participants' responses to it. In the following section I will use the example of two participants – Monika and David- illustrating the dialogical process shaping the organization of religious *I*-positions. I have selected two participants who differ considerably in terms of their initial positions taken in relation to the Catholic Church.

Different Views on Religion

Monika is a young professional working in recruitment agency. At the time of data collection Monica had been living in United Kingdom for six years and was attending a marriage preparation course run by the Catholic Church. She considered religion as important aspect of her life, but her religious life was not church–centred;

she attended church only twice a year and was critical of the church's teachings. David, a young man with a similar length of migration, was working as a kitchen porter. Contrary to Monika, he described himself as a religious person and a church goer, attending Sunday mass twice a month. The matrices constructed by Monika and David were very similar with regards to the external and internal social positions they included in their repertoires. Both of them included external *I*-positions representing close members of their families and spouses ("My mother", "My father", "My brother", "My partner", "My wife") and a few internal positions related to marriage; Monika listed "I as wife," "I as mother,", whereas David chose "I as husband," and "I as father". There was however a difference in terms of inclusion of positions related to religion. Whereas Monica did not include any, David added "God" and "I as Catholic" into his matrix, and rated them as relatively prominent. Quantitative analysis of David's matrix indicated a close relationship between the external positions of "God" and "My grandmother". These two positions had very similar prominence rating profiles in relation to all of his internal positions and appeared in close proximity in the PCA plot. In his narrative David revealed that he was raised by his grandmother, a devout Catholic. In the discussion David acknowledged his grandmother's influence on his faith development and recognized that whenever he looks at his actions with his grandmother's eyes he also applies the valuations based on the moral prescriptions of his religion. For David both "God" and "My grandmother" were positions representing important significant others in his life. This is reflected in the high prominence of internal positions evoked by these external positions.

The greatest differences between Monika and David can be observed within internal personal positions; in Monika's repertoire the highest prominence was given to "I as I am" and "I as able to make sacrifices", while in David's the most prominent positions were "I as I am," "Optimist," and "Pole." This pattern of similarities and differences seems to confirm the postulated influence of the specific research context, in this case the context of a marriage preparation course for Polish migrants in the UK, on the constellation of *I*-positions reflected in matrices built by participants. It is also consistent with the theoretical conceptualisation of personal (e.g. I as resourceful) and social positions (e.g. I as a wife). Personal positions remain relatively independent of the situational context, while social positions become re-shuffled in such a way that the ones that are most relevant in a particular context come to the fore (Hermans & Hermans-Konopka, 2010).

What the Participants Discovered

During the discussion which followed the matrix construction, some participants were able to reflect on the role the audience plays in the constant positioning and repositioning processes within the self. Talking about his choice to include "God" into this repertoire, David stated that the matrix may have been different if it was constructed in a different context.

> I mean like now, we are all sitting here, attending this marriage preparation course, yes? If we were sitting somewhere, I don't know, in the pub or with some strangers, perhaps we would not want them to know that we are Catholics and whether God is important to us or not. We would omit these points, because of, let's say because of who we are sitting with, what kind of company we are in.

The absence of positions related to religion in Monika's repertoire was consistent with her views and opinions voiced during the group discussion. One possible interpretation is that during the construction of the matrix, Monika silenced all positions related to religion because of the conflict between her intention to get married in church and her rejection of Catholic teachings on marriage. Analysis of Monika's input into the dialogue suggested that her views on marriage and family were in stark opposition to the religious interpretation presented by the priest during the course. Gradually, as critical voices toward Catholic discourse on marriage became expressed more frequently by other participants of focus group, Monika started to talk more openly about her views assuming a critical positon. Monika strongly objected to the church's view on premarital sex and birth control. In her narrative she moved from her own experience to the story of her aunt:

> But this is sick, as I understand the previous meetings we have attended … We have been a couple for seven years now and he says to us … he [the priest] wants me to stop living in sin. Chastity? Excuse me, but if I stop sleeping with my partner today it will not change anything in the eyes of the church, or God. My six years-long sinning will stay. It will not change anything, it is nonsense. What has happened has happened. And if I will be living in chastity now until the wedding it will not change anything, not for myself. So I think priests have strange ideas. For me it is some kind of waffling. When I hear this sort of talking, I am shaking inside, I feel like leaving and slamming the door. This priest sits here and says, "No contraception." I am very sorry, but my aunt was like that: no contraception, and bowing in front of the altar. She ended up with 11 children and three weeks before the birth of the last one, her husband left her. The local parish priest was visiting her only once a year, and only to collect the money. He never asked if she had any money. She lived like that because the church said this is how you should live. But she lived in poverty with all these children. And no church came to help.

The rejection of gender roles, as they are constructed by church, was also reflected in Monika's PPR matrix, by the place of the internal position "I as mother". Monika included it into her repertoire but ascribed very low prominence to this position. It did not correlate strongly with any other position, and did not "attract" any personal positions reflecting socially constructed attributes of a "good mother" (for example, there is no strong correlation between "I as mother" and "I as sacrificing"). A possible interpretation is that Monika initially silenced her views of motherhood as undesirable in the context of marriage preparation course. After giving voice to her position as someone opposing church teachings on marriage, Monika was able to reflect on the conflict between two positions: that of someone attending catholic marriage preparation course and that from which she rejects the church's discourse on marriage. She was also able to resolve that conflict by ascribing a very practical meaning to her participation in the course. She stated it was a mere formality, a condition she needed to fulfil in order to be able to have a church wedding: "I am here only because I need this piece of paper, the certificate stating that I have attended". She accepted that church will be present in her marriage and family, but on her own terms:

> If only the church was … I don't know, there are so many things made up, stretched, and I will not go to church each Sunday and bow in front of the altar. I believe in God and I accept many things, but as far as the future is concerned … I can say today that my children will be baptized, they will receive First Holy Communion and all sacraments, which they have to receive, but for sure I will not force them to be part of the church.

Such conflict was not experienced by David. In his repertoire the positions "I as Catholic," "I as father", and "I as husband" correlated strongly with each other. This suggests that unlike Monika, David endorsed a position of marriage course participant at the beginning of the research procedure. It was a position with a voice when David joined the discussion on birth control. In his response to another participant who stated that the church is not flexible in its approach to contraception, David questioned the moral grounds of that objection:

> Is it us who should accommodate to the faith, or should faith be accommodated to our needs? […] I am not saying here that church is right. But on the other hand, from a priest's perspective … if everyone tried to bend the church's rules to their own needs … you could say I need something today, so I have stolen a piece of that thing.

Having heard Monika's views on the birth control and the story about the single mother raising eleven children on her own, David changed his initial position. In response to Monika's voice, he stated with regard to the church's teaching on the use of contraception that "this approach is stupid." Engagement in the dialogical exchange with other course participants allowed David to move from his initial, orthodox position and give voice to counter-positions.

The Value of Dialogue

Both Monika and David reflected on the value of dialogue and the influence of real others who are dialogue partners in a given context. For them, the marriage preparation course in the form they experienced in their local parish did not offer any space for dialogue. Monika described the priest running the course as being unable to neither see the problematic nature of the situation of a single mother raising eleven children nor acknowledge the practical challenges of marriage, given the rejection of any forms of birth control. For her the priest represented an authoritarian voice talking from an abstract position rather than a partner in dialogue able to relate to people entering marriage and becoming parents.

> I would like to see a priest who has a wife and 15 children. Then I would say to him, "Come on, make more babies."

David highlighted the contrast between a typical session of the marriage preparation course with the focus group situation. Addressing me, as a researcher, he stated:

> You are conversing with us, you engage in a dialogue with us. The priest is conducting a monologue. He may ask one odd question, or two, and this would be about knowing catechism by heart, or something like that. He wouldn't ask us, "What do you think about this issue or that issue?" He keeps mumbling for an hour.

For David, just like for Monika, the setting of the marriage preparation course restricts or makes it impossible for participants to engage in dialogue. Like Monika, he questioned the possibility of a priest becoming a partner in the dialogue. For him it was not the inability of the priest to see marriage from the position of a married person, but his attitude, which prevents dialogue from any position. From David's point of view the preparation course exemplifies the unbalanced social power dynamics, whereby the priest has a voice and delivers a monologue, while course participants are expected to be passive recipients, silenced, and unable to question his position or express their points of view. As stated by Sullivan (2012) "dialogue is born out of inequality between self and other" (p. 4), however, as this study illustrates, when the inequality and distance are too broad, dialogue becomes impossible. Confrontation with the authoritarian discourse of a religious institution can silence positions in the individual repertoire that are in disagreement with the church. In Monika's case the silenced positions were given a voice when other course participants became dialogical partners instead of the priest and the power imbalance was neutralized. In that new context, she was able to approach the tension between conflicting positions in a more dialogical way and to work toward a compromise.

The PPR Focus Group method used in this study produced rich data suggesting that reacting to the uncertainty inherent in migration experience, young polish migrants might turn to religion. Confronted with institutional religion they are able to engage in dialogue and creatively re-organize their repertoires in order to resolve emergent conflicts (Krotofil, 2012)

Conclusion

DST is developing into a bridging theory which integrates various multidisciplinary perspectives into a complex framework with finely refined conceptual apparatus. The theory has a breadth fostering a great variety of empirical applications; accordingly, it is impossible to devise a single method to capture and measure all the processes and characteristics of the self described within the dialogical self model. In applying methods derived from DST, it is, therefore, critical to assess how well the method is embedded in the theory and question (1) what aspects of dialogical self are captured by a given method and (2) what parts of it are being omitted.

Advantages of the Method

The PPR Focus Group method is based on the notion of self as fundamentally dialogical and facilitates the analysis of intra- and interpersonal processes stimulating reflection on one's own self. The focus group component in this integrated design places participants in a situation of real, observable encounters with the other and captures "dialogical moments of transformation" (Jasper et al., 2011). The method not only has the potential of capturing, but also generating innovative moments characterised by an appearance of alternative *I*-positions which challenge the dominant voices within the self; this process, therefore has the potential to transform self-narratives as they are expanded and elaborated (Gonçalves & Ribeiro, 2012). This is illustrated in the case studies discussed above. In the context of marriage preparation courses run by the Catholic Church, a gradual shift from the *I*-position of a course participant expressing agreement or conflict with the traditional view of the church toward a more independent position can be observed, as participants engage in dialogue with each other. When a fellow course participant becomes the dialogue partner, instead of the priest running the course, the dialogue is liberated from the "social language" of the Catholic Church. The role of the expectations and views projected by participants on the priest, or the researcher diminishes, giving them more freedom to express their own views. The interaction becomes truly dialogical exchange of lived ideas, full of personal judgements and values.

Limitations of the Method

Individual interviews most likely will yield more in-depth data and it seems that individual discussions with a psychologist carried out over a prolonged period of time may be better suited to study the intimate realm of the individual's self. The focus group method has been criticised for a lack of depth in the generated material. As Monard (2013, p. 352) notes, "focus group interviews may give an impression of negotiations of identity, but the group context may not be appropriate for studying the depth and nuances of individual identification as well as tabooed aspects of identification". It can be argued, however that, contrary to this view, group dynamics might serve to break taboos and foster openness. The presence of other group members who share similar experiences or viewpoints can discourage idealised accounts adjusted to meet social expectations. Even one individual who is prepared to discuss their experiences in a "tell it as it is" and realistic manner can challenge those participants who tend to give more censored or idealised accounts (Jarrett, 1993). Certainly, the exploration of participants' views in a group discussion involves the risk that one or more individuals may dominate the discussion and silence the voices of others. In most focus group sessions it can be observed that some people remain silent for the duration of the discussion. In such case the researcher is left with an individual matrix providing very detailed information on positions included in the personal repertoire, but is unable to fully interpret that data. It requires skilled and experienced researcher to minimise this effect.

Required Skills

The researcher moderating the focus group takes on the role of the dialogue facilitator. Effective facilitation is a key factor in the collection of rich and valid material and one of the main challenges the facilitator faces is the creation of a nonthreatening environment that encourages all participants to engage in the discussion (Stewart & Shamdasani, 1990). The researcher has the task of guiding participants through questions in a way that creates dialogical space "…in which they feel accepted as dialogical partners and feel the freedom to express their experiences from their own point of view" (Hermans & Hermans-Konopka, 2010, p 181). The questions posed to the group need to be context specific, but open, encouraging participants to explore the subject from various internal and external positions and to interact dialogically with fellow participants. The quality and type of data generated in focus group interviews is greatly influenced by how directive the moderator is. In the PPR Focus Group method, the facilitator is required to be constantly alert to guide the discussion about different aspects of the self and pursue any 'leads' that have the potential to bring new *I*-positions into the dialogue. This method therefore, as with its original version, requires commitment from both the participants and researchers. The professional experience of the facilitator and familiarity with specific groups of participants gives advantages in the cooperative enterprise of self exploration (Hermans, 2001).

When to Apply

Focus groups allow the researcher to combine the micro level of interaction advocated by symbolic interactionism with macro level of social processes, including economic, political, or policy contexts (Barbour, 2007). The method endorses the notion of self as extended and is not blind to the context and situation in which the research is being conducted. Positioning is one of fundamental processes identified in DST and means that the researcher should pay close attention to the situational context of research procedure. The theory postulates that "[…] the process of positioning and being positioned determine to a large degree which voices are actualised, what they have to say, and under what circumstances they are constrained in their expression" (Hermans & Hermans-Konopka, 2010, p. 227). Controlling the context in which participants engage in dialogue allows the researcher to gain some insight into positioning/repositioning within the self as it is confronted with the voices of others and engages in dialogue with them.

Due to the specialisation of research, methodological combinations across the qualitative–quantitative divide remain largely unexploited. The PPR method is a strong example of a mixed method approach which offers an opportunity for in-depth analysis, employing quantitative and qualitative tools. The use of Likert scale allows for the quantification of the prominence of *I*-positions; the analysis of the correlations between the positions can be very informative, as it often reveals the hidden associations between the positions and enables participants to explore less accessible relationships between their positions and to gain access to the less conscious layers of the self. The qualitative analysis facilitates better understanding of these relationships. The method produces an overview of the self as a member of different groups, performer of different roles and as a specific individual possessing a number of qualities. It also reveals important patterns in which an individual relates to others. Focus groups create an opportunity for participants to simultaneously manage their individual identities and make a collective representation, providing insights into the construction of meaning (Callaghan, 2005). The results produced through the application of this method are, to a large extent, idiosyncratic. The method is not standardised, but it is useful in exploring patterns of identification and looking at individuals as localised in a particular socio-cultural space, embedded in social dialogues.

PPR Focus Group method can be used with specifically defined subgroups to study the "distribution of identities" and identify similar patterns within self structure across different people and their relation with shared group experiences and histories. Although the data discussed in the group may lack the complexity on the individual level, group discussions provide useful material for the analysis of more general patterns observed on a group level and give insight into how the collective voice of a particular group is being shaped in socially situated dialogues with others. The method is particularly useful when applied to generate collaborative narratives that reflect shared patterns of dominant positions within the self in contested or marginalised groups. In this procedure, participants engage in a research process which serves not only to generate data, but is also in many ways affirmative. It creates a context where individuals can express who they are using their own terms (by adding *I*-positions of their choice to the matrix) and negotiate their positions with others sharing a similar socio-cultural space. One of great advantages of the PPR Focus Group method is its' flexibility. The method is general and sufficiently open to be applied in many fields including developmental, clinical and cultural psychology, as well as psychotherapy. The list of internal and external positions presented to participants can be modified to facilitate the study of particular subgroups or experiences.

The PPR Focus Group method can be refined in future research by adding the longitudinal element whereby participants construct another personal repertoire matrix immediately, or sometime after the focus group discussion. Incorporating longitudinal design into the modified PPR method would allow the researcher to systematically examine the permanency of changes in structure and content of self over time and shed light on how different voices encountered in social world become voices within self.

References

Bandlamudi, L. (1999). Developmental discourse as an author/hero relationship. *Culture and Psychology, 5*, 41–65.

Barbour, R. (2007). *Doing Focus Groups*. Thousand Oaks, CA: Sage.

Callaghan, G. (2005). Accessing habitus: Relating structure and agency through focus group research. *Sociological Research Online, 10*(3).

Dahl, H. M. (2009). New public management, care and struggles about recognition. *Critical Social Policy, 29*(4), 634–654.

Duggleby, W. (2005). What about focus group interaction data? *Qualitative Health Research, 15*(6), 832–840.

Gonçalves, M. M., & Ribeiro, A. (2012). Narrative processes of innovation and stability within the dialogical self. In H. J. M. Hermans & T. Gieser (Eds.), *Handbook of dialogical self theory* (pp. 301–318). Cambridge, UK: Cambridge University Press.

Hermans, H. J. M. (1999). Dialogical thinking and self-innovation. *Culture and Psychology, 5*, 67–87.

Hermans, H. J. M. (2001). The construction of personal position repertoire: Method and practice. *Culture & Psychology, 7*, 323–365.

Hermans, H. J. M. (2002). The dialogical self as a society of mind. *Theory & Psychology, 12*(2), 147–160.

Hermans, H. J. M. (2003). The construction and reconstruction of a dialogical self. *Journal of Constructivist Psychology. Special Issue on the Dialogical Self, 16*, 89–130.

Hermans, H. J. M. (2008). How to perform research on the basis of dialogical self theory? Introduction to the special issue. *Journal of Constructivist Psychology, 21*(3), 185–199.

Hermans, H. J. M., & Dimaggio, G. (2007). Self, identity, and globalisation in times of uncertainty: A dialogical analysis. *Review of General Psychology, 11*, 31–61.

Hermans, H. J. M., & Hermans-Jansen, E. (1995). *Self-narratives: The construction of meaning in psychotherapy*. New York: Guilford Press.

Hermans, H. J. M., & Hermans-Konopka, A. (2008). Dialogical self theory: Introduction to the special issue. *Studia Psychologica, 8*, 5–10.

Hermans, H. J. M., & Hermans-Konopka, A. (2010). *Dialogical self theory*. Cambridge, UK: Cambridge University Press.

Hermans, H. J. M., Kempen, H. J. G., & Van Loon, R. (1992). The dialogical self: Beyond individualism and rationalism. *American Psychologist, 47*, 23–33.

Hosking, D. M. (2011). Telling tales of relations: Appreciating relational constructionism. In themed issue: Responses to social constructionism & critical realism in organization studies. *Organization Studies, 32*(1), 47–65.

Jarrett, R. L. (1993). Focus group interviewing with low-income minority populations: A research experience. In D. L. Morgan (Ed.), *Successful focus groups: Advancing the state of the art* (pp. 184–201). Newbury Park, CA: Sage.

Jasper, C., Moore, H., Whittaker, L., & Gillespie, A. (2011). Methodological approaches to studying the self in its social context. In H. J. M. Hermans & T. Gieser (Eds.), *Handbook of dialogical self theory* (pp. 319–334). Cambridge, UK: Cambridge University Press.

Karniell-Miller, O., Strier, R., & Pessach, L. (2009). Power relations in qualitative research. *Qualitative Health Research, 19*, 279–289.

Kluger, A. N., Nir, D., & Kluger, Y. (2008). Personal position repertoire (PPR) from a bird's eye view. *Journal of Constructivist Psychology, 21*, 223–238.

Krippendorff, K. (1980). *Content analysis: An introduction to its methodology*. Beverly Hills, CA: Sage.

Krotofil, J. (2012). Religion, migration, and the dialogical self: New application of the personal position repertoire method. *Journal of Constructivist Psychology, 26*(2), 90–103.

Lucius-Hoene, G., & Deppermann, A. (2000). Narrative identity empiricized: A dialogical and positioning approach to autobiographical research interviews. *Narrative Inquiry, 10*(1), 199–222.
Madriz, E. (2000). Focus groups in feminist research. In N. K. Denzin & Y. S. Lincoln (Eds.), *Handbook of qualitative research* (pp. 835–850). Thousand Oaks, CL: Sage.
Marianski, J. (2003). Parafia szansa przemian polskiego katolicyzmu [The parish as a prospect of change in Polish Catholicism]. *Socjologia Religii, 1*, 183–206.
Mascolo, M. F., & Bhatia, S. (2002). The dynamic construction of culture, self and social relations. *Psychology & Developing Societies, 14*(5), 55–89.
Monard, M. (2013). On a scale of one to five, who are you? Mixed methods in identity research. *Acta Sociologica, 56*(4), 347–360.
Polkinghorne, D. E. (1995). Narrative configuration in qualitative analysis. *Qualitative Studies in Education, 8*(1), 5–23.
Ricoeur, P. (1984). *Time and narrative* (Vol. 1). Chicago: University of Chicago Press.
Sages, R., & Lundsten, J. (2015). *Meaning constitution analyses: A penomenological appraach to research in human sciences*. Retrieved from: http://www.iaccp.org/drupal/sites/default/files/spetses_pdf/22_Sages.pdf
Salgado, J., & Hermans, H. J. M. (2005). The return of subjectivity: From a multiplicity of selves to the dialogical self. *E-Journal of Applied Psychology, 1*, 3–13.
Skinner, D., Valsiner, J., & Holland, D. (2001). Discerning the dialogical self: A theoretical and methodological examination of a Nepali adolescent's narrative. *Forum: Qualitative Social Research, 2*(3).
Stewart, D. W., & Shamdasani, P. N. (1990). *Focus groups: Theory and practice*. Newbury Park, CL: Sage.
Sullivan, P. (2012). *Qualitative data analysis using a dialogical approach*. Los Angeles, CA: Sage.
Valsiner, J. (2007). *Culture in minds and societies*. New Delhi, India: Sage.
Van Dijk, T. A. (2001). Critical discourse analysis. In D. Tannen, D. Schiffrin, & H. Hamilton (Eds.), *Handbook of discourse analysis* (pp. 352–371). Oxford, UK: Blackwell.

Chapter 7
Dialogical Culture Coaching

Jutta König and Kate Clarke

Increasingly in our globalizing world, individuals are confronted with cultural diversity in their environments and/or grow up in different cultural contexts due to enhanced demographic, cultural, economic, ecological and military interconnections and technological advancements in transport and media. By now approximately two-thirds of the world's population is either bi- or multilingual, yet within clinical psychology, organizational and management theories relatively little attention is paid to the effect that being multilingual has on identity, emotions and mental health, (Jones & Bradwell, 2007). In many organizations as well as in coaching and therapeutic settings it is still largely a manager or professional with relatively little intercultural experience dealing with an increase of clients with so-called hybrid identities.

Refugees, economic migrants, expatriates and their children, global nomads and third culture kids (Pollock & van Reken, 2001), as well as second and third generation migrants have hybrid identities which means that they see the world through more than one cultural frame of reference. More often than not in organizations and therapeutic settings this surplus of vision is largely ignored, whereas if engaged in dialogue it can enhance creativity in the workplace or bring about innovative personal solutions to identity issues.

In this chapter we will describe the stepping-stones towards the development of the Personal Emotional Account of Cultural Experience (PEACE) methodology and a dialogical culture coaching approach that does justice to the diversity of cultural self-positions that populate the self of many contemporary citizens with hybrid identities that speak more than one language.

J. König (✉)
Moving Experience, Loosdrecht, The Netherlands
e-mail: movingexperience@planet.nl

K. Clarke
Clarke & Esser, Rotterdam, The Netherlands

H. Hermans (ed.), *Assessing and Stimulating a Dialogical Self in Groups, Teams, Cultures, and Organizations*, DOI 10.1007/978-3-319-32482-1_7

Consequences of Global Migration: Closing, and Opening as Stages in an Intercultural Learning Process

On the 9th of November 2014 Germany celebrated the 25th anniversary of the coming down of the Berlin wall. Since the fall of that wall however, many other walls have gone up: a wall on the Southern Boarders of Europe, regularly causing the drowning of boat refugees from Africa, a wall between America and Mexico and a wall between Israel and Palestine to mention but a few. In spite of the walls that are being erected to prevent people from seeking out a better perspective in life for themselves, and to protect the interests of national cultures, the volume of intercultural contact is increasing rapidly on a global scale. According to Hermans:

> Individuals and groups open or close themselves, depending on their needs, interests, anxieties or uncertainties. The increasing interdependence of globalization has separation or localization as it's counterforce, in the service of their vested interest and demarcation of their own identity … This creates a field of tension in which individuals, groups and communities position themselves and others as part of the current process of civilization. (Hermans, 2015, p.29)

According to Bennet, M. (1993b, p.29) groups and individuals open and close themselves, depending upon the stage in their developmental process of intercultural learning and sensitivity. He sees isolation, separation, denigration, superiority and minimization of cultural differences as a natural first reaction when individuals are confronted with the increased complexity of a different culture. These reactions are seen as the ethnocentric stages in a developmental model of intercultural sensitivity. These stages of ethnocentrism, or closing, are followed by ethno-relative stages where respect for behavioral and value differences, empathy, pluralism, contextual evaluation and constructive marginality prevail. Ethno-relativity implies an opening towards and an appreciation of difference as individuals and societies learn to navigate the increased complexity with which they were originally confronted. With increased experience of another culture, and the rebuilding of social networks in the new environment familiarity and appreciation grow. We shall show that dialogues between personal cultural positions and dialogues between individuals of different cultures facilitate movement from ethnocentric towards ethno-relativist stages of the intercultural learning process.

Hybrid Identities

Many individuals with hybrid identities seek coaching or therapy for varying reasons. Some feel ‘caught’ between their two cultures as, for example, a woman who, on the one hand, is encouraged by the host culture to develop herself through education and work and, on the other hand, feels the duty to stay at home to conform to the cultural expectations of her family and husband. Other clients hear from their Dutch managers that they are too emotional and must learn to be more to the point and direct. Many Dutch, known for their 'directness', have trouble with cultures in which information is passed on through more circular, indirect forms of communication. Often cultural behavior is misread e.g. seeing an Iranian's modesty as meekness and passivity (König, 2008). This, beside other subtle and blatant forms of discrimination, could be one of the reasons why clients with hybrid identities have difficulty finding jobs that fit their talents and ambitions (Ghorashi & van Tilburg, 2006; Verkuyten, 2005). Many of these clients feel angry, depressed and rejected.

Another frequently heard request in coaching is from clients seeking new jobs who struggle with the question: 'in which country do I want to work and in which language?'. This particular question mirrors the ever-present internal push and pull between the personal cultural contexts that make up a hybrid person's concept of home. There is always a 'there' and 'then', and a 'here' and 'now' and often in life-transitions, the theme of 'home' and 'rootlessness' emerges which can be anxiety provoking. Hybrid clients often complain that they do not feel helped in their therapy or coaching sessions and we also hear coaches and therapists who themselves feel ineffective and "lost" when dealing with multicultural clients.

Radhakrishnan writes about what he calls 'diasporic hybridity'. In his book *Diasporic Mediations* (1996) he talks about how, in the United States, ethnic groups living in the U.S.A. are named by joining their ethnic background by means of a hyphen with the word American. He himself is described as an Asian-American and asks an intriguing question:

> How does authenticity speak for itself: as one voice or as many related voices…When someone speaks as an Asian-American, who exactly is speaking? If we dwell in the hyphen, who represents the hyphen: the Asian or the American, or can the hyphen speak for itself without creating an imbalance between the Asian and the American components?…Which has the power and potential to read and interpret the other on its terms? If the Asian is to be Americanized, will the American submit to Asianization? (Radhakrishnan, 1996, p. 211).

His questions illustrate the complexity of the relationship between cultural voices. He suggests themes of dominance and submission emerging between personal cultural voices, which could undermine a sense of authenticity. He mentions a voice in the space between cultural voices, and wonders what this voice is saying. He points toward the need to help hybrid individuals explore the dialogues between their personal cultural voices.

Dialogical Culture Coaching

The Dialogical Culture Coaching approach was developed to help practitioners, clients, managers and employees to understand and work with the complexity and multiplicity of cultural voices, which comprise both hybrid identities and globalizing contemporary societies. It is based on the theory of the dialogical self (Hermans, 2001; Clarke, 2003) and the Personal Emotional Account of Cultural Experience methodology (PEACE) (König, 2009, 2012).

According to König, the internal dialogues between personal cultural positions, which are so familiar to cultural hybrids are theoretically caught in the dialogical theory of the self (Hermans, 2001) which is rooted at the intersection between the psychology of the self in the tradition of William James and the dialogical school of Mikhail Bakhtin.

> … The dialogical self challenges both the idea of a core essential self and the idea of a core essential culture. It conceives of self and culture as a multiplicity of positions among which dialogical relationships can be established. It allows for the study of self as 'culture inclusive' and of culture as 'self inclusive'. At the same time, this conception avoids the pitfalls of treating the self as individualized and self-contained, and culture as abstract and reified. The theory of the dialogical self accentuates the fact that culture and self are deeply intertwined and acknowledges history, body and social environment as intrinsic features of a developing person localized in time and space. (König, 2009, p.101)

The self is seen as composed of many different *I*-positions that have their own voices and stories and are positioned in the landscape of the mind. A dialogue between positions allows new meanings to emerge and has the potential to innovate the system of the self (Hermans, 1999). The achievement of the dialogical self theory is that it becomes possible to "conceptualize and study the complexities between personal cultural positions which for years have gone largely unnoticed in the psychological field." (König, 2009, p.104).

A First Stepping-Stone: Dialogues Between Personal Cultural Positions, the In-Between and the Meta-position

Any hybrid person can identify a host of personal cultural *I*-positions depending on the number of countries and cultures to which they have been exposed (König, 2012). Bhatia and Ram (2001) stated that these cultural voices are expressions of embodied and historically situated selves that during acculturation processes are constantly involved in negotiations, arguments and discourses with other voices within the self and with the contextual environment. König's research shows that when a dialogue is conducted between cultural positions, new insights occur in one's personal system of meaning. The intricacies of these negotiations, arguments and discourses become more evident to the person. This results in a greater ability to deal with one's own diversity and enhances the acculturation process (König, 2012).

König discusses two other positions in the personal intercultural dialogue, the in-between position (König, 2012) and the meta-position (Hermans, 2003), which are described in the following paragraphs.

The "In-Between" Position in the Process of Acculturation

Once a person, group or society is confronted with a new culture, the process of acculturation begins. Bennett, J.M. (1993a) sees acculturation as an ongoing *process* between two responses to living on cultural margins, which she calls encapsulated and constructive marginality. Encapsulated marginals experience disintegration and ambiguity between shifting cultures, have difficulty in decision-making, feelings of alienation and self-absorption, no recognized reference group, and never feel at home. From a constructive marginal position, cultural hybrids have a more positive outlook on life. Constructive marginals have self-differentiation, well developed boundary control and are able to make choices. Instead of alienation they experience a sense of dynamic in-betweenness and authenticity. In this position, they are intrigued by complexity and always feel at home. Encapsulated and constructive marginality represent two extreme positions in the process of acculturation on the boarder zones of different cultures.

Because the connotation of the word 'marginality' is often negative, we prefer to use the term in-between (König, 2009; Said, 1994). The "in-between position" is the hyphen in Radhakrishnan's example of the Asian-American. It is a position where one is neither here nor there, of being in transition in between cultural points of reference.

In her research König (2009) invited her research candidates to formulate a statement from an in-between position. She discovered that the in-between position is a way to discern where individuals position themselves in their acculturation process from encapsulated to constructive in-betweenness. Table 7.1 shows statements voiced by the in-between positions of her research candidates and illustrates the concepts of encapsulated and constructive in-betweenness.

Table 7.1 Encapsulated and Constructive in-between statements (König, 2012)

Name	Encapsulated in-between statements
Lisa	Having to choose between my English mother and Dutch friends at school gave me a horrible position. Where was I?
Filoster	As I write this I still feel vulnerable and easily wounded.
Lelie	At home it was always different from others. Family far away, isolation.
Bibi	There is a large sometimes burdensome responsibility in holding US citizenship.
	Constructive in-between statements
Luc	I as a cosmopolitan adapt easily.
Django	I adapt myself to the expectations and behavioral norms of the other. (All / Germans embrace and Dutch do not. Male friendships are defined differently in Germany: in the Netherlands they are more taboo.
Bibi	I speak and take action where I can to influence US policy and speak and take action every day to support the coming together of people across differences of language and culture.
Mr. Buwono	In between my different cultural backgrounds I find myself to be the integrator of them, sort of harmonizer.

The encapsulated in-between statements show disintegration between different cultures, loose boundary control (Lisa), alienation and isolation (Lelie), conscious of self (Bibi) and troubled by ambiguity (Lelie).

The constructive in-between statements show self-differentiation, well developed boundary control and wisdom about different cultural norms and values, (Django), adaptability and flexibility (Luc, Django), the ability to integrate different perspectives (Mr. Buwono) and empowererd activism (Bibi) to help people to experience the positive aspects of the coming together of individuals with different norms and values.

Our research and practical experience (Clarke, 2003; König, 2012) show that dialogical processes enhance the well-being of people with hybrid identities, reduce uncertainty and help to move a client from encapsulated to constructive in-betweenness. Dialogue is a way to melt personal walls in an individual's cultural identity structure and create more creative combinations between personal cultural positions.

The Meta-position

According to Hermans (2003), a meta-position permits a certain distance towards other positions and is important for facilitating the therapeutic reorganization of the self. It is a way of dealing with complexity, deficit knowledge and ambiguity and provides an overarching view so that several positions and their organization can be seen simultaneously.

To counteract the sense of fragmentation that hybrids often experience, given the complexity of multiple personal cultural positions, König (2009) invited her clients to voice a statement from a meta-position or, as she calls it, a bird's eye view statement. They did this by looking at all the previous statements they had formulated and written out on cards: the personal cultural positions, the dialogical repositioning statements between two personal cultural positions and the in-between statement. Her hypothesis was that a meta-position could be helpful in moving from encapsulated to constructive in-betweenness. In Table 7.2 a number of the meta-position statements are described as voiced by her research candidates.

A number of the sentences speak of "little pieces strewn", "multiple influences united in universality", "a rich mosaic of colour sounds and smells" implying that the meta-position brings together scattered parts. In two sentences the meta-position was made up out of two different languages. The words in italics are the translation of the original language, implying an integrative quality between linguistic contexts. It also leads to an evaluation of several positions and their organization and makes it possible to devise future strategies as the statements by Lisa, Alice, and Filoster suggest. It helps the individual to discern the importance of one or more positions for future development and facilitates the creation of a dialogical space in which positions and counter positions entertain significant dialogical relationships. A metaposition is crucial to facilitating reflection, devising new strategies and enables a client to position himself differently in his position repertoire.

Table 7.2 Meta-position statements (König, 2012)

Kate	I feel like a sort of mid-Atlantic Russian Jewish immigrant who speaks a sort of mid-Atlantic English and doesn't really belong anywhere "little pieces of myself strewn all over the world".
Ginger	Multiple influences are united in a universality, *that certain underlying things in which you believe remain stable in spite of different influences.*
Filoster	I have adapted and am wary. If I take "calculated risks" I can feel more connected.
Mr. Buwono	From the bird's eye view position I see a rich mosaic of colour, sounds and smells
Bibi	Nationalism and multi-nationalism are uneasy global bedfellows
Lisa	I just want to be myself and people will have to accept that, *c*I like to be busy with myself like this. It makes me feel safer.
Elise	What belongs to what and who to where?
Alice	I acknowledge that I have not done myself justice.
	Even if the context does not ask I wish to feel whole
Mimi	The Surinamese is far away, oh poor Surinamese!
Henri	I feel a great richness in cultures, societies, history, landscapes and mores.

A Second Stepping-Stone: The PEACE (Personal Emotional Account of Cultural Experience) Methodology

A next step in the development of the Dialogical Culture Coaching approach was the development of the PEACE methodology (König, 2012) to explore the personal cultural position repertoire of cultural hybrids on an emotional level.

For this emotional exploration the Self-Confrontation Methodology (SCM) was used (Hermans & Hermans-Jansen, 1995). The client is invited to score each statement on a five point scale using a standard set of 24 affects, as described in Table 7.3. The rationale underlying this procedure is that when a person values something, he

Table 7.3 Standard list of 24 affect terms

1. joy (P)	13. guilt (N)
2. powerlessness (N)	14. self-confidence (S)
3. self esteem (S)	15. loneliness (N)
4. anxiety (N)	16. trust (P)
5. satisfaction (P)	17. inferiority (N)
6. strength (S)	18. intimacy (O)
7. shame (N)	19. safety (P)
8. enjoyment (P)	20. anger (N)
9. caring (O)	21. pride (S)
10. love (O)	22. energy (P)
11. self-alienation (N)	23. inner calm (P)
12. tenderness (O)	24. freedom (P)

Hermans & Hermans-Jansen (1995, p. 277)

or she always feels something about the valued object. In order to do this quickly and efficiently a computer programme has been developed. Alternatively, pen and paper materials are available.

The PEACE methodology, as does the Self Confrontation Method, appeals to the self-organizing capacity of the person. Both methods invite the person to organize and articulate their world into a differentiated meaningful whole. The client as knower is invited to investigate, in cooperation with the interviewer, the self as known. The difference between the SCM and the PEACE methodology is that the latter focuses on stories voiced from an individual's cultural perspectives and explores an individuals' cultural complexity.

In valuation theory (Hermans, Hermans-Jansen, & van Gilst, 1985) the statements with their affective connotation are called "valuations". This procedure ultimately enables the measurement of the psychological concepts of self-enhancement (S) and contact and unity with the other (O) and helps to investigate and clarify the valuation system of cultural voices and it's organization into a complex whole at a certain moment in time in a certain contextual environment. Figure 7.1 illustrates the general types of valuations that can be generated depending on their particular affective profile.

The valuation of Strength and Unity (+SO) is one of the eight different types of valuation shown in Figure 7.1. We use it as an example to demonstrate how valuations are computed following the methodology devised by Hermans & Hermans-Janssen (1995, p. 42).

Strength and unity valuation +SO	S	O	P	N	
I as an English person feel at home in England	20	20	40	20	+SO

1. Index S is the sum score of the four affects expressing self-enhancement (self-esteem, strength, self-confidence, pride). In this valuation a maximum of 5 points for each affect was scored resulting in a score of 20.
2. Index O is the sum score of four affects expressing contact and union with the other (caring, love, tenderness and intimacy). A maximum of 5 points was scored for each affect resulting in a score of 20.
3. Index P is the sum score of eight positive (pleasant) affects (joy, satisfaction, enjoyment, trust, safety, energy, inner calm and freedom). A maximum of 5 points for each affect was scored resulting in a score of 40.
4. Index N is the sum score of eight negative (unpleasant) affects (powerlessness, anxiety, shame, self-alienation, guilt, loneliness, inferiority, anger). A maximum number of points for each affect was scored resulting in a score of 20.

Note that the sum scores of the S and O indices range from 0–20, the P and N from 0–40. For each valuation the P:N ratio can be studied. This indicates the wellbeing that an individual experiences in relation to the specific valuation.

If $P-N>10$ then + Wellbeing is positive

If $N-P>10$ then − Wellbeing is negative

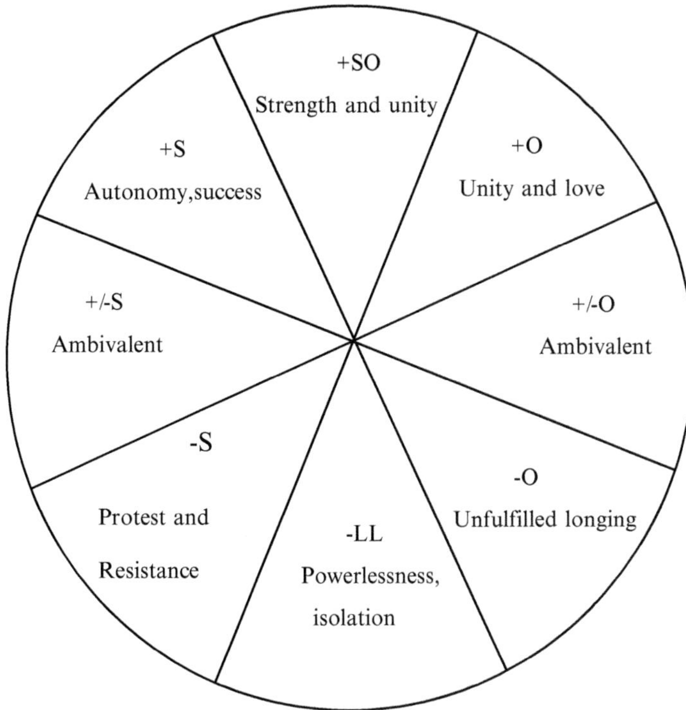

Fig. 7.1 A variation of Hermans and Hermans-Jansen's (1995) original figure with types of valuations

If P = N then +/− Wellbeing is ambivalent

The positive and negative feelings determine if one feels positively, negatively or ambivalently about a certain specific valuation.

Valuations are organized by combining the sum scores for feelings grouped under S, O, P, N into eight different affective types (+S, −S, +/−S, +O, −O, +/−O; +SO,−LL) which provide information about the affective quality of each valuation, and the organization of the affective system as whole.

The different types of valuations are illustrated by the following examples:

Autonomy and success valuation + S	S	O	P	N	
I as a Dutchman am very down to earth.	12	7	22	3	+S
S − O > 5 and P − N > 10					

Protest and resistance valuation − S	S	O	P	N	
I as a third culture kid never belong anywhere completely.	9	0	4	20	−S
S − O > 5 and N − P > 10					

Strength and unity valuation + SO	S	O	P	N	
I as an English person feel at home in England	20	20	40	20	+SO
S > 12 and O > 12 and P – N > 10					

Contact and unity valuation + O	S	O	P	N	
I as a German like to embrace my male friends when I meet them or leave them (as an Egyptian as well).	9	15	21	11	+O
O – S > 5 and P – N > 10					

Unfulfilled longing valuation – O	S	O	P	N	
In my job I am regarded as a native speaker of a country that I haven't lived in for many years and this can be awkward at times. (in between)	7	12	13	23	–O
O – S > 5 and N – P > 10					

Powerlessness and isolation valuation – LL	S	O	P	N	
I acknowledge that I have not done myself justice.	4	5	4	27	–LL
S < 8 and O < 8 and N – P > 10					

The PEACE Methodology: Step-by-step

Here follows a step-by-step procedure for the PEACE (Personal Emotional Account of Cultural Experience) methodology in which the previously described stepping-stones are integrated. This procedure may be used flexibly depending on the spontaneous flow of clients stories.

Step 1: Ask the client which cultures they call their own

The way in which an individual identifies personal cultural positions seems to be related to idiosyncratic choices and decisions made during the evolution of the personal life story. Cumulative lived experience adds to the prominence of a certain cultural position within the position repertoire. Many clients define their personal cultural positions by the countries they have lived in or by their parents' cultural background (König, 2012).

Step 2: Invite the client to write each personal culture on a separate card

e.g. I as Dutch on one card; I as Egyptian on another; I as British on a third card etc.

Step 3: Invite the client to conduct a dialogical repositioning exercise between two cultural positions of choice

First the one cultural position voices a sentence (write this on a separate card).

Then the other cultural position voices a response to the first statement (write this on a separate card).

Then the first cultural position voices a response to the statement that the second position voiced. (write this on a separate card).

Step 4: Invite the client to formulate a statement from an in-between position (write this on a separate card).

Step 5: Invite the client to look at all the statements on the cards and formulate a meta-position or bird's eye view statement (write this on a separate card).

Step 6: Clients are then asked to add two questions: 1) How do I feel in general and 2) How would I like to feel ideally (write these two sentences on separate cards).

Step 7: Clients are then invited to rate on a five-point scale how often they experience each of twenty-four specific feelings for each of their personal cultural positions, dialogical repositioning statements in-between and meta-position statements.

By following these steps an intrapersonal dialogue between cultural positions is developed and it becomes possible to measure the affective state of the different sentences voiced by different positions in the personal cultural position repertoire.

Step 8: Once the valuations have been computed it is important to reflect on them together with the client to discover the latent personal meanings of the valuation scores.

The following case study gives a practical example of the construction and workings of the PEACE methodology (König, 2012, p.261).

A Case Study Illustrating the PEACE Methodology: Filoster

Filoster, 55 years old, was born in The Netherlands. His parents divorced when he was very young and he grew up moving regularly between his German mother's grandmother in Germany during the holidays and his father in The Netherlands. He now lives in The Netherlands and works as a coach, consultant and entrepreneur in a variety of businesses. Growing up in The Netherlands in the aftermath of the Second World War, Filoster remembers vividly how he was beaten up because he was a German boy. In Table 7.4 we see the affective profiles of three personal cultural positions.

Filoster's Dutch position shows the affective profile of strength and unity (+SO), while his German and migrant position both show the affective profile of powerlessness and isolation (–LL). This clearly shows that personal cultural positions are in fact situated in power relationships within the self. An emotional valuation of -LL may literally mean that a personal position is being oppressed or reduced to powerlessness and isolation by a different voice in the system.

Table 7.4 Culture valuations Filoster

Culture valuations Filoster	S	O	P	N	Valuation type
I as Dutch	15	12	29	5	+SO
I as German	3	0	4	19	–LL
I as a migrant	0	0	10	24	–LL

Table 7.5 Repositioning valuations Filoster

Repositioning valuations Filoster	S	O	P	N	Valuation type
I am extremely careful about unveiling my German background here in The Netherlands.	9	5	19	23	+/–
I as a Dutchman avoid sharing details about my German roots as much as possible.	13	2	20	11	+ S
I have not yet solved a sense of distrust, which I developed early in my life.	5	0	0	19	–S
As I write this I still feel vulnerable and easily wounded. (in-between position).	4	3	0	21	–LL
I feel homeless, in the past much more than now, lonely. (in-between position)	6	4	3	30	–LL
I have adapted and am wary (meta-position).	13	2	21	5	+S
If I take "calculated risks" I can feel more connected (meta-position).	16	12	33	5	+SO
In general I feel	19	16	32	9	+SO
Ideally I would like to feel	19	18	39	1	+SO

> Many of the social processes, like dialogue and fights for dominance that can be observed in society at large also take place within the self as a "society of mind". The self is not considered as an entity in itself, as pre-given, with society as a facilitating or impeding environment, but rather as emerging from social, historical processes that transcend any individual-society dichotomy or separation. (Hermans & Hermans-Konopka, 2010, p.1)

When we look at the sentences Filoster formulates in his repositioning exercise (voiced from two cultural positions) we see how carefully he hides his German identity in the context of the Netherlands (Table 7.5).

In his first repositioning statement he speaks from his German position about how careful he is about unveiling his German background in the Dutch context and values this statement with affective ambivalence ((+/–) with P=19 and N=23). Apparently, the hiding of the German position causes more negative than positive affect and could be considered to be an energetic leak, as positive and negative emotions hold each other in sway. The Dutch position states that he avoids sharing details about his German roots as much as possible. This strategy provides the Dutch position with a score of autonomy and success (+S) but at the price of hiding and disenfranchising other seemingly incompatible personal cultural positions. Apparently in order to be successful in The Netherlands, he must hide his German and migrant positions, which may be the cause of his affective ambivalence. Again in this sequence it would seem that one cultural position (Dutch) dominates his other (German) cultural position.

His German position then comments that he has not yet solved a sense of distrust, which he developed early in his life. He feels protest and resistance (−S) about still not having solved this sense of distrust. This emotional charge may help to move his oppressed German and migrant positions out of their area of powerlessness and isolation in the future.

Filoster formulates two statements from an in-between position. His German and migrant positions have the same −LL valuation of powerlessness and isolation. He speaks of feeling vulnerable, homeless and lonely, emotions which could also be related to his state of moving back and forth between Germany and The Netherlands after his parents divorce.

From his bird's-eye-view position he realizes that he has adapted and is wary and in a second statement from this position he seems to devise a new more effective strategy of taking calculated risks in order to feel more connected with his bicultural being in The Netherlands.

This procedure helps him to understand how he deals with his conflicting cultural positions in the context of the post war years in The Netherlands and Germany. It helps him to make sense of his personal complexity and emotions by discovering a new strategy "taking calculated risks" which help him to feel more connected.

His general sense of wellbeing carries the affective valuation of contact and unity after this reflection on his cultural positions, which is more positive than the initial scores of powerlessness and isolation for his German and migrant positions. This sequence shows that conducting a dialogue between personal cultural positions, voicing an in-between position and viewing the personal meaning system from a meta-position, brings about an integrative quality, which increases wellbeing (+S and + SO).

With this process it is possible to witness the shifting emotional dynamics of the dialogical self as it flits between different cultural positions within the self. We see how a structured process of reflexive meaning making can facilitate personal innovation in between cultural contexts. In this way the complexities of personal cultural positions are conceptualised, explored and related to the subtle power of collective discourses in their broader sociological context. The dialogues in the social domain are mirrored in the dialogical self of migrants and internal power structures between personal cultural positions are related to dominant discourses in society.

Central to recent developments in the theory of the dialogical self is that the self works as a mini-society, analagous to the macro-society (Hermans, 2014, p. 135). The dialogical self theory provides a comprehensive social-scientific theory that incorporates the deep implications of the process of globalization and its impact on individual development. "…In a world that is increasingly interconnected and intensely involved in historical changes, dialogical relationships are required not only *between* individuals, groups and cultures, but also *within* the self of one and the same individual" (Hermans & Konopka, 2010, p.1). It therefore becomes extremely important to become aware of these mirrored internal dialogues in order to transform them and to then transform the limiting dialogues in society by challenging them.

Using the PEACE methodology as described above enables hybrid individuals to explore their stories from the perspective of each cultural position and from the in-between and meta-positions. The emotional scores make it possible to discern power differences between personal cultural positions, and often shows how deeply self and society are intertwined. When voices in a society object to a culture the individual has the tendency to reject or silence that cultural voice in his self-system, to comply with the norm. The PEACE methodology makes it possible to become aware of these power politics. Personal cultural voices are revalued and new constructive relationships between cultural positions emerge. Dialogical processes facilitate intercultural learning and cultural hybrids can then raise their voices as cultural change agents to promote the learning of others. A sense of peace and connectedness between and within individuals is made possible through this approach.

A Variation: Expanding Dialogue and Initiating Behavioral Change

The PEACE methodology can also be used in a more experiential way by exploring past, present and future stories of different cultural positions. This process of analysis, in which different cultural positions are invited to take a position in a room and voice their stories, deepens the dialogue and facilitates the development of new behavior in the hybrid client. This can be seen as a further step towards creating a dialogical culture coaching approach.

The following case study (König, 2012, p. 261) describes a client from Suriname who had arrived in the Netherlands for his vocational studies at the age of seventeen. He had become a teacher, then a headmaster at a black school, and later moved into a prominent position in a municipality, where he supervised building projects. In our first session he talked about how depressed he felt, he said "there is no sun in my life". A dear friend with whom he had been planning a trip to Suriname had recently passed away.

In a variation of the PEACE methodology described above, I asked the client which cultural positions he called his own (step 1). He answered Dutch, Cosmopolitan and Surinamese cultural positions. I invited him to find a place in the room for each of these positions and let them speak, from their past, present and future perspectives (a variation of step 3, here three cultural voices are invited to tell their past, present and future stories).

It can be helpful to use the following questions to trigger the stories when the client is invited to step into the first cultural position.

Past	Has there been anything of major significance in your past life that still continues to exert a strong influence on you?
Present	In there in your present existence any person or circumstance that exerts a significant influence on you?
Future	Do you foresee anything that will be of great importance for or exert a major influence on your future life?

Hermans and Hermans-Jansen (1995, p. 35)

The coach's role in this phase is to witness the client's stories as voiced from the different cultural positions as carefully as possible, and to invite the client into a different position as the story wears itself out.

In his Dutch schoolteacher position the client stood at a huge whiteboard and began a lecture using pen and paper. For his Surinamese position he went and sat in the sun in the window opening. His whole body posture changed, "I am relaxed, I see many different people from different cultures and know exactly what their customs and habits are", he said, smiling contentedly. For the cosmopolitan position he chose to sit at a table in the middle of the room. He became very philosophical in this position, speaking of the importance of the liberal arts to foster global consciousness. After he had voiced these positions, I invited him to find a position in the room from where he could look at all of these positions, the meta-position (step 5). From that position he felt compassionate towards the Surinamese position and realized that he had lost that part of his personality, as his system had been dominated by the Dutch schoolteacher position for such a long time. Ultimately, he founded his own company and worked in The Netherlands and Suriname supervising building projects, and developing a number of cross-cultural ventures.

This methodology is ideal for working with hybrid clients in relation to their coaching questions on work, career or life as they feel themselves recognized in their unique cultural and emotional make-up. Reflecting on the different dialogues voiced by different cultural positions from the perspective of the meta-position leads to a clearer sense of personal identity, increases perspective, a sense of agency and well being in clients. The emotional component of personal cultural positions sheds a light on how different personal cultural positions are organized in the self system. The Dutch position is often related to study, work, and success and sometimes to love life (Clarke, 2003). Often clients realize that the stories told from a non-Dutch position are long lost stories or reserved for private and/or family life. They are frequently related to shame and secrecy, sometimes idealized and never talked about.

> Often a cultural position's voice that is incongruous with the environmental discourse is silenced and hidden (e.g. Germans in the Netherlands). Silencing or disenfranchising dissonant personal cultural voices can over time lead to an identity crisis, energetic leaks or burn out. We have seen that with an increased consciousness of how culture is manifest in personal identity development, individuals become freer to construct and choose which elements of culture they wish to maintain or change in their respective cultural fields. (König, 2012, p. 262)

Needless to say, that from a managerial and organizational perspective, this method is invaluable, as it is a useful instrument to stimulate diversity by consciously inviting dissonant cultural voices into the conversation. As a way of preventing energetic leaks and burnout in hybrid clients, it can also lead to more wellbeing and creativity in organizations.

The Dialogical Culture Coach

In order to work effectively with this method, the coach must be able to create a safe space in which a client can explore his personal cultural voices. A safe space is created by listening carefully and non-judgmentally to the stories voiced by the different personal cultural positions of an individual. Working in this way with clients who have a mix of cultural backgrounds preferably requires a coach who has experienced an intercultural learning process and moved from an ethnocentric to an ethno-relative mindset. The first step towards an ethno-relative mindset and intercultural sensitivity is becoming aware of one's own cultural baggage. The second essential step is realizing that one's own cultural viewpoint is not central to everyone's reality.

The pitfalls (Bennett, 1993, in Rosinski, 2003, pp. 30–32) on the path from an ethnocentric to an ethno-relative mindset are often difficult to recognize in oneself as coach. This makes intervision sessions with colleagues so important when working with clients from different cultures. In intervision sessions the coach becomes aware of the pitfalls that are part of this process. The most common pitfall is ignoring, or even, denying differences. A second pitfall of an ethnocentric mind-set is to recognize difference but to value it negatively. Feeling a sense of superiority or finding yourself thinking your culture is better and more advanced than the other are characteristics of this pitfall. A third pitfall is recognizing the differences but minimalizing their importance. As Rosinski states, 'minimization is characterized as ethnocentrism because people bury differences under the weight of similarities… cultural differences are trivialized' (Rosinski, 2003, p. 33).

Erin Meyer, author of the book *The Culture Map* (2014), who has conducted extensive studies on intercultural communication, sums up the attitude of the ethno-relative and sensitive coach as "being able to put yourself in the client's shoes, be humble and be curious" (Meyer: blog; www.erinmeyer.com, 2014). For the coach or manager the shifting perspective from ethnocentric towards ethno-relativism is a developmental process that is exciting but can also be confusing and frustrating.

This dialogical culture coaching method is ideal for exploring the complexities of personal cultural positions that are so familiar to individuals with a hybrid identity. This can be in a coaching, psychotherapeutic, or organisational setting. Increasingly in our global village, individuals have hybrid identities because they were born in a different country than their parents, have parents coming from different cultures or because they grew up in different cultures as a global nomad and have encorporated different cultural perspectives into their identity.

It is also especially important for managers working in organisations that are becoming increasingly diverse to realise that many of their employees have different cultural voices and positions. It is essential to invite these cultural voices into the office, so that their different points of view can enrich the diversity of the workplace and enhance creativity, out of the box thinking and open new business markets. It can also prevent individuals wasting their precious energy to adjust and adapt to a given norm, and help them to feel welcome in all their cultural diversity. In the workplace people of different cultural backgrounds can meet and learn to adapt to each others cultural frames of reference, simultaneously strengthening bonds in society.

Conclusion

The cases described in this chapter show that constructions of the dialogical self in the dialogical culture coaching approach offer one of the most exciting possibilities to capture more faithfully the human potential for self-creation and self-transformation in between cultural contexts. The PEACE methodology has the potential to show how the discourses of the dominant culture have been internalized into the personal meaning system, how personal cultural voices may be dominated and even annihilated by the discourses adopted and incorporated from the dominant culture, and how they can be reintegrated and transformed.

From this overview we clearly see that people grow to value cultures with which they have had personal or visceral experience, in the sense that they call these cultures their own. This shows quite clearly that living in different cultures results in valuing more than one culture and that cultural loyalty is not necessarily restricted to one's culture of origin. By reflecting on the embodied emotional chords of personal cultural positions, repositioning dialogues, in-between and meta-position valuations the PEACE methodology facilitates the emergence of new meanings in the personal meaning system.

Dialogical culture coaching combines the internal emotional narrative with the external narrative mode in a self-reflective meaning-making mode of inquiry. The person is approached as someone capable of self-reflection and as an expert on the content of his/her experiences. The active, methodological, and well structured stimulation of the process of self reflection within the framework of a dialogical model helps to narrow the gap between assessment and change and may function as a bridge between personality psychology, culture coaching and psychotherapy. In this chapter we have described case studies that reflect the dialogical culture coaching approach. We hope that many professionals in (career) coaching, psychotherapy and organisations that work with hybrid clients will feel inspired to learn to work in this way with their bi- and multicultural clients who have hybrid identities and multicultural frames of reference and to participate in intervision sessions to become aware of their own cultural blind spots.

References

Bennett, J. M. (1993a). Cultural marginality: Identity issues in intercultural training. In R. Michael Paige (Ed.), *Education for the intercultural experience* (pp. 109–137). Yarmouth, ME: Intercultural Press, Inc.

Bennett, M. (1993b). Towards ethnorelativism: A developmental model of intercultural sensitivity. In R. Michael Paige (Ed.), *Education for the intercultural experience* (p. 30). Yarmouth, ME: Intercultural Press.

Bhatia, S.,& Ram, A. (2001). Rethinking "acculturation" in relation to diasporic cultures and post-colonial identities. *Human Development, 44*, 1–18.

Clarke, K. (2003). Met jezelf in gesprek gaan: De Zelfkonfrontatiemethode en burn-out (Talking with yourself: The self-confrontation method and burn-out). In R. Van Loon and J.Wijsbek (Eds.), *De Organisatie als Verhaal* (The organization as a narrative) (pp. 176–195). Assen, The Netherlands: Van Gorcum.

Ghorashi, H. & van Tilburg, M. (2006). "When is my Dutch good enough? Experiences of refugee women with Dutch labour organisations. *JIMI/RIMI, 7*(1), 51–70.

Hermans, H. J. M. (2015). Human development in today's globalizing world: Implications for self and identity. In L. Arnett Jensen (Ed.), *Oxford handbook of human development and culture* (pp. 28–42). New York: Oxford University Press.

Hermans, H. J. M. (1999). Dialogical thinking and self innovation. *Culture and Psychology, 5*(1), 67–87.

Hermans, H. J. M. (2001). Mixing and moving cultures require a dialogical self. *Human Development, 44*, 24–28.

Hermans, H. J. M. (2003). The construction and reconstruction of a dialogical self. *Journal of Constructivist Psychology, 69*, 89–127.

Hermans, H. J. M. (2014). Self as a society of *I*-positions: A dialogical approach to counseling. *Journal of Humanistic Counseling, 53*, 134–159.

Hermans, H. J. M., & Hermans-Jansen, E. (1995). *Self narratives: The construction of meaning in psychotherapy*. New York: Guilford Press.

Hermans, H. J. M., & Hermans-Konopka, A. (2010). *Dialogical self theory*. Cambridge, UK: Cambridge University Pres s.

Hermans, H. J. M., Hermans-Jansen, E. & van Gilst, W. (1985). *De Grondmotieven van het menselijk bestaan: Hun expressie in het persoonlijke waarderingsleven* (The basic motives of human existence: Their expression in personal valuation). Lisse, The Netherlands: Swets and Zeitlinger.

Jones, S., & Bradwell, P. (2007). *As you like it: Catching up in an age of global English*. London: Demos.

König, J. R. (2008). *Birds of passage, disillusion and surprise*. Heemstede, The Netherlands: Van Assema for Van Ede & Partners.

König, J. R. (2009). Moving experience: Dialogues between personal cultural positions. *Culture and Psychology, 15*, 97–119.

König, J. R. (2012). *Moving experience: Complexities of acculturation*. Amsterdam: VU University Press.

Meyer, E. (2014). *The culture map: Breaking through the invisible boundaries of multi-cultural business*. New York: Public Affairs. Blog: www.erinmeyer.com.

Pollock, D. C. & van Reken, R. (2001). *Third culture kids, the experience of growing up among worlds*. London/Boston: Nicholas Brealy Publishing.

Radhakrishnan, R. (1996). *Diasporic mediations*. Minneapolis, MN: University of Minnesota Press.

Rosinski, P. (2003). *Coaching across cultures*. London/Boston: Nicholas Brealey Publishing.

Said, E. W. (1994). *Representations of the intellectual: The 1993 Reith Lectures*. London: Vintage Original.

Verkuyten, M. (2005). *The social psychology of ethnic identity*. New York: Psychology Press.

Chapter 8
The Team Confrontation Method (TCM)

Peter Zomer

As illustrated throughout this book, concepts taken from Dialogical Self Theory (DST) offer a fertile ground for the development of practical methods. The present chapter offers an introduction into a DST-based method for team coaching: the Team Confrontation Method (TCM).

The practice of team coaching concentrates on fostering team effectiveness, by helping team members to address issues that hinder it. In today's corporate environment, teams take a central role in the production of goods and services. Their collective intelligence (Woolley, Chabris, & Pentland, 2010) is capable of tackling complex challenges like innovation, crisis management or problem analysis. Woolley et al. found that teams are effective when team members have a high average social sensitivity, an equal distribution of conversational turn-taking and a high proportion of females in the team. Admittedly, it may be that individuals often prove to come up with superior solutions to those provided by teams. For teams run the risk of social loafing, i.e. team members exerting less effort when they work in a group than when they work alone (Pennington, 2002). But teams have at least the *potential* to make effective use of a rich presence of diverse resources and talents. There is a whole industry dedicated to team learning, aimed to tapping into this potential of diversity.

Proper team coaching is therefore regarded as something very valuable in present corporate surroundings. It can make the difference between average teams and good teams, and between good teams and great teams.

A colleague of mine called a team 'a wild beast that doesn't want to be tamed', and indeed, practicing team coaching can be like riding a rodeo horse. A team's group dynamics is often unpredictable and sometimes even malignant. It requires a lot of the team facilitator, who should be streetwise and authentic at the same time.

P. Zomer (✉)
Zomer & Cornelissen, Tilburg, The Netherlands
e-mail: peter@zomer-cornelissen.nl

H. Hermans (ed.), *Assessing and Stimulating a Dialogical Self in Groups, Teams, Cultures, and Organizations*, DOI 10.1007/978-3-319-32482-1_8

The practice of team coaching tends to be eclectic. Teamcoaching practitioners select interventions from a practical body of knowledge that is shared with other practitioners. Their connoisseurship of when and how to intervene is taken as the key predictor of success in improving a team's group dynamics. But connoisseurship is intuitive and lacks a clear structure: the interventions of practitioners often seem coincidental and their logic is hard to transmit. Against this background, the Team Confrontation Method (Zomer, 2006) is meant to provide the team coaching practice with a tried and tested, protocolled way of facilitating team learning. Success becomes less dependent on sheer connoisseurship. The method adds to it by providing a protocol and philosophy that is science-based and tested. The basic ambition that triggered the development of the TCM is to make success in team coaching more likely.

In the present chapter, I aim to give an introduction to the method. I'll start with an overview of its theoretical basis; after that, I present the design of the method; then I illustrate the workings of the method with a case; and finally, I address some important issues about its use in the section "Discussion".

Theoretical Basis

The TCM (Zomer, 2006) derives its principles and core concepts from the Self Confrontation Method (SCM) and the related Valuation Theory (VT) (see Visser's contribution in this book, Chap. 2, this volume). The SCM is a method for individual self-development that is used in psychotherapy and counselling / coaching. It is, together with the VT framework, well described in Hermans and Hermans-Jansen (1995). Other concepts of the Team Confrontation Method are taken from Dialogical Self Theory (DST) of which good introductions are provided by Hermans and Hermans-Konopka (2010) and Hermans & Gieser (2013). As the reader undoubtedly knows by now, Valuation Theory and Dialogical Self Theory study the functioning of the self and the role of meaning-making processes connected with it.

The Self-Confrontation Method (SCM) proves very helpful not only because of its concepts but also by its way of working. Individuals are invited to actively investigate their experience and the meanings they give to it, and use the resulting insights for self-development. Special emphasis is laid on the role of the SCM facilitator, who is not a neutral (or distant) bystander who conducts the investigation from an outsider's perspective, but rather a personal helper who assists the individual in his self-investigation.

For the grounding of the Team Confrontation Method (TCM), I extended central concepts of VT and DST (valuation, affect and voice) from the individual to the collective level of functioning. Especially the work of Karl Weick (1979, 1995) proved helpful for making this framework extension possible. His view on sense-making as a way by which collectives organise their world is reminiscent of Hermans's view on meaning-making as a way by which individuals structure their world. Weick provided me with some propositions of collective functioning that describe essences of what happens in collectives like teams, such as: 'Norms are transmitted in groups through collective stories; these stories depict general expectancies from the individual member, by the group', and 'Collective stories coordinate group action'. Weick's work made it possible to understand in what ways collective stories and collective behavior (and thus, 'effectiveness') are connected. Collective stories provide useful empirical material that can be meaningfully connected with the issue of team effectiveness.

The presented conceptual framework contains the concepts collective valuation, collective affect, and collective voice.

- A *Collective valuation* is a concise description of relevant experiences of the team, that are meaningful and valuable for those who have experienced them. It is put in one or two sentences about what happens (or happened) to the 'We' of the team. An example: 'We were disappointed when the customer told us that he chose our competitor for doing the job instead of us.' Collective valuations are units of meaning, the smallest 'particles' of the collective stories that team members share about their world.
- A *Collective affect* is a feeling experienced by team members in the name of their team. Team members share affective tones when they jointly experience a situation *as team members* (not as individuals). An example could be a shared feeling of being disappointed, or of anger. Consider the situation when your country is out from the Soccer World Cup. Unfortunately this happens every fourth year, except when you happen to be German. I have personally experienced this collective sadness too many times.
- A *Collective voice* is a voice with which the team speaks 'as one person' in the contact with the outside world, or in the contact among the team members. It can be considered as a collective position. For instance, in a team of advertising agents, the voice of 'The Creative' may be shared by all of the team members in a more or less equal way: it is this 'We-position' that sees possibilities everywhere and makes the team members behave creatively toward each other and towards the outside world. Collective voices tell the collective stories that enjoy full credibility to each team member. Collective voices could be considered 'responsible' for the behavioral patterns that are common in the team, and they correlate highly with them. By means of their collective voices, team members express that they expect each other to behave in a certain way.

These concepts help the TCM to *assess* the quality of the collective functioning of the team members. But the TCM also makes use of concepts that help to *improve* their collective and individual functioning. The theoretical basis for interventions aiming for improvement is provided by the work of many different authors, such as, again, Weick (1979), but also Mead (1972 [1934]), Bakhtin (in Morris, 1994), or Bohm (1996). The here presented conceptual framework contains the concepts of deviant voice, pattern breaching, dialogue and reorganization of collective valuations.

- A *Deviant voice* is a voice that tells stories which deviate from the collective stories practiced in the team. It can be considered as a position taken by a minority, and ventilates viewpoints that run counter to the current mainstream thinking, feeling and acting in the team. The advertising agents might have 'The Accurate' as their deviant voice, which potentially provides an alternative narrative about their world. Deviant voices are seldomly used openly by the team members. But the deviant voice will become more prominent in the team when patterns of cooperation are broken (see following item in this list); a deviant voice can even *make* the pattern break.

- *Pattern breaching* is the breaking of patterns of cooperation. Patterns of cooperation are maintained by the active use of collective voices and hang together with collective stories. Counterproductive patterns can be broken with the aid of lever deviant voices that open up new experiences and behavioural possibilities.
- *Dialogue* is the careful and respectful joint investigation of the common experience, and of the viewpoints of each team member. It is a rare attribute of a team's functioning, but actively fostered in the process of carrying out a team investigation with the TCM. Dialogue helps to find out what the patterns of cooperation are in the team, and what the possibilities are for the team to break them.
- *Reorganisation of collective valuations* is the process of new affective connotations and meanings becoming attached to the team's collective valuations, of new valuations coming to the team's awareness, and old valuations disappearing from it; and the change of deviant valuations into collective valuations or vice versa.

The Method: Design Choices and Protocol

Before sharing the protocol of the method, I start this section with a listing of its fundamental design choices. The design of the TCM shows a clear family resemblance to the SCM. This means that it has, next to a similar conceptual framework, a special emphasis on self-investigation and the role of the facilitator as a personal helper instead of a neutral 'white-coat' investigator. The method also emphasizes the central importance of 'subjective meaning' instead of 'objective truth'. Finally, the method aims at the investigation of collective phenomena in the team. I now present the basic design choices that lie at the root of the TCM, starting with its focus on the patterns of collective functioning.

Assessing Collective Behavior

Of course, coaching a team doesn't simply mean coaching its individual members, since only that would not help the team run more smoothly as a whole. Team performance is essentially a *collective* performance, dependent on the quality of the *relationships* between team members instead of solely on their individual qualities. Team members who approach their common objective from the perspective of the group as a whole, tend to interrelate their actions with care. Each of them really acts *as a member of the group* and not as an individual (Weick, 2001). Proper team coaching should take this core characteristic of team performance seriously into account. Therefore, when I designed the Team Confrontation Method, I decided to make it concentrate primarily on the quality of interlocking behaviors, or patterns of cooperative behavior, rather than on the personalities of the different team members.

Triggering the Team's Self-Investigation

To describe the behavioral patterns in a team, one could basically choose between two options. *Either* one observes the cooperative behavior in the team from an outside perspective, as with the Interaction Process Analysis of Bales (1970) or the related SYMLOG method (Bales & Cohen, 1979). In these methods, a critical assessment is done by a neutral consultant using twelve categories which cover the behaviors occurring in group interaction. Result is a score for each of the categories that is to be interpreted, or compared with scores of other teams or of the same team in the past. *Or* one gets the team members to derive their behavioral patterns from a thorough analysis of their own reported experience. In case of the TCM, the second path is taken. In a similar way as in the Self Confrontation Method (SCM), reports of team members' experiences with their mutual cooperation are collected and assessed for their accompanying affect patterns. Their joint interpretation of the resulting data makes the team members realize what is going on in the team and conclude how their typical cooperative behaviors are hanging together. The outcome of their investigation is a mapping of these behavioral patterns in a 'system diagram'. In such a diagram, a team describes for example its pattern of long-winded discussions leading to an experience of time–pressure among the team members, leading to a strongly felt irritation, then leading back again to long-winded discussions. The diagram maps a repetitive pattern occurring in the team. With such a system diagram, and the work done in preparation of it, the team's awareness is raised of behavioral patterns that should urgently be altered. Its sense of urgency grows as well as its felt responsibility to act. The method enhances the team members' ownership of the desired change.

Having the TCM Facilitator as an Aid

Because of the active role of the team members in the investigation, the TCM could be considered as a method similar to action research (e.g., Greenwood & Levin, 1998), where a group of people investigates a question of shared interest, aided by a facilitator who is experienced in conducting research. As in action research, it is central that the TCM facilitator on the one hand, and the team members on the other, share responsibility for the quality of the investigation. They are supposed to consciously and conscientiously fulfil the obligations connected with their roles. The team members should openly share their experiences and show their willingness to critically assess their own functioning. The facilitator should offer a method to the team for conducting the investigation and help them to use it in a sound and safe way; 'sound' meaning that the investigation produces reliable outcomes, and 'safe' that it guarantees safe circumstances for all people who are involved in the investigation. When the team and its facilitator work well together, the biggest gain is a fruitful combination of global and local knowledge. The team's experience (local knowledge) becomes more meaningful by the facilitator's reference to generic phenomena that occur in teams. Vice versa, the facilitator's knowledge about and experience with teams (global knowledge) is checked and enriched by the specific empirical circumstances of the team. The cooperation between these two parties is key. If they don't cooperate well, the quality of the investigation and its outcomes is hampered.

Making Meaningful Interpretations

The reader will probably recognize the constructivist nature of the TCM. After all, the method is orientated towards the collection and generation of *meanings* constructed by the team members. Every user of the method should realize that the TCM Facilitator is not the outside observer who should determine what the 'truth' is about the team and impose it on the team members. The conclusions that the team and its facilitator draw should be 'meaningful' in the local context of the team in the first place. If the team members don't recognize the meanings suggested by the facilitator, then he should accept this and look, together with the team, for more valid meanings. This involves a facilitating style that is best characterized by activities like listening, following, reflecting; truly implying a 'gentle investigation'.

The TCM Protocol

In Zomer (2006), the Team Confrontation Method is put forward as an integral whole. The design process leading up to this result is checked against and enriched by the benchmark of design methodology. In the design, the function of the method is leading: the TCM should be a tool for assessing and improving collective and individual functioning in teams, or more briefly, a tool for collective learning.

Figure 8.1 shows an overview of the protocol. It consists of eight steps, the first three to be taken on the first team meeting day, the second three (4 to 6) to be taken on the second meeting day, and the last two (7 and 8) in the period thereafter.

- Step 1 in the protocol is to determine a question of inquiry. The team members jointly formulate it, with the assistance of the TCM Facilitator. E.g., 'What change is desirable and possible for us, in order to acquire more customers and secure continuity?', or 'What are our energy leaks?'.

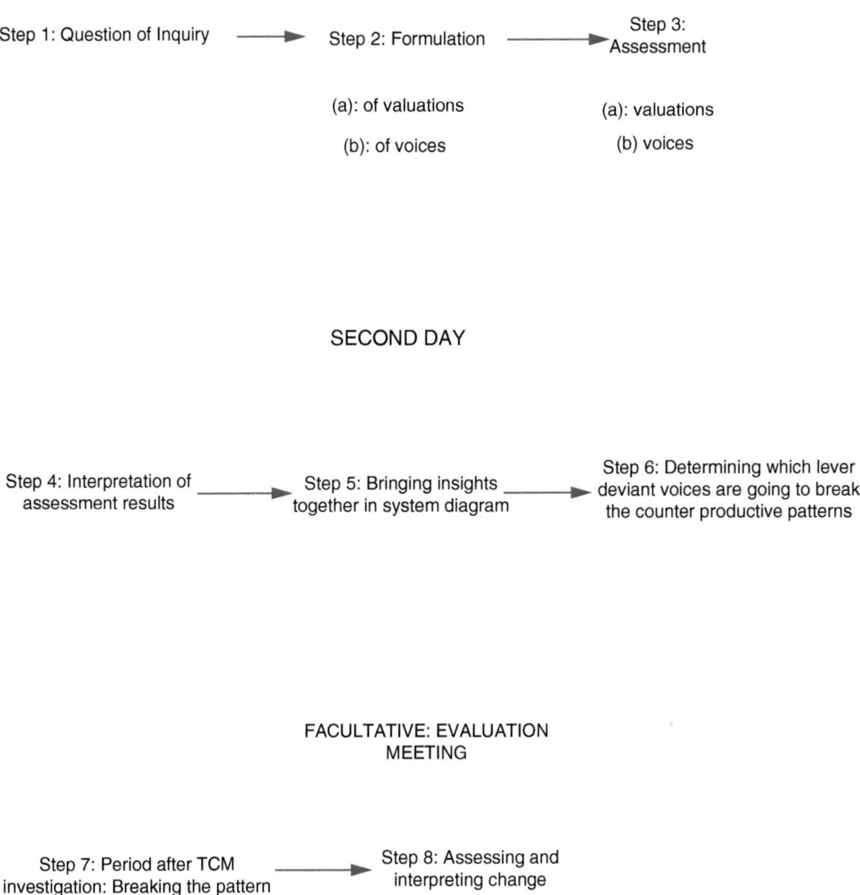

Fig. 8.1 The steps in the TCM protocol

- Step 2 is to formulate:
  - (a) collective and deviant valuations. The team members are invited to write experiences on a flip chart that are relevant in the light of the question of inquiry. The team is asked to formulate some collective valuations (that the members expect to be shared by a majority in the team) and some deviant valuations (that they expect to be shared by only a minority in the team). E.g., 'We experienced stress when Harry asked Sally for commitment to our factory's continuity' or 'We devote so much time to analysis and planning that we don't get ourselves to the real work'.

- (b) collective and deviant voices. The team is asked to first indicate which collective voices are, according to them, active in the daily functioning of the team. E.g., 'The Creative' or 'The Enthusiast'. Then, team members are asked to indicate the unique positive contribution of each of the other team members; in this way, a list of possible deviant voices is produced, also as an input for the assessment. E.g., 'The Accurate' or 'The Serious'.

- Step 3 is to carry out a quantitative assessment of two aspects of the team's functioning.
  - Firstly, an assessment of the *affective connotations of valuations*. With the aid of a questionnaire (usually completed online), the team members indicate what affective connotations the valuations have to them. They indicate the intensity of individual feelings – individual affect, i.e. feelings that they experience individually (e.g., 'I feel happy'), and of group feelings – collective affect, i.e. feelings that they attribute to the group (e.g., 'The team feels powerless'). It is possible that the assessment shows that for a valuation the average individual feelings differ significantly from the average group feelings. E.g., team members discover that they fool themselves and each other by commonly projecting an experience of anger to the group, which is actually not there (or not so strongly) in the individual team members' experience. Here, the dominant group dynamics are unmasked: the team members think that there is a lot of anger in the team and act accordingly (for instance by taking the conflict very seriously and making it more problematic), whilst the actual anger among them is much lower. The group dynamics add fuel to the conflict. With the aid of the results of the assessment, it is possible to have a good dialogue about the affective overtones of important experiences. Such a dialogue produces new meaning and makes the daily experience more meaningful.
  - Secondly, an assessment of the team's *multivoicedness.* A team consists of a 'polyphony' of voices that produce, with each other and in dialogue, a set of (collective and deviant) stories about the team's collective experience. One voice, for instance 'The Critical' may be used by the team members to tell stories of ineffectiveness of the team or team members (E.g., 'We have regularly made mistakes with security issues'). Another voice, 'The Rational', may be responsible for stories of clear cause-effect relationships (E.g., 'Each time when we make this planning of operations, the desired outcome is not being produced'). As explained before, there are collective voices and deviant voices. The assessment among the team members shows which voices prove to be collective and which of them deviant; some voices unexpectedly prove to be collective, others are unexpectedly deviant. This is information of central importance, since collective voices contribute decisively to the team's collective behavioral patterns, including the ones that are counterproductive.

- Step 4 is to jointly interpret the assessment results, and to make the functioning of the team transparent by the ensuing discussion about the meaning of the evidence.

This brings to the surface what is happening inside the team below the level of manifest team functioning. E.g., 'Evidently we raise the bar too high and then get quickly disappointed' or 'Evidently we cannot let go and put a lot of strain on ourselves'.

- Step 5 is to bring these insights about the team's functioning together in a system diagram. This diagram describes the recurring patterns of cooperation in the team. Some of these are counterproductive and may be the cause of the team's ineffectiveness.
- Step 6 is to determine which patterns should be broken and changed, and with the aid of which lever deviant voice this could be done. These patterns are named (e.g., the 'Alone in the world loop', describing how team members repetitively function in isolation from their colleagues and forget to support each other), so that it will be easy for the team members to remind each other of the pattern after the TCM sessions.
- Step 7 is to experiment with new, pattern breaking behavior. This step is done in the period after the TCM sessions. The lever deviant voices are included actively and purposefully in the team's dialogue and cooperation. E.g., 'The Creative' as a lever to break a pattern of overly conservative behavior in the team. After all, every overly conservative team does contain voices that are creative and willing to do things differently.
- Step 8 is to do a reassessment of collective valuations, collective affect and multivoicedness, in order to determine what changes have taken place since the time of the first assessment. In this way the success of the team investigation can be assessed. One could expect that after the investigation and the ensuing period of pattern breaching, collective stories and their affective overtones will have been changed, and lever deviant voices have become stronger.

The here described sequence of steps will take about 6 months.

Case: Application of the Team Confrontation Method

I will now give an example of the application of the TCM Protocol. Each of the steps that are described above are illustrated here.

The Situation

A management team of a chemical factory, consisting of five group leaders working on the shop-floor in a five shifts system, three members of the supporting staff, and the team leader, had been complaining for some time about bad mutual relations. Team members kept on wrangling with each other about operational decisions in the factory. It often happened that individual members made decisions without consulting the other members. This mostly occurred during night shifts when a member worked alone. A decision would typically affect other team members, who then, in the following shifts, would react with indignation. It proved that also in regular meetings of the team, the team members could often not find agreement about what decision to make.

The team wanted to do something about it, and asked a colleague of mine to facilitate. He carried out individual talks with each of the team members and organized a team meeting, in which the participants mainly discussed operational problems and actions to tackle them. These interventions gave him an initial insight into some patterns of cooperation and communication. Even though he had the insight, he did not succeed in communicating it to the team. He had too much been an 'outside observer'. When it became clear that his interventions had been insufficiently effective, the decision was made to use the TCM with myself as the facilitator. It was expected that this method would allow the team to do its *own* investigation, to produce its *own* insights by giving attention to the undercurrents in the daily cooperation that really mattered, and thus to achieve real change.

Steps 1 and 2: Question of Inquiry and Formulation of Valuations

During the first Team Confrontation meeting, the question of inquiry was jointly formulated: 'How can we make a decision that has the support of us all?' Subsequently, the team members formulated some collective valuations, listed in Table 8.1. The valuations show collective experiences of how difficult it was to make a joint and supported decision. This showed by detailed and lengthy discussions and disagreements about who should have done what at which moment in time. The typical way to behave in such discussions was to be unnaturally strict and precise. The team members labelled this as 'business-like' and 'objective', but in fact it was cumbersome and demanded lots of energy.

Table 8.1 Collective valuations of the Chemical Factory Team

Valuation
1. We look at problems in a business-like way, instead of getting carried away emotionally.
2. When a decision is made by the person, this person feels ownership. Example: not calling the boss when you have a problem in the nightshift.
3. The communication among ourselves is not satisfactory.
4. After our initial exclusion of hiring the Petroil man, he was hired anyway, in spite of the foremen having thought up a cheaper alternative. After some time, the Petroil man was deemed too costly.

Valuations describe collective experiences of the team members

Step 3a: Assessment of Collective Affect

Also the affective connotations of these valuations were measured. It was the affective connotations of valuation 3 that caught the eye, describing the experience of each of the team members working in a vacuum. The measurements indicated a much lower score on trust as a group feeling than on trust as an individual feeling: the team members attributed little trust to the group, whilst they experienced individually more of it. The assessment outcome was surprising to them and helped them to understand that it was merely group dynamics (influencing each other) that had worsened a pattern of mutual distrust. The actual trust was much higher, as was confirmed in the ensuing investigative discussion among the team members.

Step 3b – Assessment of Multivoicedness

During the first meeting, the team members came up easily with three collective voices (see Table 8.2) and five deviant ones.

Especially 'the Critical' (which was, according to the team, 'the voice who puts question marks') was found typical of the team. Other voices also showed to be collective, such as 'the Objective' and 'the Problem Solver'. Deviant voices were among others the 'Maintainer of Relations' and 'the Acceptor', more reasonable voices with more openness to cooperation.

Table 8.2 Collective and deviant voices in the Chemical Factory Team

Collective voices
The Critical
The Problem Solver
The Objective
Deviant voices
The Maintainer of Relations
The Acceptor
The Enthusiast
The Long-term Planner
The Flexible

Collective voices describe the team members' collective positions; deviant voices describe the positions of minorities in the team

Step 4: Joint Interpretation of Assessment Results

After my presentation of the assessment results in the TCM report, the team sat together to interpret them. The significantly lower score on trust as a group feeling than on trust as an individual feeling was a topic of conversation. The team members realized that they had created a negative collective truth ('Evidently, we talk each other into a problem of distrust'). The actual mutual distrust as experienced by the individual team members was not so high. Based on different striking assessment results, they could also draw other conclusions about undercurrents in the mutual cooperation, e.g. 'evidently we don't take enough time for mutual calibration' (time pressure) and 'evidently, in our team you are never sure about how colleagues will react to the solution that you have come up with yourself' (insecurity about own solution). Based on other assessment results the team members drew more conclusions: 'Evidently, we are very critical toward each other' (mutual criticism) and 'Evidently, we want to consider issues very objectively here' (repeating discussions). It was as if the team members had looked into a mirror. They could open up about themselves, discuss what was meaningful about their experiences and look their problem into the eye.

Step 5: Making a System Diagram

The interpretations of the assessments were put in themes (e.g., mutual criticism), which were subsequently taken as variables in a system diagram. With this diagram, the team members made basically a description of the patterns in their cooperation.

In the diagram, the team members recognized a 'Wrangle loop' (Fig. 8.2) that described how team members kept on criticizing and wrangling with each other, thereby diminishing the common resolve. *Mutual criticism* led to less (joint) *decisiveness*, less decisiveness led to more *experienced time pressure*, and more time pressure led to the situations wherein individuals, feeling isolated from their peers, chose for themselves how to respond adaptively to the circumstances in the factory (*flexible response to what situation needs*), thus causing again the criticism of the colleagues. In the diagram, it became visible how this problem could have become worse and worse.

Step 6: Determining Which Pattern Should Be Broken

This loop in the cooperation behavior was according to the team members perpetually present as well as counterproductive. In order to break this undesirable pattern, the team members determined which collective voice in the team was responsible

Fig. 8.2 A system diagram of the 'Wrangle Loop'. Diagram describing the repetitive pattern of cooperation: mutual criticism leading to less decisiveness, less decisiveness leading to more experienced time pressure, more experienced time pressure leading to more flexible ad-hoc responses to situations, more flexible ad-hoc responses leading again to more mutual criticism

for it, and which lever deviant voice would probably be capable of breaking it. The team members pointed at the Critical as the collective voice responsible for the dysfunctional pattern. The Critical corresponded with their attitude to criticize to the core each of the decisions that one of their colleagues had been making without their explicit consent, even when it was made in relative isolation in a nightshift. They chose as a lever deviant voice the Acceptor that was not so much used, but supposed to be well able to break the unwanted pattern of cooperation. This voice would be capable of stopping the endless pleading about decisions and show the reasonableness necessary for breaking the pattern. In a dialogue, the team explored in which type of situations the Acceptor would do things differently. The team members listed these situations and made resolutions with the aim to make the team function differently in these situations. Herewith the reflection phase (steps 1 to 6) was finished.

Step 7: Experimenting with New, Pattern Breaking Behavior

The team members had the feeling that they had thoroughly addressed what their problem was and how it could be solved. They should let the lever deviant voice of the Acceptor do his work. The Acceptor would acknowledge that independent operational decisions were never intended to harm the colleagues, or lazily made with indifference to the consequences for them. Instead, the Acceptor would recognize that the decisions were made under time pressure, in eager need for the agreement of others. In using this voice, team members would also accept that their decision would have consequences for the others, thus enhancing the quality of their decision.

After about 4 months, the team members evaluated the progress in this jointly carried out experiment of 'Making the Acceptor exert more influence in the daily cooperation'.

Step 8: Evaluation by Reassessment of Collective Valuations, Collective Affect and Multivoicedness

During a last meeting, the team members were asked to indicate their progress or stagnation. I wanted to find signs of collective learning: whether ineffective patterns were actually broken and whether they were replaced by new, effective patterns. I also wanted to find out if there had been unforeseen side-effects.

The team members pointed out that the work itself was as hectic as it had been before the start of the TCM trajectory, and that mistakes were still made in the mutual communication; but that this all had become less a cause for upheaval. They reported that the Acceptor had clearly become a prominent voice within the team, which was also confirmed by the assessment. Mutual trust had increased: 'We don't treat each other so grumpily anymore. We accept an explanation when something has gone wrong. Before, I also didn't trust the explanation.' Another team member, referring to another example of recent miscommunication: 'If this had happened before the trajectory, the bomb had gone off. Now we talk in a respectful way, with each other, instead of against each other'. The team members didn't take things so personally anymore and did not become so quickly annoyed, even if there were continuing disturbances in the daily work. They experienced more support from each other. The 'Wrangle loop' had mostly disappeared. After a recent negative incident a team member said: 'Of course, one could criticize this easily, and before we would certainly have done that, but now I haven't really heard so much about it.'

During the evaluation, the team made a surprising discovery: 'We have never looked at our list of resolutions anymore. But what do we find out now? We have unconsciously stuck to it'. The TCM aims to have exactly this effect: inner voices are better levers for change than a list of resolutions. In order to realize collective change, the inner experience (the valuations, the feelings, the inner voices) of the individual team members is an essential starting point.

Discussion

The reader should be aware that there are other ways of applying the TCM conceptual framework, since the method has been developing ever since the first years of its existence. But the 'classical' protocol as illustrated above still serves as the starting point and reference for all TCM novices who embark on a trajectory to learn to use the method.

A central feature of the TCM is the fact that its main point of action is the pattern of cooperation, which is an attribute of the group. Many team-coaching approaches have attributes of the individual team member as their point of action, such as personality characteristics, individual expectations or individual experiences or feelings. Of course, also the TCM makes room for the facilitator's attention for individuals' uniqueness and singularities. But in the TCM investigation, the pattern that is made by the existing constellation of team members is central. Individual team members cannot be blamed for the counterproductive loops that are described in the system diagram. Such loops are a feature of the collective, though every member will have his or her share in making or maintaining these loops. Since no-one is to be pointed at as the sole guilty one, it is only the team as a whole that could be called 'guilty', and it is only the team as a whole that can break the pattern. Of course individual team members can choose their own way to break it, taking the lever deviant voice as their help, but they make it stronger by using it in orchestration with other team members when they are involved in daily action.

Below, I will address two issues. Firstly, I'll discuss the issue of choosing the right occasion to apply the TCM. Secondly, I'll list the demands that are put on the TCM Facilitator and his or her way of working.

When Should the Team Confrontation Method Be Applied, and When Should It Not?

As I have described above in so many ways, the method is a tool for collective self-investigation, reflection and learning, with the aim to improve the team's effectiveness. Customers and colleagues often ask me in what circumstances the method is helpful, and when it is better to use another method. Well, it can be considered helpful whenever team members are prepared to devote some time to a thorough self-investigation. Not in all cases are team members prepared to carry out such an investigation. Basically, I have discovered that there are two main reasons why they feel they should not: first, the team members might not experience enough safety in their team; second, the team members don't allow themselves much time for team-coaching.

As to the first factor, safety, a thorough self-investigation requires openness and the willingness to temporarily put a question mark behind own convictions and to receive feedback from colleagues. This can be very hard if the team members are in serious conflict with each other. In such cases, they are not inclined to do the patient work of self-investigation, but usually feel an urgent need to be justified, preferably by an outside party such as the facilitator. This person is then seen as a referee, a judge, who should be convinced of the own viewpoint. The need to convince others of the own viewpoint will quickly run counter to the need of thoroughness that a TCM investigation requires. In matters of serious conflict, mediation seems a better way of facilitating the team towards conflict resolution.

As to the second factor, time, a thorough self-investigation needs the patience of team members to stand still and reflect on the quality of the daily cooperation and discuss meanings, feelings, wishes, etc. Often, teams are so result-oriented that they feel a great urge to make results in an efficient manner; and a dialogue about meanings, feelings, wishes does not seem efficient to them. They prefer team-coaching meetings with a more immediate goal, usually connected to the content that the team is supposed to produce. Though the TCM is a method that is explicitly aimed at improving a team's effectiveness, the team members might feel that team building is only effective when it is concerned with the team's immediate output in terms of content. The use of the full protocol as it was explained here requires two days of the team's time, and sometimes this is seen as too much.

In many cases, team members feel sufficiently safe and not so much in a hurry. For this majority of teams, the TCM can be very helpful, because it provides structure for the team to help itself, with its own questions and its own answers.

What Is Demanded of the TCM Facilitator?

In the introduction to this chapter, I have used a characterization of what is generally needed of every team coach/ facilitator: he or she should be 'streetwise and authentic'. I have also described what makes the TCM so special (a tool for self-investigation) and what it requires of the TCM facilitator in particular: to be a 'friendly co-investigator' instead of a 'neutral bystander'. Below, I would like first to explain what I mean by 'streetwise and authentic', and then say a few words on the 'friendly co-investigator'.

With 'streetwise', I mean that you are, as facilitator, not naïve and don't let yourself be too easily fooled by team members who keep up appearances of being somebody who is nice and innocent, or hurt by team members who suggest that you or others are terribly in the wrong and should be blamed for it. Team-coaching is not like individual coaching. In processes of individual coaching, coaches or counsellors will find with almost all clients plausible backgrounds of maladaptive behavior, mostly lying back in childhood times, which makes them feel mild and understanding towards the client. Although facilitators can (and probably should) always be compassionate in working with a team as well, they also have to deal with genuine misbehavior and disrespect in the team, without the opportunity to find the reasons of such behavior. The behavior can have dire consequences for the cooperation between team-members in the meeting (or after it), and for the cooperation between the team and the facilitator. The facilitator should therefore keep a just order, for instance by referring to ground rules of conduct that the team has agreed upon in an earlier stage of the team-coaching process. The facilitator should focus on the process of the group as a whole, and try to avoid being a coach with too much attention for individual processes.

Connected with this is that he should try to foster some pace in the group process. The average participant to a team-coaching meeting tends to become impatient if the pace is too slow. He or she won't allow the facilitator to take much time for looking below every team member's surface. Therefore, a team mostly needs a dynamic facilitator, who is fast enough to bring progress and slow enough to take the needs of individual team members seriously and so to build trust. Of course, timing is significant: having a nose for what is a relevant topic on a given moment in time, and sometimes the guts to respond to this moment and jump into the unknown.

Authenticity is probably an even more important characteristic of a good team coach. He should be capable of opening up at any moment about the feelings he has in working with a team ('Jerry, I sense that you are not very satisfied after sharing your thoughts with Susan, am I right?' or 'You guys give me the creeps. I normally don't feel so uneasy in a group. What could this tell about your group? Or is it just me?'), or about the second thoughts he has ('I could think A, but I must admit that I tend to think B. Why do I think that? Do others recognize B?'). The whole craftsmanship lies of course in presenting feelings or second thoughts in a constructive way, and in not being confused about them, but to trust in them, in that they are potentially informative and useful for the process of the team-coaching. Team members want their facilitator to be transparent in order to feel safe; this will make it easier for them to open up and share feelings and thoughts in a similar way.

Under the heading 'Having the TCM Facilitator as an aid', I described above briefly what is needed of the TCM Facilitator. The TCM is a method that provides structure to the team's self-investigation. But this structure is unknown to most of the team members (they usually do a TCM investigation for the first time), and moreover, they are often not used to conduct an investigation. Therefore, the TCM Facilitator should provide the team with his (global) knowledge about how to do a reliable, valid, and/or meaningful piece of research into the team cooperation. He or she should be prepared to share the own global knowledge about methodology and group dynamics, and be open to the team's local knowledge about the facts of what happens in the team. The TCM Facilitator will find patterns in the details and propose hypotheses about such patterns, that could be accepted or rejected by the team. If accepted, the team will add facts and details to the proposed patterns. Together, facilitator and team make the outcome of the investigations more meaningful.

In sum, the TCM Facilitator should not put on a white coat and tell the team what his diagnosis of the situation is. Instead of being a bystander, he should try to be a helper in the investigation of which, in the end, the team itself is the owner.

Development of the Team Confrontation Method: Branching It Out

In the ten years past that the method exists now, about forty team-coaching practitioners have been educated in the use of the method. That is not so many. The main reason lies in the fact that the original version of the method (the protocol as presented above) makes use of numbers (statistical data), that most of my fellow-team coaches don't feel so much at ease with. Also certain types of clients (especially teams in the health care and education sectors) don't like to work with numbers. The interpretation of the TCM's statistical data is too complicated for them, even if some care is given to have them elegantly presented in a report. For those clients and colleagues alike, the original protocol of the method is cumbersome.

Furthermore, the fact that the original protocol requires the team to devote 2 days to their investigation is a hindrance. Why use 2 days if you can do team-coaching in one day? The TCM would be a more-used tool if it were shorter, or at least, if there were shorter versions available.

In the 10 years past, Dialogical Self Theory has been developing too, and there are several interesting new concepts, such as 'meta-position' and 'promoter position' (see Van Loon's chapter in this book) that are very promising for application in the context of team-coaching. The TCM could gain from these developments.

This all means that some initiatives have been taken, and are still taken, to design different versions of the method. First, some colleague-TCM Facilitators and I have developed a qualitative version of the TCM, the 'TCM alpha' (Zomer, 2014). This is a version of the method that does not use questionnaires and a statistical report (as in the original version presented above, which is now also called the 'TCM Beta'), but a sophisticated way of collecting qualitative data in the here and now of the sessions. 'Statistics-haters' are well served by this development, and the chance for the method to do its good work will grow accordingly. Second, we have developed some one-day versions of parts of the TCM, the 'TCM light' versions. There is a version where the team concentrates on making a system diagram of the mutual cooperation; another lets the team concentrate on its multivoicedness, and another, still in progress, will focus on the team's stories and the meanings that they contain. With these light-versions, the TCM will be more accessible to teams that don't feel the room for taking two days off from work. The TCM light is still a TCM, since the conceptual framework as it is presented above in the section 'Theoretical basis' lies behind it. These recent developments show that different ways of applying the method are possible, and that the method in fact starts to branch out into different applications and forms.

Final Reflection

Dialogical Self Theory's concepts serve as a lens for looking at the team's reality and functioning. To be fair, DST is not yet very well elaborated into the realm of the collective functioning, although Hermans is currently making a step forward into that direction (Hermans, in press), and Zomer (2006) offers some conceptual support with the concept 'deviant voice'. However, as said above, developments in DST seem to be quite promising for the field of team-coaching. The coming years will show some activity of myself and my colleagues in tapping into that potential.

References

Bales, R. F. (1970). *Personality and interpersonal behavior*. New York: Holt.

Bales, R. F., & Cohen, S. P. (1979). *SYMLOG: A system for the multiple level observation of groups*. New York: Free Press.

Bohm, D. (1996). *On dialogue*. London: Routledge.

Greenwood, D. J., & Levin, M. (1998). *Introduction to action research: Social research for social change*. Thousand Oaks, CA: Sage.

Hermans, H. J. M. (in press). *The society in the self: A theory of inner democracy.*

Hermans, H. J. M., & Gieser, T. (Eds.). (2013). *Handbook of dialogical self theory*. Cambridge, UK: CambridgeUniversity Press.

Hermans, H. J. M., & Hermans-Jansen, E. (1995). *Self-narratives: The construction of meaning in psychotherapy*. New York: Guilford.

Hermans, H. J. M., & Hermans-Konopka, A. (2010). *Dialogical self theory: Positioning and counter-positioning in a globalizing society*. Cambridge, UK: Cambridge University Press.

Mead, G. H. (1972). *Mind, self and society: From the standpoint of a social behaviorist*. Chicago: University of Chicago Press. [original 1934]

Morris, P. (Ed.). (1994). *The Bakhtin reader: Selected writings of Bakhtin, Medvedev, Voloshinov*. London: Edward Arnold.

Pennington, D.C. (2002). *The social psychology of behaviour in small groups*. Hove: Psychology Press.

Weick, K. E. (1979). *The social psychology of organizing* (2nd ed.). New York: McGraw-Hill.

Weick, K. E. (1995). *Sensemaking in organizations*. Thousand Oaks, CA: Sage.

Weick, K. E. (2001). Collective mind in organizations: Heedful interrelating on flight decks. In K. E. Weick (Ed.), *Making sense of the organization* (pp. 259–283). Oxford, UK: Blackwell.

Woolley, A. W., Chabris, C. F., & Pentland, A. (2010). Evidence for a collective intelligence factor in the performance of human groups. *Science, 28*, 686–688.

Zomer, W. J. P. (2014, 19–22 August). *A concrete case of scientist-practitioner cooperation in dialogical self theory: The making of a TCM alpha*. Paper presented at the 8th international conference on the dialogical self, The Hague.

Zomer, W. J. P. (2006). *The team confrontation method; Design, grounding and testing*. Dissertation, Radboud University, Nijmegen, The Netherlands.

Chapter 9
SCM-Organization: A Method for Assessing and Facilitating Organization Dialogue and Development

Richard van de Loo

Introduction

Creating a sense of urgency for the need to change is the first step in the process of reorienting a team or organization. However, such a step is often not easy to make. De Caluwé and Vermaak (2003) address the struggle between internal forces for continuing the old, familiar routines and structures and the forces that champion renewal. In their view the main source of this struggle lies in the informal organization. They use the metaphor of the iceberg to highlight that this informal organization is almost completely hidden, as only a small part is visible above the surface. The visible part literally is ‘the tip of the iceberg”.

The question now rises whether it is possible to get an insight in the forces and emotions that hide below the surface. However more insight alone is not enough for change. In another publication, De Caluwé and Vermaak (2004) address the importance of dialogue based on different paradigms and perspectives for organizational vitality, and therefore for organization development. This triggers the theoretical and methodological connection between organization dialogue and organization development.

In this chapter we explore the possibilities and the limitations of Dialogical Self Theory (DST) as a means to get more insight in those forces and emotions hiding below the surface. We also investigate how this theory can contribute to organization dialogue. After this we explore to what extent a DST based Method (SCM-Organization) can support organizations in their organization dialogue and development. The last paragraph presents a discussion of the implications of this method and explores lines for further development of this approach.

R. van de Loo (✉)
Meijer Consulting Group, Utrecht, The Netherlands
e-mail: richard@meijercg.nl

H. Hermans (ed.), *Assessing and Stimulating a Dialogical Self in Groups, Teams, Cultures, and Organizations*, DOI 10.1007/978-3-319-32482-1_9

Dialogical Self Theory in an Organizational Context

Dialogical Self Theory, as formulated and developed by Hubert Hermans in a long and impressive range of publications, has its main focus on the individual person (e.g. Hermans, Kempen, & Van Loon, 1991; Hermans & Kempen, 1993; Hermans and Giesser, 2012). Most of the cases and examples in these publications refer to individuals, although not isolated from their context. Hermans' view on the self is based for one part on the fundamental distinction made by William James between I and me. James' distinction broadens the concept of self to the surrounding world, represented by elements like 'my children, my work, my colleagues, my books, my projects and hobbies'. To this concept of self Hermans added the notion that this surrounding world is not to be conceived as an object, but as a subject in the extended self. Therefore, as another I that makes dialogical relations possible (Hermans, 2014).

In order to elaborate the construct of dialogical self, Hermans refers to Bakthin's methapor of the polyphonic novel. In the polyphonic novel different, even opposing, characters, each with their own voice and unique view of the world act in autonomous ways. In Hermans'view the dialogical self operates in the same way. Different *I*-positions act in the self, each rooted and positioned in the personal history and actual context of the person, like 'I as father', 'I as employee', 'I as assertive' and 'I as hesitating'. For a better understanding of the central concept of dialogical self in this chapter, we will present three key-features or qualities of this concept in the next sections: multi-voicedness, context and dynamics.

Multivoicedness

The self can be conceived as 'a dynamic multiplicity of *I*-positions or voices in the landscape of mind' (Hermans & Dimaggio, 2007, p. 36). This 'society of *I*-positions' (Hermans, 2014) creates the multivoicedness of the self and also its potential for internal dialogue (Hermans, 2001). In the aspect of multiplicity the construct of dialogical self resembles the concept of 'inner team' of Schulz von Thun (2008) or the approach of Voice Dialogue (Stone & Stone, 2007). However, according to Rowan (2012), approaches like Voice Dialogue run the risk of reification of selves as sub-personalities. In DST the self is to be understood as a process of positioning and re-positioning and not as a process between different sub-personalities.

In an organizational context the concept of multivoicedness of the self addresses some highly interesting and relevant *I*-positions that a person can activate, such as: I as a professional, I as a leader, I as a victim of reorganization, I as a partner or opponent of management. In DST these positions are defined as internal positions, because they belong to the internal domain of self (Hermans, 2014; Raggatt, 2012). However, an internal position like 'I as an opponent of management' already reflects an external element: management. Therefore, *I*-positions cannot be isolated from their context. The contextual dimension of Dialogical Self is the topic of the next paragraph.

Context

I-positions are often triggered by certain contexts. For example: as a teamleader I have a different message (voice) than as a member of the works council. Another way in which the context is present and active in the self is by external *I*-positions, defined as 'the other in the self' (Raggatt, 2012, p. 31). In an organizational setting relevant others as external *I*-positions are for example: my boss, my best colleague, my employees, my most demanding customer, my most dangerous competitor. The contextual dimension creates an extended self that incorporates other positions and perspectives. It broadens and deepens the internal as well as the external dialogue (Hermans & Kempen, 1993). The self is not only located in space but also extended in space. Without context the development of the self would be impossible, as will be explained in the next section.

Dynamic Quality

Multivoicedness and context facilitate movement from one *I*-position to another. This movement creates the opportunity to explore different and even opposing views in a process that is called positioning and counter-positioning (Hermans & Hermans-Konopka, 2010; Raggatt, 2012). This process stimulates the internal as well the external dialogue and therefore leads to a better understanding of other, even opposing, parties. The process of positioning and counter-positioning can also result in a repositioning to a totally new or a so-called third position that integrates two or more former opposing *I*-positions (Hermans & Hermans-Konopka, 2010; Raggatt, 2012). This potential to construct new positions especially represents the developmental or dynamic quality of self. Figure 9.1, inspired by Hermans (2014, p. 141), visualizes the concept of self in terms of DST including the three before-mentioned key features.

The two circles in the middle represent the self, divided in an internal domain of *I*-positions and an external domain in which meaningful others or entities are located with their (internalized) message and voice in the self. Those others and those entities are also part of the context or outside world. The boundaries between the internal and external domain of self and between self and context are permeable. Because of this, movement in the total field is possible and facilitates development in terms of the construction of new positions. In line with others (Lindegger & Alberts, 2012; Wijsbek, 2009; Zomer, 2006) we believe that the concept of dialogical self as multivoiced, contextual and dynamic at the individual level, also has a meaning at the collective level: a team, unit or organization and even community.

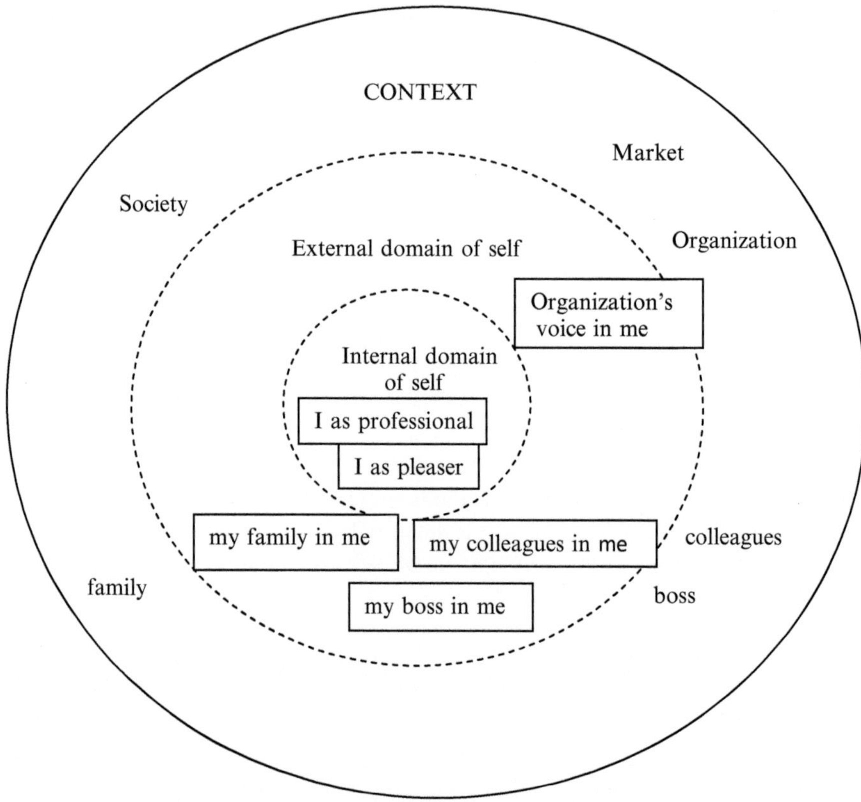

Fig. 9.1 The dialogical self as multivoiced, contextual and dynamic

The Concept of Dialogical Self on a Collective Level

Collective stories in organizations operate as unifying frames of reference. They create meaning and direction in the daily stream of actions and experiences of all workers (Gabriel, 2000). For most workers building a cathedral is a far more inspiring story than working under a burden of producing and transporting a maximum of stones. Without a shared, collective story an organization cannot exist. But, an organization that cultivates only one, dominating story can't exist either. It loses its flexibility to react and adapt adequately to changing conditions and challenges. Organizations need both homogeneity and heterogeneity. In his study about long-existing companies De Geus (1997, p. 9) identified one factor that refers to homogeneity as distinctive of a long life as a company: cohesion and identity. Two other factors in his study referred to heterogeneity: tolerance and decentralization, and sensitivity for the environment. Companies which lose heterogeneity and diversity in their boardroom, staff and shop floor run the risk of tumbling into the pitfall of groupthink (Janis, 1982).

In the next section I will explore the applicability of the concept of dialogical self at the collective level. This exploration is a stepping stone to the description of an DST-based method for assessing and facilitating organization dialogue.

Multivoicedness on an Organizational Level

Especially organizations with a lot of professionals such as a hospital, a law firm or an accounting firm have to deal with a lot of internal multivoicedness. But in fact all bigger organizations have to deal with multivoicedness. This is a serious challenge for most organizations. Workers have different assumptions about their work (Schein, 1992, p. 274) and they have different interests and power. Pluriformity and heterogeneity seem to be relevant conditions for innovation and problem solving. For example, Hafsi and Turgut (2013) found a significant relation between diversity of age and gender in the boardroom and social performance. According to De Caluwé and Vermaak (2004) the combination of different or multiple thinking strategies generates a better process of decision making and change in organizations. The reality, however, is often stubborn. Dissonant voices are often experienced as difficult to handle. Escalation into a conflict is then close (Lencioni, 2002). Let us look at Fig. 9.2. It visualizes the situation of two parties which are locked in their own paradigms.

Figure 9.2 illustrates the situation of two monolitic blocks standing right next to each other: the triangulars and the squares. The multivoicedness is in reality more univoicedness, because there is no listening involved. The boundaries are therefore drawn as impermeable or closed. In a deeper sense, the dialogue fails, because the

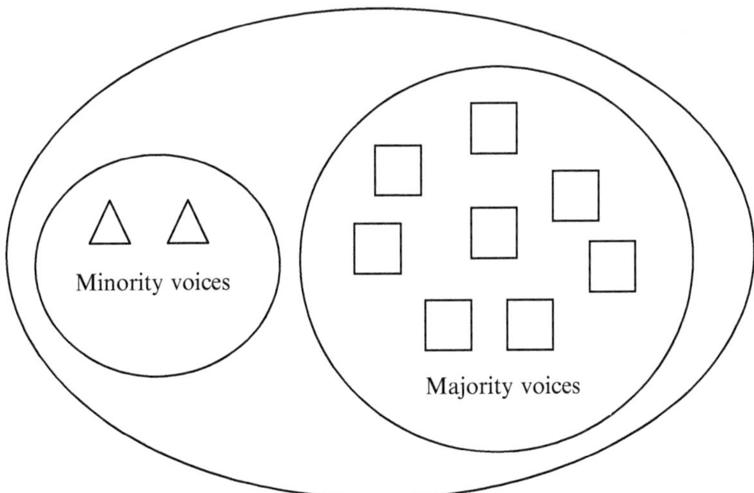

Fig. 9.2 Two parties in monological discussion

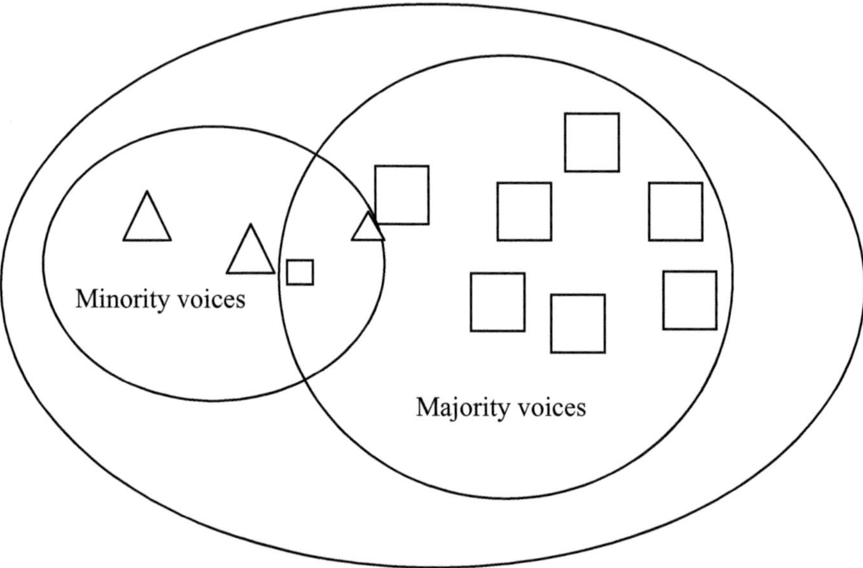

Fig. 9.3 Two parties in dialogical exchange

minority voices are suppressed. In other words: Figure 9.2 shows a problematic environment. Now let us look at Fig. 9.3. It takes into account the concept of dialogical self.

As Fig. 9.3 illustrates at first sight, reality is often not as black and white. In both camps one dominant voice is accompanied by a second voice (*I*-position) that represents the opposing party, visualized as a little square or triangle. This second position shows that this member has some sympathy and understanding for the opponent position of the majority voices. The fact that members belonging to one group or party can have multiple and even opposing *I*-positions, illustrates how internal and external dialogue are intertwined and how positioning and counter-positioning are part of the dialogical process. Not only in processes of change (De Caluwé & Vermaak, 2004), but also in the everyday processes of cooperation, multiplicity in terms of multivoicedness enriches decision making and communication. Of course, there is the risk of ambiguity or a Babel-like confusion leading to desintegration in the end or to what Weick (1976) calls 'loosely coupled systems'. But this happens only in situations in which unifying elements and forces are lacking. However, maybe the most important indicator of space for multivoicedness is the emergence of a common feeling of WE. According to Hosking (2004), this feeling is the result of building new narratives and constructing new common realities together. For Hosking, organization development is in essence a relational process with questioning and listening as basic elements. In our view, organization development is also a dialogical process. In this process the external dialogue is not restricted to the 'other party', because the broader context is included and involved. This will be discussed in the next section.

Context

In line with DST, we believe that 'sensitivity for the environment'(De Geus, 1997) can be viewed and operationalized as a constructive dialogue between the members of an organization and their context. But sensitivity is not enough to create a dialogical process. A dialogical process needs reciprocity. This means that the context is involved and participating in the dialogical space between the members of a group. This statement is not as simple as it looks. Traditionally the focus of psychology was on the individual person and not on the context. There were exceptions of course such as Lewin's field theory (see for an introduction: Hall & Lindzey, 1970, pp. 209–257) or the movements of environmental and ecological psychology (for reviews see Wicker, 1979, and Morris, 2009). In all of these theories the interaction between person and context is typically conceived in terms of a S-R or an input–output model with the person as 'mediator' between context and behavior. The problematic relation in psychology between person and context is also reflected in the well-known Person-Situation Debate (see for example Epstein & O'Brien, 1985; Fleeson & Noftle, 2009). Kindermann, Th.A & Valsiner (1995, p. 2) advocate that human development is not the 'result' of the individual or the context as determinants, but of the interaction between person and context. The concept of *I*-positions in DST may give a deeper insight in how this interaction operates. That it is in fact not only an interaction between person and context, but also between group and context. This interaction also refers to the dynamic or developmental aspect of DST on the collective level, as will be demonstrated in the next section.

Dynamic Quality

Organization development supports organizations in their effort and wish to establish a more effective interaction with the outside world. This section explores the possible contribution of DST to organization development. However, our focus is not the 'entire system' in terms of Cummings (2004, p. 25), which includes the organizational structure, but primarily the organizational culture. In line with the metaphor of the iceberg, it is the part below the surface that gets our special attention.

In our view dynamic in terms of Dialogical Self Theory is operating at a collective level, especially in the dialogical process. Two ways of development can be distinguished in this process. The first way is that a group collectively constructs a new story that supports the process of framing and reframing certain key-items or conflicting issues in the group. However, we believe that a new group or organization story is the outcome of a second and (in our view) more fundamental development, namely a change in group position. If 'suppressed or marginalized voices' (Hosking, 2004, p. 273) get more space in the new story or become even the majority-voice, then this development could be explained in terms of DST at a collective level. A group can move from an old to a new position by a process of co-creating a new paradigm. The move to a totally new group position will give energy and focus, because all members of a group have then moved to this position, instead of making a compromise between majority and minority.

Another highly interesting aspect of the dialogical process becomes visible here: the connection between individual and collective development. The process of positioning and counter-positioning can contribute to a structural position shift in *I*-positions at the individual level. The accumulated shift at the individual level can in turn cause a shift in the overall group position at the collective level. This kind of development can be viewed as the outcome of collective learning in a cognitive sense or even as the outcome of double loop learning (Argyris, 2004). The co-creation of a new, common reality is not only a stepping stone to change and development, but also to trust among persons and among groups. There is empirical evidence that this kind of collective learning has a positive effect on team performance (Lodders, 2012). By developing the domain of collective learning organizations utilize and develop the talents of their employees. In this way they create conditions for innovation and entrepreneurship.

DST seems especially promising in giving insight in the process of organization dialogue leading to the construction of new realities together. In the next paragraph we will focus on a method for assessing and creating this dialogical process.

A Method for Assessing and Creating Organization Dialogue

Hubert Hermans developed a method of self-investigation and self-knowledge, the so-called Self Confrontation Method (SCM). For a first introduction of the method we refer to the chapter of Jutta König in this book and to Lyddon, Yowell, and Hermans (2006). A detailed description of the method is given by Hermans and Hermans-Jansen (1995). Up to now the SCM is applied by a growing number of certified practitioners in the field of individual coaching and therapy. The SCM has proven its applicability in the domain of personal development (e.g., Hermans & Poulie, 2000) and career development (e.g., Van de Loo, 1992). In an empirical study Van Geelen (2010) demonstrated the positive influence of this method on the self-image of persons with a chronic fatigue-syndrom.

A relatively new field of application of this method is its application on a collective level. A first description of the so-called SCM-Organization is given by Wijsbek (2003), who used this method for assisting organizations in the development of a corporate identity. A special contribution to the field is the Team Confrontation Method (TCM), developed by Zomer (2006; see also his chapter in this book) for the assessment and improvement of collective and individual functioning of a team. In the next section I will explore the applicability of the SCM-Organization for assessing and stimulating organization dialogue. I will therefore explain the method using the three key-features of DST at the collective level presented earlier: multivoicedness, context and dynamic quality.

Table 9.1 Some questions for formulating and structuring the collective story

What is the mission statement of your team/organization?
Give a short, representative impression of the actual co-operation/communication in your team?
Can you give an example of a recent success realized by your team?
Can you give an example of a recent failure of your team?
Is there something that pre-occupies the team now?
What are the most important purposes, targets, challenges for now/the near future?
Is there an image or object that has a special meaning for your team/organization?

Assessing Multivoicedness on the Collective Level

Multivoicedness in a group or between groups is always centered around certain issues and topics in their actual story. As a narrative approach SCM-Organization is constructed to explain these topics and issues in a systematic and structured way. Like a person in an individual SCM, a group or several groups are invited to formulate the key-issues and topics in the actual situation. Best practice is that a small, representative preparatory committee is formed to tell their story. This is done in co-operation with a consultant trained in the SCM-Organization. By means of a structured interview the consultant supports this committee to formulate the relevant issues in the team or organization. The consultant can use a set of questions to help the preparatory committee to identify the relevant themes and topics. See Table 9.1 for an example of these questions.

In general a number of 16 to 20 statements is enough as answers to these questions. The then constructed list of statements is a custom-made, unique instrument that highlights the key-issues in a team at that moment. This list provides food for thought and stimulates reflection within the team. A list of statements, however, gives no information about how these statements are evaluated at the group level. Is there homogeneity or heterogeneity in the total group regarding the key-issues and to what extent? Especially this aspect of the evaluation on the group level is highly interesting for orchestrating the organization dialogue. Therefore, SCM-Organization assesses how the statements are evaluated by the respondents. This is operationalized in the same way as in the individual SCM (Hermans & Hermans-Jansen, 1995).

All participants are invited individually to rate their feelings regarding each statement on line. For this purpose custom-made software was developed. Each statement is presented separately on a screen in combination with a list of feelings. The respondent is invited to indicate to what extent each feeling regarding the statement is experienced. The rating-scale has a range of 0 (= not at all) to 5 (= very much). A much-used list of affect terms contains 24 feelings, categorized in four sub-scales: Self-Enhancement (S-motive), Contact and Union with the Other (O-motive), Positive feelings (P) and Negative feelings (N). For a description and explication of these four scales we refer to Hermans and Hermans-Jansen (1995). Table 9.2 presents a frequently used list.

Table 9.2 List of 24 feelings (affect terms) in SCM-Organization

S-motive	O-motive	Positive affect	Negative affect
Self-esteem	Caring	Joy	Loneliness
Strength	Involvement	Trust	Powerlessness
Self-confidence	Solidarity	Enjoyment	Anxiety
Pride	Warmth	Inner calm	Anger
Freedom	Collegiality	Enthusiasm	Inferiority
Energy	Affection	Pleasure	Disappointment

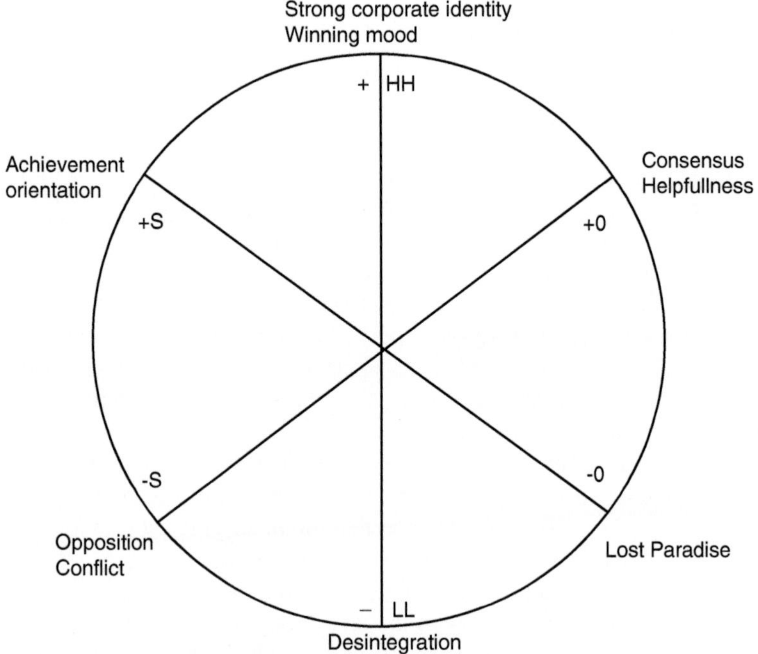

Fig. 9.4 A circular model of six different types of dominating culture
+S refers to high S, low O, high P and low N; +HH refers to high S, high O, high P and low N; +O refers to high O, low S, high P and low N; –O refers to high O, low S, low P and high N; –LL refers to low S, low O, low P and high N; –S refers to high S, low O, low P and high N

The totals of each sub-scale (sum-scores) can vary between 0 (6×0) and 30 (6×5). In an oral or written briefing to all participants the consultant can explain that this part of data-collection is strictly confidential, that each respondent will get an individual report of his or her profile and that only anonymous information will be shared with the group. These requirements stimulate the respondents to show their real feelings regarding each issue.

Hermans (1992) placed the four dimensions S-motive, O-motive, Positive and Negative in a circular model, leading to six different types of valuation. In the same way collective statements can be classified in a comparable circular model, as shown in Fig. 9.4.

It is important to note that the distribution of the statements in the circular model is based on the average ratings of the feelings of the total group. If there are two groups, information on differences between the distribution of the statements in the circular model can be used as input for the organization development. The circular model is helpful in getting an indication of the dominating culture in a group. If, for example most statements are evaluated as +S, then this pattern can indicate for a strong achievement orientation in the group. A pattern of –O refers to longing for what has been lost. For example: a former unit that has been located elsewhere in the organization. There is of course no direct relation between a certain pattern and the actual culture in the group. The statements, which are the basis for the evaluation, are always a selection of a larger amount of issues. Therefore, interpretations have to be made with care. Best practice is that the group itself does the interpretation and formulates conclusions.

Within-group multivoicedness can be illustrated by comparing individual feeling patterns regarding a certain statement with each other. If there is not enough trust to share this collectively, then it is possible to present these data anonymously. At least in this way the participants can be informed about the homogeneity or heterogeneity in the group regarding certain key issues. Without knowing exactly who contributed a certain evaluation or who has a dissonant position, this kind of feedback is highly informative for the group and stimulates dialogue.

Context

SCM-Organization has at least two ways to incorporate relevant elements and aspects of the context in the organization story. First: some statements may refer directly to entities or persons (e.g. a specific customer, competitor, supplier) outside the organization or within the organization, such as other departments. Second: some statements may reflect the voice and message of that external party to the group (e.g., “The board of direction insists strongly on cost-reduction”). Of course it is neither possible nor necessary to include all relevant external relationships in the list of statements. The consultant and the preparatory committee can make a selection in line with the key question of the group for intervention. Broadening the context is also stepping stone for development. The developmental or dynamic aspect of SCM-Organization is the subject of the next section.

Dynamic Quality

It is often confronting for the participants of the group to see the constructed list with all themes and topics that unify or separate them. Assessing, communicating and sharing how the participants evaluate these topics are other ways to intervene in the dialogical process that creates momentum. This does not automatically result in learning and development. As stated in this chapter and stressed by a whole range of authors (e.g. Argyris, 2004; Boonstra, 2004; Lodders, 2013; Wierdsma, 2004), it is an open and critical dialogue within a group and between groups that stimulates learning and development. SCM-Organization helps to orchestrate this dialogue. I will present how this dialogue can be structured based on best practices. Because SCM-Organization is an open method, there is not one prescribed way of structuring this dialogue.

To share all the information with the group, the preparatory committee and consultant organize a workshop. A one-day workshop is usually sufficient for sharing the first feedback. Of course more workshops are necessary to stimulate, guide and evaluate the dialogue. With the aid of a statistical program the collected data of the individual evaluations is aggregated and reported to the group.

The role of the consultant is to present the material in such a way that the participants become familiar with it. The participants are invited to discuss the meaning of remarkable signals, which is often a challenging task for them. This division of roles places the group in an active position of analyzing their own situation and deciding on its consequences. The collected data and statistical information have diagnostic value, but don't generate a fixed diagnosis. They provide input for a process of sharing information, views, feelings and perceptions. Only in this way the process of collective construction of new meanings and frames of reference can start as stated by Hosking (2004) and Wierdsma (2004). Working with subgroups or even duos first gives more space to less dominating or prominent voices and an opportunity to be heard and to grow.

If two groups are participating in the workshop, it is possible to make a specific general report for each group. If there are remarkable differences between these groups regarding the evaluation (i.e. the feeling pattern S,O, P, N) of certain statements, then best practice is not to ask each party to explain their views but to ask all participants of both groups to collectively focus on the feeling pattern of that party and to try to explain the considerations associated with these results. In this way participants with a different or even opposing view become more familiar with the perspectives of the others. In turn, group members of the 'other' or even 'dissonant' side feel empowered by all the attention for their view and voice. This working script illustrates how the central process of positioning and counter-positioning (Hermans & Hermans-Konopka, 2010) can be operationalized in a simple exercise. Other scripts are possible, for example: participants move to a specific point in a given space and share their arguments and feelings from that position.

As will be illustrated in the case description, sharing, analyzing and interpreting of the assessment results by the participants themselves is the heart of SCM-Organization. In the case description the focus will therefore be on collective construction of meaning.

A Case Illustration of SCM-Organization

The presented case (see also Van de Loo, 2012) concentrates on two different groups in a hospital unit. One group consists of four unit managers. The other group, the medical staff, consists of four medical specialists. Unit management and medical staff shared the wish to improve their co-operation and to develop a more shared view on their organizational structure. This common wish was a basic condition for the consultant to accept their request for support. The focus of this case description is how SCM-Organization can be applied to support organizations in their organization dialogue. The three key-features context, multivoicedness and development will be especially highlighted in this illustration.

As a first step a preparatory committee was formed consisting of representatives of both groups and the consultant (the author of this chapter). This committee constructed a list of about 20 statements concerning the key issues in this unit. The second step was to invite all participants to evaluate the statements online. As a third step the preparatory committee organized two workshops for the two groups combined. These two meetings of one day each, about a month apart, were planned to discuss the results of the evaluation and to make plans for the future.

Context

With the aid of the consultant the preparatory committee constructed a list of 21 sentences, all referring to key issues in the actual context of both groups in the hospital unit. A criterium for the selection of contextual elements was their relevance for the actual co-operation and organization development of this unit. Here are some examples of these contextual elements:

- The mission statement of the unit.
- The regular communication structure between managment and medical staff.
- Their own contribution to the policy of this unit.
- The plans for clinical pathways.
- The common feeling within the unit.
- The co-operation between management and medical staff.
- The actual emphasis on production and efficiency by the general management of the hospital.

The issues, represented by these contextual elements, were framed in short sentences in such a way that they could be combined with a list of feelings for evaluation. In this case it was a list of 24 feelings (see Table 9.2). The main question for the respondents was: *How do I experience the actual communication structure between management and medical staff?* Both groups received the same question and the same list of feelings, because this was the best way to compare the results of both groups with each other. Compared to standard general questionnaires for work experience, the constructed list was experienced as customer-friendly. The questions referred to the specific und unique topics in the unit and were formulated in their own, specific language. The familiarity of the constructed list stimulated the committment of the respondents to evaluate the statements. This was done online, individually and without mutual consultation. How the collected material gave input for the organization dialogue will be demonstrated in the next section.

Multivoicedness

About one week after evaluating the statements a first meeting was organized with all the eight participants to discuss and share the results. The way they were seated in the conference room was a remarkable indication of the 'temperature' between the two groups: on one side the medical staff, on the other side management. The lack of trust at the beginning was also made clear by the provocative announcement of one of the participants that his joining us for dinner after the meeting depended totally on the outcome of this day. How different the perception of the groups of the same situation was, is illustrated in Table 9.3. It shows the feeling pattern connected with some key issues for both groups.

Table 9.3 illustrates that at least three key issues concerning aspects of organization development get a more negative score from the medical staff than from management. Further more the experienced feeling of S is structurally lower for the medical staff. The averages of the feeling scales S and O over all 21 statements show remarkable differences between the two groups. Overall, management experiences slightly more S than O (averages 2.6 vs 2.4 on a scale from 0 to 5). The medical staff, however, experienced more O (2.8) than S (2.5). Although producing shock and confrontation, these data provided an objective recognition of the experienced frictions and misunderstandings between both groups.

There were not only remarkable differences between the two groups. Within both groups a considerable heterogeneity regarding certain key issues appeared. For example regarding the emphasis on production and efficiency one of the managers and one of the medical specialists had a dissonant position compared to their collegues regarding the P-N evaluation. In each group the dominant voice of the other

Table 9.3 Feeling patterns of management and medical staff

	Management				Medical Staff			
Some key-issues	S	O	P	N	S	O	P	N
How do I experience my own contribution to the policy development of our unit?	18	18	17	8	14	17	13	14
How do I experience the emphasis on production and efficiency?	16	14	16	9	12	13	12	16
Clinical pathways offer challenging chances for our unit.	20	16	19	7	16	18	15	14

Note: S = feelings referring to self-enhancement; O = feelings referring to contact and union; P = positive feelings; N = negative feelings group was represented. This result came as a shock and a confrontation, because it revealed the relativity of the separation of the two opposing groups.

The next section will show some of the interpretations and conclusions made by the participants of both groups. These results are also an indication of the stimulating effect on development of the SCM-Organization.

Dynamics and Development

After sharing the results, the next step was to discuss remarkable signals in the material and their possible meaning in mixed subgroups. In the plenary session following the discussion in subgroups all participants were quite unanimous in their overall conclusion: *our co-operation can be better! Of course we have to grow in our understanding of each other* (= O-motive) *but especially in a more clear positioning of ourselves toward each other* (S-motive). It is important to note that the participants came to this conclusion and not the consultant. Especially the medical staff expressed a growing awareness of how important their own voice was for fruitful co-operation. At that moment the general manager of this unit made a very personal statement about all the difficulties and challenges of a position at the top of a complex organization. He emphasized that the help and support of medical staff and the management team were very welcome. The vulnerability expressed by the otherwise rather dominant manager created space for the medical staff, and also for the rest of the management team, to share their experiences. In terms of DST we see here how the general manager moved from an *I*-position of "I am the boss and responsible" to another *I*-position, the position of "I need support from all participants". The movement of the general manager facilitated the movement of the other participants as well.

A remaining question was how to give more expression to your own voice. One key issue referred directly to this topic. Table 9.4 presents this issue with the feeling pattern for both groups.

Table 9.4 shows that directly adressing colleagues implicated rather mixed P-N feelings for the medical staff. This finding was 'food for thought' in the discussion. Inspection of the individual feeling patterns revealed that both groups contained a dissonant voice. This heterogeneity deepened the discussion. The consultant invited the participants to collectively take an *I*-position of '*not addressing the other*'. This

Table 9.4 Evaluation in terms of S O P N of a key issue by management and medical staff

	Management				Medical Staff			
Key issue	S	O	P	N	S	O	P	N
I address a colleague directly if this colleague does not stick to his or her word or promise.	15	14	15	8	17	19	13	12

Note: S = feelings referring to self-enhancement; O = feelings referring to contact and union; P = positive feelings; N = negative feelings position felt bad for all. Then he asked to take the contrast-position of '*directly addressing the other*'. This position felt better for most participants, but for some it felt as judging the other and as a one-way communication. Another position, that resulted from the group discussion, felt far better: '*direct and open communication with each other*'. The participants said that this type of communication contributes more to a positive working climate than only addressing a specific person. In terms of DST we see a move to a third position.

Because this move was made collectively the participants could speak from a new and third group position. The collective movement made at that moment created more trust between both groups. The increased trust facilitated the discussion about plans for a better communication structure and a better division of responsibilities between management and the medical staff. Three mixed subgroups started to develop plans and suggestions for these topics. The participants also agreed on the planning of a second workshop (one month later) to share the results of the subgroups and the progress made in a more open and direct communication. And what about the seating in the conference room and staying for dinner after the meeting? Well, in the course of the day both groups were mixed on their own initiative, and all participants stayed for dinner.

In this first workshop only the group report was discussed. The team members received all their individual reports and a hand-out with an explanation of all the indices. The collected data in combination with this handout, and the input from this workshop gave starting points and direction for personal and collective development.

In the next section we will discuss this connection and give some suggestions and critical reflections on the process of anchoring insights and learning points.

Discussion

The presented approach is of course not entirely unique. For example, there are common points with the approach of Appreciative Inquiry (Cooperrider, Whitney, & Stavros, 2008) and Voice Dialogue (Stone & Stone, 2007). A distinctive aspect of SCM-Organization is the way in which it conceptualizes and operationalizes the connection between personal and collective development. Especially the process of positioning and counter-positioning at both the individual and the collective level gives promising impulses for structuring and feeding the organization dialogue.

Application Areas

If organizations have a serious wish to deepen, feed and structure their organization dialogue, SCM-Organization is a recommendable option. In situations of misunderstanding and miscommunication this method can be used to assess the extent of homogeneity and heterogeneity regarding key issues within a group and between groups. The method also has potential to clarify functional and less functional group positions. As an alternative: if a team wants to analyse functional and especially dysfunctional interaction patterns within their team, the Team Confrontation Method (Zomer, 2006) is a good option (see Zomer's chapter in this book). A basic condition for applying SCM-Organization is the wish to reflect and to learn both as a group and as an individual. If there are strong conflicts this method seems less appropiate. Given its connection between personal and collective development this method is particularly promising as a starting point for management development or for learning and development of employees and trainees,. If there is a wish to orchestrate the organization dialogue about aspects of organization development (e.g. perception and reception) this approach is a serious option.

Role and Qualification of the Consultant

The role of the consultant is to facilitate and structure the process of organization dialogue. The consultant has to be skilled in combining the qualitative and quantitative aspects of the method of SCM-Organization. An example: the guiding principles for formulating key issues and statistical information in the general group report and in the individual reports. A licence for the specially developed software for this method is also necessary.[1]) If the consultant also has a role in coaching individual participants, it is useful to be licensed in the SCM-Individual. Last but not least, the consultant should be familiar with group dynamics and team coaching. When applying this method, intervision with colleagues to discuss relevant signals and experiences and collectively building on new knowledge and applications is certainly useful.

Anchoring Insights and Connecting Collective and Individual Learning and Development

It is an illusion to think that everything can be changed in one or two sessions in a group or team. Changing routines and behavior patterns is complex and requires follow up. By creating moments for self-evaluation monitoring the development can be partly done by the participants themselves. Creating conditions for personal development (e.g. intervision, personal and team coaching) is a responsability for management. We believe that SCM-Organization has a strong potential for connecting collective learning points, agreed on collectively by a group as an outcome of organization dialogue, with learning points at an individual level. Individual learning profits from individual coaching, based on the individual SCM-report.

[1]The author developed a training course for SCM-Organization together with Anne-Marie Benschop. Information about this and other SCM- and DST-training courses can be found on the webiste of the Dutch SCM-Association: www.zkmvereniging.nl

Research and Development

Further research and practical experience in the application of SCM-Organization is desirable. Especially for team development not only affect terms but also behaviourial scales are highly informative. In future research it is necessary to evaluate this approach more systematically. Carter and Hawkins (2013, p. 184) observe that there are very few studies on the relationship between team coaching and team performance. The same authors also observe that our knowledge of the effect of specific team coaching interventions is limited. Finally, it is an interesting challenge to explore the combination of SCM-Organization with other DST-based methods that have been developed for studying the self in relation to its social and especially organizational context (Jasper, Moore, Whittaker, & Gillepsie, 2012).

Acknowledgement I wish to thank Hubert Hermans for his helpful comment on the manuscript version of this chapter.

The SCM-Organization training course also includes a license to the special software needed for the application of this approach.

References

Argyris, C. (2004) Double-loop learning and organizational change: Facilitating transformational change. In: J. J. Boonstra (Ed.), *Dynamics of organizational change and learning* (pp. 389–401). Chichester, UK: Wiley.

Boonstra, J. J. (2004). Conclusion, some reflections and perspectives on organizing, changing and learning. In: J. J. Boonstra (Ed.), *Dynamics of organizational change and learning* (pp. 447–475). Chichester: Wiley.

Carter, A., & Hawkins, P. (2013). Team coaching. In J. Passmore, D. B. Peterson, & T. Freire (Eds.), *The Wiley-Blackwell handbook of the psychology of coaching and mentoring* (pp. 175–194). Oxford, UK: Wiley.

Cooperrider, D., Whitney, D., & Stavros, J. (2008). *The appreciative inquiry handbook: for leaders of change*. San Francisco: Berrett-Koehler.

Cummings, Th. (2004). Organization development and change; Foundations and applications. In: Boonstra, J. J. (Ed.), *Dynamics of organizational change and learning* (pp. 25–42). Chichester, UK: Wiley.

De Caluwé, L., & Vermaak, H. (2003). *Learning to change: A guide for organizational change agents*. Thousand Oaks, CA: Sage.

De Caluwé, L., & Vermaak, H. (2004) Thinking about change in different colours; multiplicity in change processes. In: J. J. Boonstra (Ed.), *Dynamics of organizational change and learning* (pp. 197–226). Chichester, UK: Wiley.

De Geus, A. (1997). *The living company; habits for survival in a turbulent business environment.* Boston: Harvard Business School Press.

Epstein, S., & O'Brien, E. J. (1985). The person-situation debate in historical and current perspective. *Psychological Bulletin, 98*, 513–537.

Fleeson, W., & Noftle, E. E. (2009). The end of the person-situation debate: An emerging synthesis in the answer tot he consistency question. *Social and Personality Compass, 2*, 1667–1684.

Gabriel, Y. (2000). *Storytelling in organizations: Facts, fictions and fantasies*. London: Oxford University Press.

Hafsi, T., & Turgut, G. (2013). Boardroom diversity and its effect on social performance: Conceptualization and empirical evidence. *Journal of Business Ethics, 112*, 463–479.

Hall, C. S., & Lindzey, G. (1970). *Theories of personality*. New York: Wiley.

Hermans, H. J. M. (2014) Self as a society of *I*-positions: A dialogical approach to counseling. *Journal of Humanistic Counseling, 53*, 134–159.

Hermans, H. J. M. (2001). The dialogical self: Toward a theory of personal and cultural positioning. *Culture & Psychology, 7*, 243–281.

Hermans, H. J. M., & Dimaggio, G. (2007). Self, identity, and globalization in times of uncertainty: A dialogical analysis. *Review of General Psychology, 11*, 31–61.

Hermans, H. J. M., & Giesser, T. (Eds.). (2012). *Handbook of dialogical self theory*. Cambridge, UK: Cambridge University Press.

Hermans, H. J. M., & Hermans-Jansen, E. (1995). *Self-narratives. The construction of meaning in psychotherapy*. New York/London: The Guilford Press.

Hermans, H. J. M., & Hermans-Konopka, A. (2010). *Dialogical self theory: Positioning and counter-positioning in a globalizing society*. New York: Cambridge University Press.

Hermans, H. J. M., & Kempen, H. J. G. (1993). *The dialogical self, Meaning as movement*. San Diego, CA: Academic Press.

Hermans, H. J. M., & Poulie, M. F. (2000). Talent and self-narrative: The survival of an underachieving adolesecent. In F. M. van Lieshout & P. G. Heymans (Eds.), *Developing talent across the lifespan* (pp. 277–298). Hove, UK: Psychology Press Ltd.

Hermans, H. J. M., Kempen, H. J. G., & Van Loon, R. J. P. (1991). The dialogical self: Beyond individualism and rationalism. *American Psychologist, 47*, 23–33.

Hosking, D. M. (2004). Change works, a critical construction. In J. J. Boonstra (Ed.), *Dynamics of organizational change and learning* (pp. 259–276). Chichester, UK: Wiley.

Janis, I. L. (1982). *Groupthink: Psychological studies of policy decisions and fiascoes*. Boston: Houghton Mifflin.

Jasper, C. A., Moore, H. R., Whittaker, L. S., & Gillepsie, A. (2012). Methodological approaches to studying the self in its social context. In: H. J. M. Hermans & T. Gieser (Eds.), *Handbook of dialogical self theory* (pp. 319–334). Cambridge, UK: Cambridge University Press.

Kindermann, Th.A., & Valsiner, J. (1995) Individual development, changing contexts, and the co-construction of person-context relations in human development. In T. A. Kindermann & J. Valsiner (Eds.), *Development of person-context relations* (pp. 1–9). Hillsdale, NJ: Lawrence Erlbaum.

Lencioni, P. (2002). *The five dysfunctions of a team: A leadership fable*. San Francisco: Jossey-Bass.

Lindegger, G., & Alberts, C. (2012). The dialogical self in the new South Africa. In H. J. M. Hermans & T. Gieser (Eds.), *Handbook of dialogical self theory* (pp. 215–233). Cambridge, UK: Cambridge University Press.

Lodders, N. (2013). *Teachers learning and innovating together; Exploring collective learning and its relationship to individual learning, transformational leadership and team performance in higher vocational education*. Doctoral dissertation, University of Twente, The Netherlands.

Lyddon, W. J., Yowell, D. R., & Hermans, H. J. M. (2006). The self-confrontation method: Theory, research and practical utility. *Counselling Psychology Quarterly, 19*, 27–43.

Morris, E. K. (2009). Behavior analysis and ecological psychology: Past, present and future. A review of Harry Heft's ecological psychology in context. *Journal of the Experimental Analysis of Behavior, 92*, 275–304.

Raggatt, P. T. F. (2012). Positioning in the dialogical self: recent advances in theory construction. In H. J. M. Hermans & T. Gieser (Eds.), *Handbook of dialogical self theory* (pp. 29–45). Cambridge, UK: Cambridge University Press.

Rowan, J. (2012) The use of *I*-positions in psychotherapy. In: H. J. M. Hermans & T. Gieser (Eds.), *Handbook of dialogical self theory* (pp. 341–355). Cambridge, UK: Cambridge University Press.

Schein, E. H. (1992). *Organizational culture and leadership*. San Francisco: Jossey-Bass.

Schulz von Thun, F. (2008). *Six tools for clear communication; the Hamburg approach in English language*. Hamburg, Germany: Institut für Kommunikation.

Stone, H., & Stone, S. (2007). *The basic elements of voice dialogue, relationship and the psychology of selves; Their origins and development.* Albion, UK: Voice Dialogue International. www.voicedialogue.org

Van de Loo, R. P. J. M. (1992). *Verheldering van loopbaanperspectief, ontwikkeling en toepassing van een programma voor loopbaanoriëntatie op basis van de zelfconfrontatiemethode* [Clarification of career-perspective; development and application of a program of career orientation based on the self-confrontation method]. Assen/Maastricht, The Netherlands: Van Gorcum.

Van de Loo, R. P. J. M. (2012). De stem van de dissonant: Stimulering van meerstemmigheid en dialoog bij teamontwikkeling [The voice of the dissonant: Stimulation of multivoicedness and dialogue in teamdevelopment]. In: F. Meijers (Ed.), *Wiens verhaal telt? Naar een narratieve dialogische* loopbaanbegeleiding [Whose story counts? Towards a narrative dialogical career coaching] (pp. 219–236). Antwerpen, Belgium: Garant.

Van Geelen, S. M. (2010). *Understanding self-experience in adolescent chronic fatigue syndrome.* Doctoral dissertation, University of Utrecht, The Netherlands.

Van Loon, R., & Wijsbek, J. (Eds.). (2003). *De Organisatie als Verhaal* [The organization as story]. Assen, The Netherlands: Van Gorcum.

Weick, K. E. (1976). Educational organizations as loosely coupled systems. *Administrative Science Quarterly, 21*, 1–19.

Wicker, A. W. (1979). Ecological psychology, some recent and prospective developments. *American Psychologist, 34*(9), 755–765.

Wierdsma, A. (2004). Beyond implementation: Co-creation in change and development. In J. J. Boonstra (Ed.), *Dynamics of organizational change and learning* (pp. 227–257). Chichester, UK: Wiley.

Wijsbek, J. (2003) De organisatie als verhaal [The organization as story]. In R. Van Loon & J. Wijsbek (Eds.), *De Organisatie als Verhaal* [The organization as story]. (pp. 76–106). Assen, The Netherlands: Van Gorcum.

Wijsbek, J. (2009). *De dialogische organisatie* [The dialogical organization]. Assen, The Netherlands: Van Gorcum.

Zomer, P. (2006). *The Team Konfrontation method: Design, grounding and testing.* Doctoral dissertation, Radboud University Nijmegen, The Netherlands.

Index

H. Hermans (ed.), *Assessing and Stimulating a Dialogical Self in Groups, Teams, Cultures, and Organizations*, DOI 10.1007/978-3-319-32482-1

CPI Antony Rowe
Chippenham, UK